Praise for *Truly Great Prima...*

I'm a simple soul and I'm always looking fo. .....s to bring abstract ideas like 'quality first teaching' to life. Terms like these are talked about a lot; rarely are they exemplified. What John has done in *Truly Great Primary Teachers* is to identify and profile the work of individual teachers to help me to get some purchase on QFT. As I read these accounts of teachers who are having a profound impact on their pupils both academically and personally, I realised I can learn from each of them: the way they develop rapport with their classes, the way they pitch the lessons high, the way they include every child. And, above all, the delight they take in weaving it all together. This is such a heart-warming, unique lens on the profession. We can all take something from these wonderful profiles of brilliant professionals.

Mary Myatt, educational consultant

Truly Great Primary Teachers explores the multifaceted nature of effective teaching and considers how it can be measured. The book highlights how truly great teachers are committed to reflective practice and continuous learning, creating environments where pupils thrive academically and socially. The influence of these highly effective practitioners extends beyond measurable test scores; they cultivate a genuine love for learning, as well as confidence, resilience, intrinsic drive and curiosity in their pupils – all of which are harder to quantify, but vitally important. Through first-hand examples, John illustrates how high-quality pedagogy, coupled with a focus on personal growth, empowers pupils to grasp complex concepts that contribute to them making great progress in their learning at levels that they, themselves, hardly thought possible.

Em Ward, Head Teacher, Ravensthorpe Primary School, Peterborough

In *Truly Great Primary Teachers*, John Tomsett captures the human element of what makes great teachers 'truly great'. Through detailed profiles and personal anecdotes, we are provided with a fascinating look at their unique approaches to teaching and learning, their commitment to continuous improvement and, most importantly, what it is like to be a pupil in their classroom. We experience the dedication and passion of these inspiring individuals who make such a difference to the communities they are part of and can fully appreciate the thought processes behind the successes they achieve with their children.

Dan Oakes, Head Teacher, St Bartholomew's Primary School

This is a book for everybody interested in improving the lived experience of pupils in the classroom. From system leaders to those just stepping out into the early stages of their career, *Truly Great Primary Teachers* tells the story of how teachers change lives. Pupils from low-income backgrounds are typically more sensitive to the quality of education they experience. In the classroom, for me, this is about the triumvirate of strong subject knowledge, expert pedagogy and the understanding of childhood coupled with the ability to build strong relationships with and between pupils. It is the building and securing of relationships with pupils, who may be experiencing a range of academic and social challenges, all within the exposed environment of the classroom, that makes teachers truly special. This book brings to life how teachers have a profound impact on learners and their colleagues. It tells a story of what makes a truly great teacher.

Marc Rowland, adviser for improving outcomes for
disadvantaged learners for the Unity Schools Partnership

This is a must-read for all educators. *Truly Great Primary Teachers* drives home the importance of the purposeful relationships that sit at the heart of great teaching. It also celebrates the individual identity that each teacher brings to the classroom. John has beautifully told each teacher's story, creating a window into their world, whilst connecting the reader to the teacher's colleagues and pupils in the interwoven interviews. Rarely does a book share the raw realities of day-to-day teaching, whilst detailing the personal motivations that drive teachers to teach. It is both a privilege and a joy to read something that reminds us all why teaching is such a great profession and how truly great teachers make a difference to young people's lives by making their classrooms places where learning is irresistible.

Andrew Rhodes, Primary PGCE Lecturer and Professional Tutor,
University of Manchester, Director of Redefining Education Ltd

THIS MUCH I KNOW ABOUT

TRULY GREAT PRIMARY TEACHERS

(AND WHAT WE CAN LEARN FROM THEM)

JOHN TOMSETT

FOREWORD BY PROFESSOR ROB COE

Crown House Publishing Limited

www.crownhouse.co.uk

First published by
Crown House Publishing Limited
Crown Buildings, Bancyfelin, Carmarthen, Wales, SA33 5ND, UK
www.crownhouse.co.uk

and

Crown House Publishing Company LLC
PO Box 2223, Williston, VT 05495, USA
www.crownhousepublishing.com

Image p. 236: from J. Goodrich, *Responsive Coaching: Evidence-informed Instructional Coaching that Works for Every Teacher in Your
School* (Woodbridge: John Catt Educational, 2024). permission kindly received from John Catt Educational.
Quote pp. 239–240: from G. Duoblys, Michael Young: What we've got wrong about knowledge and curriculum, *TES*
(21 September 2022). Available at: https://www.tes.com/magazine/teaching-learning/general/michael-young-
powerful-knowledge-curriculum. Permission for use kindly received from G. Duoblys.

EU GPSR Authorised Representative
Appointed EU Representative: Easy Access System Europe Oü, 16879218
Address: Mustamäe tee 50, 10621, Tallinn, Estonia
Contact Details: gpsr.requests@easproject.com, +358 40 500 3575

British Library Cataloguing-in-Publication Data

A catalogue entry for this book is available from the British Library.

Print ISBN: 9781785837456
Mobi ISBN: 9781785837562
ePub ISBN: 9781785837579
ePDF ISBN: 9781785837586

LCCN 2025931346

Printed and bound in the UK by
Gomer Press, Llandysul, Ceredigion

This book is dedicated to Mary Myatt, who has taught me more about the school curriculum these past few years than she would ever know!

Foreword by Professor Rob Coe[1]

I suspect this book, and its accompanying title *This Much I Know About Truly Great Secondary Teachers (and what we can learn from them),* may have come into being partly because of a misunderstanding, a failure of communication. As John describes in the introduction, it arose from a presentation Raj Chande and I gave about our National Institute of Teaching project to try to estimate value-added scores for individual teachers (anonymised) in order to learn more about what great teaching is and how it develops. John was in the audience and something about the idea of reducing the rich complexity of teaching to a single number seemed to grate with him – perhaps not unreasonably. He asked a question that I interpreted as challenging, and I am sorry to say I responded a bit confrontationally, trying to put him down and close down the challenge. As a result, I missed the opportunity to find common ground, to understand his concerns and to explain why what we were trying to do was not quite what he thought. My bad. But from that bad, came a brilliant thing: a pair of books.

This Much I Know About Truly Great Primary Teachers (and what we can learn from them), alongside its accompanying title *This Much I Know About Truly Great Secondary Teachers (and what we can learn from them),* is a wonderful celebration of the complex and beautiful art of classroom teaching. It brings to life the ways great teachers coordinate great learning in classrooms with a set of vivid case studies. The chosen examples cover a range of school types, social contexts, pupil ages and subjects. Each teacher is unique in the way they teach, and in how they talk about teaching; each has found their own way; each is brought to technicolour life in John's vignette. But they also have some common characteristics and behaviours, as John draws together, summarising what we can learn from them in the final chapter.

---

1   It is worth noting that the introduction to the primary version of this book is identical to the introduction to the secondary version.

I first started thinking in a systematic way about what great teachers do when writing the report *What Makes Great Teaching?* in 2014.[2] The Sutton Trust and Gates Foundation had co-organised a conference in Washington DC at which they wanted to bring together some of the best teachers and school leaders from around the world. Lee Elliot Major had asked me to lead on creating the report that became *What Makes Great Teaching?* and to present it at the conference. I first knew John as one of the early edu-bloggers and through Twitter, and by that point was working with him directly as part of an Education Endowment Foundation (EEF)-funded project to evaluate the impact of training school research leads to interpret and apply research evidence, led by Huntington School where he was the head teacher (Research leads Improving Students' Education – RISE).[3] I think I nominated John to be invited to Washington as part of a small group of outstanding school leaders from England. My memory is that the report and its messages had a somewhat luke-warm reception in Washington. Although our hand-picked delegates from England liked it, the majority of teachers there were from the USA and other places where the role of research evidence in teaching was not yet established. *What Makes Great Teaching?* went on to become the Sutton Trust's most downloaded research report, by some margin, and has since featured in the recommended reading for all trainee teachers in England through the *Initial Teacher Training and Early Career Framework.*[4]

In the report we defined effective teaching by its impact on valued student outcomes, acknowledging that a range of different outcomes could be valued (for example, academic attainment in examinations, future education and career trajectories, along with impacts on students' attendance, behaviours and attitudes). We also considered, in

2   R. Coe, C. Aloisi, S. Higgins and L. Elliot Major, *What Makes Great Teaching? Review of the Underpinning Research* (London: Sutton Trust, 2014). Available at: https://www.suttontrust.com/wp-content/uploads/2014/10/What-Makes-Great-Teaching-REPORT.pdf.

3   See: https://educationendowmentfoundation.org.uk/projects-and-evaluation/projects/the-rise-project-evidence-informed-school-improvement.

4   Department for Education, *Initial Teacher Training and Early Career Framework* (January 2024). Available at: https://assets.publishing.service.gov.uk/media/661d24ac08c3be25cfbd3e61/Initial_Teacher_Training_and_Early_Career_Framework.pdf.

some detail, other approaches to evaluating the quality of teaching, including: classroom observations, by peers, principals or external evaluators; student ratings surveys; principal (or head teacher) judgement; teacher self-reports; analysis of classroom artefacts and teacher portfolios. We presented the evidence about the convergence of these different approaches and concluded that 'their predictive power is usually not high'. To illustrate the strength of the relationships typically found in the best research studies, we gave a hypothetical example: 'if we were to use classroom observation ratings to identify teachers as "above" or "below" average in their impact on student learning we would get it right about 60% of the time, compared with the 50% we would get by just tossing a coin. It is better than chance, but not by much.'

Part of the reason classroom observation correlates only weakly with student progress measures is that observing classrooms is a lot harder than it seems. Most teachers and school leaders have a clear idea what great teaching looks like. When they watch a lesson, they have a strong sense that they can interpret what they see and hear, and that they can judge how good it is. In my experience, it is very hard to convince them that their judgements may not be as accurate as they intuitively feel. And yet, these judgements are mostly wrong.[5]

Among the reasons why it is so hard to judge effectiveness from observation is that many of the things that make a difference to students' learning are not visible, and even those that are may not be on display in any particular lesson. This creates a challenge for any researcher who wants to develop an evidence-based protocol for lesson observation and it applies to all the existing instruments (some of which we reviewed in *What Makes Great Teaching?*). But for teachers and school leaders, who are not trained and accredited in using a validated protocol and rely on their intuitive judgements, there is a further reason: different teachers do not completely agree about what great teaching is. As we said in the report, 'It might seem obvious that this is

---

5   See, for example, R. Coe, Classroom observation: it's harder than you think, *Cambridge Insight* [blog] (9 January 2014). Available at: https://www.cem.org/blog/classroom-observation.

already well known: we surely know what great teaching looks like … In fact, there is some evidence that an understanding of what constitutes effective pedagogy – the method and practice of teaching – may not be so widely shared, and even where it is widely shared it may not actually be right.' A small section of the report pointed out some examples of 'popular teaching practices not supported by research evidence' to illustrate that describing great teaching is not just common sense. But the press release led with 'many common practices can be harmful to learning and have no grounding in research'[6] and I recall doing multiple radio and television interviews explaining the dangers of 'lavish praise for students'.

All of this is perhaps a slightly long-winded way of saying that identifying great teachers is tricky and trying to describe what they do that makes them great even more so. Many excellent researchers over the last 50 or more years have tried to do both, and yet our knowledge remains partial and uncertain. It is one of those questions about which practitioners will mostly feel frustration that researchers are making it so complicated. Surely, we know what great teaching is and is it really that hard to describe it? To which researchers may reply that, certainly, it is not hard to do it badly, but doing it well is very hard indeed.

What Makes Great Teaching? reviewed and quality-assured a wide range of research evidence about the components of teaching quality and presented an outline framework to summarise it. When I started working for Evidence Based Education in 2019, we thought it would be useful to update the review. But we soon realised that a summary of research findings about effective teaching, however authoritative and accessible, is not enough to help teachers to do more of it, more faithfully, more sustainably, more effectively and at greater scale. For that, we needed a more diverse set of tools to support a coherent approach to professional development, hence the *Great Teaching Toolkit.*

---

6   Sutton Trust, Many popular teaching practices are ineffective, warns new Sutton Trust report [press release] (30 October 2014). Available at: https://www.suttontrust.com/news-opinion/all-news-opinion/many-popular-teaching-practices-are-ineffective-warns-new-sutton-trust-report/.

Nevertheless, the foundation of that Toolkit is an updated Evidence Review.

The *Great Teaching Toolkit: Evidence Review*[7] sets out a model for great teaching, based on the best currently available evidence. The highest-level summary clarifies that great teachers do four fundamental things:

1   Understand the content they are teaching and how it is learnt

2   Create a supportive environment for learning

3   Manage the classroom to maximise opportunity to learn

4   Present content, activities and interactions that activate their students' thinking

Each of these four broad dimensions is then split into a total of 17 elements:

1   Understanding the content

    1.1. Deep and fluent content knowledge

    1.2. Curriculum knowledge: sequencing

    1.3. Knowledge of tasks, assessments and multiple explanations

    1.4. Knowledge of student thinking: misconceptions

2   Creating a supportive environment

    2.1. Relationships with students and cultural sensitivity

    2.2. Student–student relationships and climate

    2.3. Promoting learner motivation

    2.4. High expectations, challenge and trust

3   Maximising the opportunity to learn

    3.1. Managing time and resources to maximise productivity

---

7   R. Coe, C. J. Rauch, S. Kime and D. Singleton, *The Great Teaching Toolkit: Evidence Review* (Sunderland: Evidence Based Education, 2020). Available at: https://evidencebased. education/great-teaching-toolkit-evidence-review/.

Of course, these are just headlines, very abbreviated descriptions of complex practices that are, at best, inadequately captured in words. To be well-defined, in addition we need exemplification (rich and varied examples and non-examples) and operationalisation (clear processes for assessing whether an example represents the target practice). A big challenge with descriptors is that we can think we mean the same things by the same words when we actually have quite different understandings in practice, especially when the descriptors are quite abstract and general, as they inevitably must be.

The purpose of sharing this framework here is twofold. The first is to note that there is a lot of overlap between what the evidence suggests are the practices most associated with effective teaching and the practices described in the following chapters. John summarises ten behaviours of truly great teachers in the last chapter and I would say they are all represented in the model, and that other features of their teaching, described in the individual chapters, are also represented. Overall, I would say we are in pretty close agreement about what great teachers do.

The second reason is that each detailed vignette, based on an observation of one lesson and discussions with the teacher, their colleagues and pupils, brings these characteristics to life in a way no general framework can. We are left with a much richer picture of not just what these teachers do, but why: the choices and adaptations they make and the principles that guide them. In short, we need both: a generic, research-grounded framework, and specific, detail-rich descriptions of real examples.

So, does a single, numerical value capture everything that is worth knowing about great teaching? Of course not; no one has ever claimed it could or should. This might be an example of the perfectionist fallacy, that because something is not perfect it must be useless. Of course, most things are in-between. The key is to understand what uses and interpretations are valid.

In the assessment, measurement and psychometric tradition in which I was trained as a researcher, validity is not seen as a property of a particular score or measure. Instead, validity applies to specific uses and interpretations of that measure. Before we can judge whether it is appropriate to use assessment data (from a variety of commercial, bought-in assessments, school-made assessments, and national assessments and examinations) to estimate the impact of a teacher on pupils' learning, we need to know the purpose: what will it be used for and what caveats are attached to its interpretation?

In the presentation that provoked John to put down a marker for truly great teaching, we were perhaps not as clear about this as we could have been. In our project, teacher value-added scores will be used for research purposes only, with fully anonymised data. We have a clear agreement with the teachers, schools and trusts who have provided the data that no consequences (good or bad) can be linked with these value-added scores. Moreover, the analysis we have done so far makes it clear that, even if people wanted to use the scores for things like selection, reward or performance management, scores for individual teachers are mostly not really accurate enough to support those uses. Scores are probably accurate enough for us to find large-scale statistical patterns, which is what we have set up the project to do. We want to learn more, in a systematic and rigorous way, about what great teachers (i.e. those who help their students to learn more) do, know and believe and about how they became great, and how we can help all teachers to be more like them.

The teachers whose work is celebrated in the chapters of this book also contribute to the wider project. Not only do they spend their days doing the most inspiring, challenging and important job in the world, educating the next generation, but by sharing their practice with us in these pages, they illuminate the world of truly great teachers. Most of them seem to think that they are nothing special, that they just do their job and that many others do the same. While the last part of this may be true – there are many more truly great teachers who could have been featured – the first part is not: they are truly special, awe-inspiring individuals, and we all have a lot to learn from them.

Rob Coe

Preface

In order to write the teacher profiles that comprise this book, I visited each teacher's school during the Autumn term 2024. The schedule of visits was completely random, but what I learnt about these truly great teachers built over time. Consequently, I have ordered the profiles chronologically. They can be read one-by-one as individual narratives, or from beginning to end to give a more holistic sense of how my understanding of the professional behaviours common to these teachers grew.

All the teachers featured here work in primary schools, except for Mary Cawley, who is a special school teacher. Even though her school's pupils are of secondary age, the school is not designated a phase of education. She features here, as well as in this book's sister publication, *This Much I Know About Truly Great Secondary Teachers (and what we can learn from them)* because what we can learn from Mary's work is, I would suggest, applicable to all teachers in any setting.

Acknowledgements

In my experience, teachers are naturally modest. They usually focus upon what they *feel* they are getting wrong in the classroom, rather than what they are doing right. Consequently, persuading a teacher to feature in a book that celebrates how well they teach is difficult. Sincere thanks goes, then, to the teachers whose stories I tell here – Maddie Jacques, Josh Pike, Nicola Curran, Faariah Jamil, Dean Salisbury, Helen Digger, Molly Medhurst, Mary Cawley and Megan Bull – for taking a metaphorical deep breath and agreeing to let me into their working lives, to see what they do so well. Inevitably, my words are an inadequate representation of their truly great teaching.

Over the years, Professor Rob Coe's impact upon my thinking has been immense. As the narrative of this book reveals, our challenging conversation about how best to judge teacher effectiveness at the researchED national conference in September 2024 spawned this book and its accompanying title, *This Much I Know About Truly Great Secondary Teachers (and what we can learn from them)*. Without Rob, neither book would have been written. For him, then, to agree to write the books' foreword reflects huge generosity of spirit on his part. I cannot thank Rob enough.

I could not have written these books without the cooperation of the teachers' head teachers, colleagues and pupils. It has been fun zipping about the country, visiting such a range of diverse schools in such a short time. I felt welcome everywhere I've been, for which I am very grateful and my conversations with the pupils will, especially, stay with me for a long time.

It is good to be back at Crown House again, a decade after my first book with them. I am keen to thank publicly David Bowman and his colleagues for having faith in me and accepting my pitch for this project. His team have worked tirelessly with me to prepare these books for publication, particularly Beverley Randell.

Finally, I must thank my wife Louise for tolerating all those evenings I was unavoidably absent, either holed up in a hotel in a far-flung corner of these Isles, or next door in my office tapping away on my laptop.

Contents

'This job of teaching is so hard that one lifetime isn't enough to master it.'

Dylan Wiliam[1]

---

1   Speaking at The Schools Network (then known as the SSAT) National Conference 2010.

Introduction

The genesis of this book, and its accompanying title (*This Much I Know About Truly Great Secondary Teachers*), is rooted in a conversation with Professor Rob Coe. At the national researchED conference in September 2024, I had listened to Rob and his colleague, Dr Raj Chande, talk about their quest to establish a single value-added progress score for a teacher's pupils, to determine that teacher's effectiveness in the classroom.

What Rob and Raj want to do is find a reliable, easily accessible metric to assess teacher quality. In 2014 I went to Washington DC with Rob and several others, including luminaries like Professor Lee Elliot Major, to launch the Sutton Trust's publication, *What Makes Great Teaching?*, in which Rob et al. defined 'effective teaching as that which leads to improved pupil achievement using outcomes that matter to their future success.'[1] It's logical, in the light of that sensible definition, to choose one pupil value-added progress score if you are searching for a single metric.

I first met Rob over a decade ago when Alex Quigley, Stuart Kime and I ran a project for the Education Endowment Foundation.[2] We spent several afternoons in my office discussing how to set up the project. Rob made my head hurt. He genuinely transformed my professional outlook. He just kept asking the question, 'How do you know?' And most times, I couldn't answer him.

When we were chatting about his single value-added progress score project, I said to Rob that I thought there were other things they might do to determine how to measure teacher quality, rather than pursue a

---

1 R. Coe, C. Aloisi, S. Higgins and L. Elliot Major, *What Makes Great Teaching? Review of the Underpinning Research* (London: Sutton Trust, 2014). Available at: https://www.suttontrust.com/wp-content/uploads/2014/10/What-Makes-Great-Teaching-REPORT.pdf.

2 See: https://educationendowmentfoundation.org.uk/projects-and-evaluation/projects/the-rise-project-evidence-informed-school-improvement.

single, numeric pupil progress data point. Rob conceded that I *might* have a point, but then he asked me, 'Well, what should we be doing?'

I said that I would think about it. And I have. A lot.

My counter to Rob and Raj's argument is that being a truly great teacher goes way beyond value-added scores. The characteristics of truly great teachers will, in my experience, result in their pupils making great academic progress. But the impact a truly great teacher can make upon their pupils' lives is surely measured in myriad ways, beyond the single metric Rob and Raj want to establish.

As you may already have realised, dear reader, the single metric Rob and Raj are pursuing sticks in my craw. Sammy Wright's remarkable book, *Exam Nation*, asks, amongst many things, how our education system became so obsessed with the single output measure of pupils' academic progress.[3] Don't get me wrong, examination success gives young people a choice about how they live their lives; that said, without wanting to provoke cries of 'the soft bigotry of low expectations', surely there are other measures of success which matter just as much, but in different ways. If we pursue a single value-added measure as the *only* outcome of education that *really* matters, then we have, perhaps, missed the point. As Bernard Andrews wrote in his provocative essay, 'How "efficiency" derailed education', 'if school encourages and enables students to be brave, kind, wise and so on, and if it does so with prudence, then it is time and money well spent.'[4]

If Rob and Raj did one thing, they got me thinking … about all the colleagues I worked with over 33 years, and about the hundreds of teachers I have had the privilege of watching teach as a peripatetic consultant since stepping down from headship. In answer to Rob's question, 'Well, what should we be doing?' I have concluded that we should try to ascertain what it is that truly great teachers do that makes

3   S. Wright, *Exam Nation: Why Our Obsession with Grades Fails Everyone – and a Better Way to Think About School* (London: Vintage Publishing, 2024).

4   B. Andrews, How 'efficiency' derailed education, *TES* (25 February 2025). Available at: https://www.tes.com/magazine/teaching-learning/general/how-efficiency-derailed-education.

them truly great. Consequently, I identified 19 teachers – eight primary and ten secondary colleagues, and a special school colleague – who I think could be described as truly great teachers and constructed a profile for each one of them. In the following pages you will find profiles of the eight primary teachers. The secondary teachers' profiles can be found in the sister book, *This Much I Know About Truly Great Secondary Teachers (and what we can learn from them)*. I have included our special school colleague in both books, as the learning from her profile is educative irrespective of phase, making it nine teacher profiles altogether in *this* book.

When it comes to pupils' attainment and progress, I too want pupils in the classes of truly great teachers to make brilliant progress and attain amazing examination grades. But any data on pupils' progress needs triangulating with other evidence. Consequently, to assure you that they are truly great, each teacher profile contains the following elements:

- A conversation with their head teacher/principal (if possible)
- Lesson observation reflections
- Interviews with pupils
- An interview with me
- Testimonials from colleagues, pupils and parents
- A summary of the traits that make them exceptional
- Pupil progress and attainment data

Having been involved in education, in one guise or another, for 54 of my 60 years on earth, I knew I couldn't include all the tremendous teachers I've known in that time. I would have featured more, but even nine is probably too many. So, my sincere apologies to all those truly great teachers I could have included but didn't, because there just weren't enough pages to go round.

It wasn't so hard finding nine truly great teachers – there are thousands of them in our country's classrooms. The challenge was to persuade them to let me include them in the book. Truly great teachers are a modest lot. They took some convincing to take part. And when a school leader asked me what I meant by a 'truly great teacher', I replied: *Nothing scientific . . . a teacher who you think is truly great, who really knows their stuff, who teaches great lessons, day-in, day-out, whose pupils get great outcomes and who is just consistently great in every sense.* Consequently, the teachers featured in this book are not intended to be representative of anything. They are merely a small group of truly great teachers I happen to know or who have been recommended to me by people I know and trust. In the words of Sir David Carter, they teach 'consistently good lessons that are well planned and progress sequentially from the previous lesson.'[5] And that's it.

In the final chapter of this book, I identify the professional behaviours common to the teachers I have featured. I contextualise my conclusions within research findings from Barak Rosenshine.[6]

Now, I am acutely aware of the problem with labelling anyone a *truly great teacher*. No teacher is flawless. *Any* teacher can teach poorly, simply because the essential raw materials of a lesson are flesh and blood, not wood and steel. In every lesson there are literally hundreds of variables, each one of which can make any *teacher* look anything but truly great. As Chris Husbands so elegantly argues, 'it's teaching, not teachers, which matters.'[7]

That said, if I had focused upon *teaching* rather than *teachers* in the book's title, it would have not represented the content of the book, nor what motivated me to write it. The book is about *teachers*, and how those teachers teach in a way that means their pupils learn. If the book was entitled, 'This Much I Know About Truly Great Primary *Teaching*', it would have suggested that it's about me and what I might think about

---

5   In a private conversation with the author.

6   B. Rosenshine, *Teaching Behaviours and Student Achievement*, no. 1 (IEA studies) (Slough: National Foundation for Educational Research, 1 November 1971).

7   C. Husbands, Great teachers or great teaching? Why McKinsey got it wrong, *IOE blog* (10 October 2013). Available at: https://blogs.ucl.ac.uk/ioe/2013/10/great-teachers-or-great-teaching-why-mckinsey-got-it-wrong/.

primary teaching, when the book is about truly great primary *teachers* and, crucially, *what we can learn from them*.

Beyond that important semantic nuance, I wanted to stress the *humanity* of the teaching and learning process. Focusing upon the teachers and what they actually do in the classroom in detail, underlined how teaching and learning is such a messy, joyful, human process. And I wanted, ultimately, to celebrate some of the best teachers I know, as I near the end of my professional career and hand the baton on to the truly great colleagues featured here.

I am both delighted and grateful that Professor Rob Coe agreed to write the foreword to this book. He provides a brilliant, forensic counterpoint to my qualitative approach. It may be that any teacher whose pupils make extraordinary progress, only make that progress because that teacher exhibits the professional behaviours shared by the nine truly great teachers featured here. The behaviours and the progress data are, perhaps, just two sides of the same coin.

Finally, the conversations that form the heart of this book have been genuinely inspiring. Gadamer said that, 'No one knows in advance what will "come out" of a conversation . . . a conversation has a spirit of its own, and the language in which it is conducted has a truth of its own so that it allows something to "emerge" which henceforth exists.'[8] We live in a world of binary intransigence. So, in the spirit of collaboration, I hope that the conversations you'll find in the following pages spark limitless discussions in schools across the country, and from those discussions clarity and truth emerge as we all work to provide our young people with the richest classroom experiences imaginable.

---

8 H. Gadamer, translated by J. Weinsheimer and D. Marshall, *Truth and Method* (New York: The Crossroad Publishing Corporation, 1991).

A Truly Great Primary Teacher: Maddie Jacques

Maddie Jacques is a Year 6 teacher at St Bartholomew's Primary School, Royal Wootton Bassett.

The school leadership's view

Dan Oakes is a sharp head teacher. He leads St Bartholomew's Primary School in Royal Wootton Bassett. I met Dan when I was helping his team use Tom Sherrington and Oliver Caviglioli's *WalkThrus* to improve the effectiveness of teaching at St Bart's.[1] I knew he had some great teachers working there, one of whom is Maddie Jacques, the subject of our conversation this morning.

---

1   T. Sherrington and O. Caviglioli, *Teaching WalkThrus: Five-Step Guides to Instructional Coaching: Visual Step-By-Step Guides to Essential Teaching Techniques* (Woodbridge: John Catt Educational, 2020).

Refreshingly, Dan tells it like it is. 'There's a personal cost to Maddie's greatness. It takes huge time and effort.' His brow furrows. 'My job is to nurture her and look after her.' He tells me her background. Maddie's Mum was a learning support assistant. Maddie began as a teaching assistant, which was followed by training with Teach First before becoming a teacher. 'When I interview, I will only shortlist people who can do the job … *genuinely* do the job. When we interviewed Maddie, I was determined that she wouldn't leave here without us appointing her! She was absolutely the right person for our school … either that, or she was a compulsive liar!' We laugh. 'The final interview was a conversation. She was happy to say that she was "not quite sure" about some answers, and that is usually a sign of a reflective practitioner.' She is in her fourth year of teaching and such is the faith Dan has in Maddie, she is now teaching Year 6.

I ask him what it was that prompted him to suggest I include her in this book. 'It's like what Graham Taylor said about David Beckham, "You look at his passing and he makes it look so simple. When he passes the ball, it always seems to go where he wants it to go. That sounds simple, but believe me, it is not." What Maddie does in the classroom looks easy, but it certainly isn't. And the progress that her children make is remarkable.' There are many factors, according to Dan, that make her the teacher she is becoming. She enjoys reading about what the evidence says might work, and making it work for her in her circumstances. She is very reflective. She is sensitive to what is going on in the room.

Year 6 is a potentially tricky year to teach says Dan, but Maddie has them exactly where she wants them. She has high expectations of the pupils. She focuses upon broadening their word hoard. She is interested in their personal and social education too. She sees the bigger picture of their lives and cares about them deeply. Parents are unfailingly praiseworthy of Maddie's work.

Finally, Dan tells of how she came in last week despite an ear infection, and how she was demonstrating to colleagues in the staff room how she was using the 'listening round an imaginary pillar' technique, where you crane your neck forward so that your good ear is turned towards the speaker. The staff room was heaving with giggles, apparently. She cares about the children deeply. She never loses sight of why she came into the profession and how, at the school gate, parents hand over their children to Maddie, entrusting her with their most precious possession for seven hours a day.

It's time to go and meet Maddie Jacques . . .

———————————

Teaching

As we walk in, Maddie is taking the register. 'Good morning, Sam.'

'Good morning, Miss', Sam replies. This respectful exchange repeats around the room.

The pupils are working on a maths starter. One boy says to Maddie, 'Me and my dad have been practising maths, Miss.'

'That's good. So, if I get some things wrong, you can help me out.' The boy nods sagely.

I notice the word of the day on the board along with its etymological and linguistic roots: Labour; Laboratory; Laborious; Collaborate; Liberate; Liberty; Liberal. Suddenly Maddie says, 'Show me 10!' Every single pupil has both hands in front of them, with their fingers outspread. 'I'm just waiting for one person.' Within a nanosecond she has complete attention. 'Please can my helpers hand out the books.' With no fuss, four pupils distribute copies of *Wonder* by R. J. Palacio. On the electronic screen comes up the question: 'Do we know what he looks like? Give me two features of his face.' They discuss in pairs and, exactly 30 seconds later Maddie gives a rhythmic clap, which the pupils repeat. Then 100% attention. She takes answers from around the room. Inference is a hard skill to teach. She explores the children's thinking and why they have said what they have said. It is a disciplined, psychologically safe environment devoid of any barriers to learning. There's full engagement and the energy levels are high. Dan was right when he said she has complete control of the room.

Maddie likes to see as many hands up as possible. Emily's hand is down. She asks Emily a question. Emily doesn't respond. She asks again, breaking the question down further. Nothing. She repeats the question. Emily has frozen. The silence verges on the uncomfortable. She reassures Emily and asks someone else, instead. For the next question she asks them to turn to their partners to share their thoughts. They all have partners, of course. No odd pupil out in Maddie's class. She makes a beeline for Emily, hears her say the right answer, whispers to her, and then when she brings the whole class round, asks Emily for her answer. Emily smiles. She has thawed out completely. Such brilliant teaching. The episode reminded me of Tom Sherrington's observation that, 'if you leave pupils out because of your anxiety about their anxiety, you're no use to them. You're not carrying them; you are leaving them behind.'[2] No one gets left behind in Maddie's class.

They do some more retrieval work. When they get to a word like 'duelling' they repeat it chorally. Every pupil gets their tongue around the word. She has 100% control. There is such a beautiful balance between behavioural control and engagement. Of course, there is such a high level of engagement because the orderly classroom allows everyone to fix upon the learning.

They complete a comprehension task, which they find when they use their iPads to log on to *Showbie*.[3] I have no idea what *Showbie* is, but delight in watching these 10-year-olds use the technology adroitly. The focus in the room is immense. Finlay exclaims, 'Miss, I've found something out.' There is an industriousness one rarely sees. I sit in this purpose built, modern room, watching the future, *now*. This is their

---

2 T. Sherrington, Reviewing lessons from the perspective of the least confident. Are you reaching them? *Teacherhead* [blog] (27 December 2021). Available at: https://teacherhead.com/2022/12/27/reviewing-lessons-from-the-perspective-of-the-least-confident-are-you-reaching-them/.

3 *Showbie* is an app used by teachers to assign, collect and review student work. See: https://www.showbie.com/.

world. A young teacher, completely on top of her craft, marshalling 28 pupils' learning using new technology efficiently. When she talks to them, she gives nothing away. She lives with the casual conversations going on around the room, because the pupils are all discussing the work. Her tone with them is insistent but kind.

I notice that some pupils are writing with their fingers on the iPads rather than typing answers. A second later, Maddie notices too. It's not what she wanted. She admits to the pupils she might have been unclear when she gave the instructions. It is always helpful when the teacher admits their own fallibility.

Her working of the room is expert. Maddie has excellent situational assessment. She has her radar on *all* the time, building an insight map across the class as to what learning is happening, pupil-by-pupil. When she is speaking to an individual, she does so from a position from where she can continue to scan the room.

Seamlessly, we move onto long division. They begin by reciting the times tables chorally, to well-known tunes:

3s – Row, Row, Row the Boat

4s – Away in a Manager

6s – Twinkle, Twinkle Little Star

7s – Bare Necessities

8s – Heads, Shoulders, Knees and Toes

9s – This Little Light of Mine

12s – If You're Happy and You Know It

It is impressive and they love it! Most importantly, the pupils know their times tables by heart. Maddie spent the last lesson ensuring the building blocks were in place for the pupils to learn the long-division process. She gives them the tools they need to become fluent – multi-plication grids last lesson and a heuristic this lesson.

She begins with the etymology of Dividend/Divisor, teaching the pupils the Latin-Anglo-Norman French-English historic roots of the word 'dividend', a word she asks the pupils to say out loud repeatedly, using robotic arm movements.

She tells them that she wants them to ask themselves two questions: 'What do you notice?' and 'What do you wonder?' She goes on: 'Long Division. It's brand new. I was practising it over the weekend and making some mistakes. You can help me with long division. We are going to practise, practise, practise. We'll go slowly, one step at a time.'

She begins with 575/23. The pupils all have a x 23 multiplication grid. She uses the visualiser, modelling the long division precisely. She has two big screens for the long/narrow classroom so that everyone can see what she is doing. She moves on to 390/15. The x 15 grid is used. She asks a bit more of the pupils. A textbook 'I do, we do, you do.' She gives nothing away. She has a pre-prepared heuristic on the left-hand side on a flip chart, to support everyone, but especially those with additional needs. 'Give me 10 when you have the answer.' She then sets the pupils questions to complete without the scaffolding. 351/39, 663/17, 552/23. 'You're going to do long division now. I'm excited! I'm going to come round and see what you're doing and showcase some good work.' She notices one boy who made an error carrying over and she helps him think it through expertly. She showcases Emily again. She celebrates doing 'our first one'. To support the subject-specific learning process, the use of the multiplication grids represent a lovely way to show the essential relationship between multiplication and division, and reminds one of the requirement to teach multiplication before division.

The lesson motors along, with pupils just getting on and Maddie coordinating all the moving parts. She is alert to everything. She has the ability to maintain running the room whilst providing targeted support for individual pupils. More showcasing. More examples, with gradated variations. She announces that they should, 'only put your hands up if you are completely stuck'. She works with the Smarties group, a scaffolded intervention for those that she feels need greater support. She is both adaptive and ambitious.

I look around the room. There is a big *Star Wars* figure on top of the bookshelf. She teaches with the door open. There is a poster, extolling the St Bart's Way: *B*e Honest; *A*im High; *R*espect Your environment; *T*reat everyone well. She suddenly says, 'Give me 10!' It's time for assembly and they are nearly late already. They stand behind chairs silently, but not quite silently enough. Despite the time pressure, she says, 'Let's try that again.' At a moment when it would have been easy not to have insisted on the perfect enactment of a pre-determined instruction, Maddie knows how important it is never to let those standards slip. Maddie shows real discipline.

Off to assembly. I join at the back with Miss Pilsworth, the teaching assistant. I remark on Maddie's energy. 'Oh, she's wonderful! She's like this every day.'

I come back briefly into the lesson after assembly and the energy levels are undiminished. Grammar terminology is flying round the room with unfailing accuracy. 'This is how I can use semi-colons to demonstrate the boundaries between independent clauses. Violet played violin; Leo played piano . . .' I take half-a-dozen pupils off to the conference room to see what they think of Miss Jacques.

What the pupils think

We don't have too long. 'She's nice. She treats us well. The lessons are fun.' I ask about the learning. 'I have a better understanding than last year. She explains things clearly.'

Another one speaks up. 'I think she's unique, passionate, friendly and respectful.' The last word piques my interest. I ask them to tell me more. 'Well, we get to give our own points of view. I was disagreeing with something she thought. She respected my point of view but still disagreed with me and Eloise. It was in geography. We said that the birth rate would go down if there was better health care and medication. Miss thought it would go up. In the end we agreed it might do either.' It's an impressive anecdote, in many ways, not the least of which is the precision with which it is recalled and the fact that the pupil feels confident to share it with me.

Indeed, they talk about feeling confident with Miss. 'She boosts our confidence. Even if what we say is wrong, Miss says things like, "I totally understand where you're coming from, but if you just think about …." It doesn't make us feel stupid and we all have a go at things in class now.' They tell me about how she chooses which people to help, how the *Smarties* get extra help in maths and the *Skittles* are more independent. They don't seem fazed at all by the identification of who needs extra support. I remember our sons sat on tables labelled by different fruits, as though that was going to disguise the fact that the tables were settled by prior attainment. Every pupil knew where they were in the academic pecking order, whilst the teachers tried to pretend there was no such ranking system. Best be transparent and base the allocation of support on equity.

Miss Jacques is fun, but still teaches them what they need to know, apparently! She is OK, as long as they have tried hard. 'I can go up to her about anything in Year 6. If I was to say I was nervous about my SATs she would help me.' SATs are on their mind already. That said, Lucy loved being a number in the number charts (I don't really understand what she means, but I go with it). And they also recall when she played football in high heels and they studied a painting called 'Jesus on the Tube'. Ordinary words like 'nice' are banned – they tell me – and she insists on extending their vocabulary. The Mayans are really interesting. They like having classroom jobs, because they make them feel useful.

According to them, Miss Jacques is: 'approachable, caring, helpful, unique, passionate, phenomenal, extraordinary'. And having watched Maddie teach, it is impossible to disagree.

IRL⁴: Maddie Jacques

John Tomsett (JT): How did you get into teaching, Maddie?

Maddie Jacques (MJ): I was raised in a household where teaching was a big thing. My mum works in a college and she supports children with special educational needs and disabilities (SEND). She'd always talked about how rewarding it was, and how you see the impact of all your efforts come to life. I think one of my secondary teachers really changed my view of education. I always struggled in school and she was awesome. She built such a good rapport with me. I remember coming into the classroom. She'd enquire about my weekend, she knew my name, she'd always ask me questions. It was the first time that I ever felt noticed, felt I'd been seen, and because of that, I wanted to make her proud. She inspired me to go to university at Nottingham to study history.

I got my first ever A in that class, ever, in secondary school. She took me aside. I remember it so clearly. She celebrated with me quietly in the corner, stressing how proud of me she was and I just felt so proud of myself in that moment. She'd built up my confidence. I felt I wanted to engage more, put my hand up more, ask questions if I didn't understand. She changed my view of school because I did really struggle, and I just wanted to be more like her.

When I graduated, I didn't know what to do with my life. My mum suggested I think about going into education because I'm quite a caring, chatty and enthusiastic person, so I got a job as a teaching assistant in an inner-city school in Nottingham. That was during COVID. I absolutely loved it. During COVID the teachers stayed at home, and us teaching assistants taught the key worker children in the classroom, and even though the size of the class was so small, it was the first time that I'd had the experience of leading in the classroom. I fell in love with it. Because it was such a small group, I was able to build a rapport with them, I got to know them well. I went from there to Teach First.

JT: **What was the training like with Teach First?**

MJ: Very intense. I think it's the best way to do it though. You're put in the classroom from day one, and you just learn as you go. At first that was quite challenging but it's just the nature of a school, things come up and you just have to deal with them. That experience was a whirlwind, but I think it was one of the best preparations I could have had; when I qualified I'd been in the classroom for two years, so I knew exactly what I'd be facing.

So, this is my first school as a qualified teacher. I was in Nottingham for two years' training and then I moved to this school last year.

JT: **What are your thoughts about how to teach?**

MJ: Building rapport with the children is really, really key to me, because I think that changed my outlook. Once I'd built a rapport with the teacher, I was far more willing and engaged and wanting to make them proud. So, that's really key to me, and that entry morning routine, greeting them on the door and checking in with them every day.

When I'm thinking of planning my lessons, I always think about their interests, no matter whether it's geography or maths I'm making sure I think, 'Oh, what did so and so tell me last week … they went to a theme park. Can I include that in my slides somehow linking it to maths?' so always – that's a big thing for me, trying to hook them in.

JT: **There's also a real level of expertise in your lessons. You pitch it high.**

MJ: Yes, I think I've learned that early on in my career. I think you set your expectations high to begin with, and you're really clear with them. I have my behaviour golden rules and I made that, I remember, with my initial tutor. She said to me, which has stuck with me, 'Be clear on your expectations. If you just have three rules for your classroom, then it's about communicating them to the children, and insisting upon them relentlessly.'

JT: **What are they, tell us the golden rules?**

MJ: They are listening (and no speaking) when the teacher's talking, no fiddling with equipment, and no getting out of your chairs. That's just stayed with me. I think the other lesson that came from that tutor was, don't be afraid of just pausing and waiting for the children to pay attention. It's completely OK to pause, and that silence from you signifies that whatever's going on is not acceptable, and it needs to stop.

JT: **The behaviour in your class is excellent. The maths was interesting today. You gave them the liberty to get it wrong in the way you framed it. Tell me about that?**

MJ: I think it's so important, especially with this cohort in my class this year. Many of them lack self-confidence, and a lot of them have really struggled with their maths last year. I've been trying to reinforce the message that mistake making is absolutely OK in this classroom, and showcasing pupils' work has really helped, because that's built their confidence massively. It's not only about celebrating good work, but when I spot a misconception, they show so much courage. They say, 'Yes, it's OK Miss Jacques, you can show this.' So, I show it with the child and work through what they could've done wrong, and we typically put our detective hats on and we think, we try and solve it together. So it's not me just saying, 'Oh, this is wrong.' It's the whole class working together, putting their detective hats on and thinking, 'Ooh, how could we improve that answer?' and that has taken a lot of work and a lot of reinforcement, but I don't think they're worried about making mistakes now, they just know it's part of the learning process.

JT: **When I interviewed the pupils, one of them said, 'She boosts our confidence, even if it's wrong. She'll say things like, "I totally understand where you're coming from." '**

MJ: Yes!

JT: **That's a phrase almost hardwired into your brain, isn't it?**

MJ: Yes, so I like to use that one, and 'Thank you for contributing.' I think it takes so much courage to even raise your hand and give an answer a go. I say to them, 'The main thing is that you are putting their best effort in.' It doesn't matter if they find it challenging or get answers wrong, or don't do as many questions as I'd set out. I just want them to put in 100% effort.

JT: **And they do, don't they?**

MJ: Yes, they do, they work really, really hard.

JT: **I didn't see any pupil off task, they're on point all the time.**

MJ: Yes, that maths test was hard. Yes, they did amazingly, and that was the first time they did long division, and that was a lot of modelling, but they all stuck with it.

JT: **You don't really need to use mini-whiteboards because you know who's understood and who hasn't, because you're round the room looking at their work all the time. Like the lad in the corner who carried an eight over instead of a sixteen ...**

MJ: Yes, I do circulate. That's been a real change for me. They've still got the whiteboards on their desk.

JT: **Used really well, mini-whiteboards are great.**

MJ: Yes, but typically if I've got one side of the room, my teaching assistant, Abby, will start checking the other side of the room. We've made a special note of who's got additional needs or pupil premium, so we know to check in straight away with those children and make sure they're getting the support they need. We review it at the end of every day anyway – who's struggled with that, who do I need to keep an eye on. So, we knew from yesterday's lesson that the girl Abby was supporting at the front really struggled, so that's why she was directed to sit with her and maybe stay with her that lesson.

JT: **Right, so you're relentlessly scanning the room – and making an assessment to help you decide what to do next.**

MJ: Yes.

JT: **Where do you learn that, because that's really sophisticated stuff?**

MJ: I'd say the WalkThrus coaching has been really effective. In our staff meetings and continuing professional development (CPD), Dan always ensures that our coaches and team leaders act out the techniques with us, so we get the experience of seeing it in action from someone who's very experienced and knows the steps really well. In Teach First, *Teach Like A Champion* by Doug Lemov was a big influence; we went through certain techniques, and lots of them have stuck with me.[5] The EEF research was also a big thing in the Teach First training scheme.

---

5   D. Lemov, *Teach Like a Champion 3.0: 63 Techniques that Put Students on the Path to College* (San Francisco, CA: Jossey-Bass, 2021).

JT: **And all that has stuck with you, because you seem incredibly well trained. You're only in your fourth year of teaching.**

MJ: Yes. This school has massively boosted my confidence. I'm a completely different teacher to the one I was in Nottingham.

JT: **Right, tell me about that.**

MJ: Dan and Rachel (the deputy head teacher) visit my classroom quite often, and they are superb at feedback. Rachel will always list things that I'm doing well and how to improve, and then she comes to see that I'm using those techniques that she suggested. They've just got such an open-door policy and I just feel happier here. That's influenced the energy I bring into the classroom. When you've done something well, they acknowledge it and they praise it, and I think it's noticed, you're noticed here, and everyone's valued. It goes such a long way when you've got a supportive senior leadership team.

JT: **How do you sustain yourself with that level of energy?**

MJ: I think that's just me. Yes, I've always been that way. I just love what I do, and I think that really comes across in how I teach. I absolutely thrive on their joy and seeing their light bulb moments, and their passion for learning, I just love it. I wouldn't say I'm doing anything in particular to keep those energy levels high. I think it's just my enthusiasm.

I love teaching Year 6. I think they're a lot more independent. I think a really good lesson that I learned teaching Years 3 and 4 is to break down instructions really clearly and carefully. I've taken that up to Year 6 with me, and if it's a lot of instructions, then I like to say, 'When I say go, I'd like you to do three things, number one, number two, number three', and then I ask them, 'What's number one, what's number two, what's number three.' Years 3 and 4 really needed that precision . . . I'm so glad I learnt it because it's enabled me to adopt that approach in Years 5 and 6.

Similarly with the phonics teaching and breaking down words, I've still got children that really struggle with their spelling and breaking down challenging words, but that phonics knowledge that I picked up and brought up to Year 6 has been really useful. I like the challenge, the stretch and being able to push the Year 6s and draw on the learning that they've done beforehand, and link new material to everything that they've learned.

JT: **They know their times tables! They love the songs …**

MJ: Oh my goodness! We had some parent feedback that was amazing. She said her daughter didn't know her times tables last year, and since coming into the class she said, 'I cannot believe that she knows her six, sevens, eights and nines now.' I just think it's such a good way to recall them quickly and it works. Yes, I love doing the songs.

JT: **Were you faking it or are you less sure about your maths?**

MJ: Yes, that was the first time that I've done long division with a class, ever, because I haven't taught it in Years 3 and 4. I plan the maths. Usually I am more confident with my maths but today especially … I wanted them to know how I felt about it, that I've gone through it, building my confidence. I was trying to reassure them.

JT: **Reciprocal vulnerability is really powerful. That's what you were showing. It helped them relax.**

MJ: Yes, when they got there, eventually, because it's so many steps, it was lovely to see their smiles.

JT: **I really liked the way you had the heuristic on the steps on the board, when you were modelling the process.**

MJ: Yes, I'll put that on my wall later so they can refer back to it in lessons to come.

JT: **What are you working on at the moment in your teaching?**

MJ: I'm working on my feedback, addressing the pupils' misconceptions. It's just so useful in addressing them there and then, in the lesson, instead of taking books in at the end and realising, 'Oh, they didn't get that!' I'm trying to be more proactive in getting them thinking about how to improve and editing their work in the moment, and giving verbal feedback. Before, I'd mark their books but find that it wasn't helping them improve. Having that conversation with them there and then is much more effective. Abby's supporting me. She's going round and giving verbal feedback as well, so they're editing as they go.

This is the first year that I have led a subject, which is history, which I'm excited about. I've been doing a lot of work looking at the curriculum, looking at progression, thinking about my own subject knowledge and building that, and looking at ways to improve what we offer here at St Bart's. I'm building my confidence in presenting to the staff, because that's not something I've ever had to do before.

JT: **So, when do you go off-piste?**

MJ: I tend to do that quite a lot! Especially with this cohort, to cater to their needs, and I know a lot of them struggle with vocabulary and science. We were looking at micro-organisms. They found that really hard, the idea that you couldn't see it. We were talking about fungi and how it has a fruiting body, but the fruiting body's not the micro-organism, because you can't see the micro-organism, the fruiting body is just the mould. They really couldn't understand that. So, we did this demonstration and, honestly, their faces just dropped. I showed them a tiny token. I said, 'OK, right, this is the micro-organism, and you're not going to be able to see it at the moment.' Then one of the boys, Harry, laid down and pretended to be a piece of bread. I put the token on top of him. I said, 'This is the micro-organism and you're not going to see it because Josh will be the fruiting body, which is the mould that's growing off it.' So, he leant over Harry, and the pupils could not believe that I was asking Josh to become a piece of mould. At the end of it, I said, 'OK, Josh, here's the bread. Which part is the micro-organism?'

'Oh, we can't see the micro-organism, Miss Jacques, because it's micro, and Josh is the fruiting body. We can see the fruiting body, but we can't see the micro-organism.' I was so, so pleased because they got it, eventually, and they were using that terminology correctly. I love doing that type of thing.

JT: **Do they love it?**

MJ: Yes, they do. We did the same in maths with place value charts. I got them all to be the numbers and we went out and demonstrated it physically with them representing numbers in different place values.

JT: **Oh, Lucy loves that, the first thing she said when I asked what they liked about being taught by you was being the numbers, 'We're the whiteboard, we become the number charts'.**

MJ: I'm really pleased. This school has a very specific lesson design, but I love putting my own take on it. It is a very modern school and using the iPads more in teaching has been a real challenge for me, but they're such a good resource for feedback and modelling, in celebrating the children's work, so I just think, 'How am I going to make that technology work for me?'

What I have done, which they absolutely love, is bring my visualiser to face them. The desk is at a bit of an awkward angle where I used to sit, and I didn't like the idea of my back being to them. There was a moment at the start of term where I'd been modelling for ten minutes about how I was going to do this beautiful artwork, and then I turned around and the board was off. I said, 'Why didn't you tell me?'

'Oh, because we don't want to interrupt you, we were being really polite', and they all had their hands up and it was so lovely, but since then, I've been moving the visualiser towards them. Those ones at the front are there for a reason. They struggle with their attention so it's good to sit with them at a desk, and they can see me doing it in real life.

JT: **Just to finish, what do you think your strengths are as a teacher?**

MJ: I'm energetic, and I love to bring the learning to life. Thinking about my history teacher back in secondary school, she made the learning so fun and memorable. I remember all these crazy statistics because she'd tell us anecdotes to go with them, and I like to bring that into the classroom too. I try to make the learning stick through bringing all that energy and all those jokes and stories – and the singing – into the classroom. I think that's what makes my teaching, hopefully, so effective. I suppose I'd also say that I'm quite empathetic, and a good communicator. I think mum is like that through her work in supporting children with SEND and I think, as I said, it's so important that I build that rapport and greet them in the mornings and check in with them, like with Emily. I could tell she had frozen, and I think it's having that empathy, knowing when to push and when not to push. I think it's coming back and building that confidence up again and making sure she feels comfortable. How to communicate effectively with them is a real thing for me, yes.

JT: **I'd say you'd know every child in that class. And you've got your radar on all the time. You're a very intentional teacher, in terms of 'I know why I'm doing this, I'm responding to that.' You're responding in the moment.**

MJ: Yes, I have those children at the forefront of my mind who I think will need support with this or that, or I know they struggled with that thing yesterday. So, I'll go to them.

JT: **You can see it all going on. Seeing your brain whirring. That's really impressive.**

MJ: Oh, thank you.

JT: **It's been an absolute joy.**

Testimonials

'We have all been on a learning journey this last year and Miss Jacques has blown us away with her commitment and dedication to ensuring each child thrives. She cares so much, and the children feel that. She has their trust. Miss Jacques has stood by a child who has at times found school and the world around her rocky and she has walked beside her, guiding her through. It is a huge achievement to get Kerri to where she is currently, and it's important to us as a family that Miss Jacques is recognised for her huge and significant contribution to Kerri's development, confidence and happiness at school. Miss Jacques is an exceptional teacher, but she is also a remarkable leader, and I have no doubts that, even though she's just getting started and will rise very high in everything she chooses to do.'

'Ashley has loved having you as his teacher and we couldn't be happier!'

'Jack has grown and been stretched in all the right areas. Reading his report, it is clear that you know our son so well and all the quirks that make him, him! Maddie, you are brilliant!'

So, what can we learn from Maddie Jacques?

I don't do sycophancy. Never have. But I do rate Dan Oakes, highly. I have a deep respect for the way he runs St Bart's. So, for him to nominate Maddie Jacques for this book, means a great deal. The thing is, everything I know or have seen of Maddie merely confirms that Dan's nomination was warranted.

One thing that strikes me about Maddie is her thoroughness. She doesn't take short cuts. She knows that to be the teacher she aspires to be takes huge commitment and effort. She makes teaching look effortless because of the effort she puts into her work. She brings an energy to the room that is relentless. Forget the iPads, Maddie is the greatest learning resource for those Year 6 pupils!

I wrote down several times when I was watching Maddie, 'This is modern teaching.' This is in a modern building, pupils are using the iPads, this is a young, modern teacher who's been trained recently. She has traits that you'd have found in the very best teachers of the last two millennia, but she's also forward-looking. You didn't have to tell me that Doug Lemov has been an influence on Maddie, because it's completely clear when watching her teach. But some people criticise the Lemov stuff because, according to them, it's robotic teaching by numbers, but Maddie has lost nothing of her individuality. The structure and discipline of her lessons is 100% Lemov, *which allows her to go off-piste*. It's not binary. She demonstrates the perfect combination of the two ends of a spectrum.

And finally, Maddie's classroom is a cynicism-free zone. What delighted me about watching Maddie teach is seeing someone at the very beginning of her career, full of the joy of the job. It is always worth remembering what an energy-fuelling experience it is to spend one's working life with young people, full of wonder about the world. One of the first A level texts I taught was Shakespeare's *The Winter's Tale*. In the first scene, we hear reports of Mamillius, the young prince, who 'makes old hearts fresh'. I felt the same being in Maddie's room, inspired by her, as a teacher at the very end of his career, passing the baton on.

Maddie Jacques' pupils' progress and achievement data

As she has only been with the school a year, Maddie doesn't have too much data to share, but what there is hugely promising:

Y4 multiplication check

- 88% passed
- 47% achieved full marks

End of year outcomes

- Reading: 58% EX, 26% GDS
- Writing: 71% EX, 6% GDS
- Maths: 65% EX, 16% GDS

Josh Pike is a Year 6 teacher and mathematics lead at Old Fletton Primary School, Peterborough.

The school leadership's view, part 1

Expert deputy head teachers who can step up to run the school when the boss takes on system-wide responsibilities are priceless. Neal Dickson is such a man. He runs Old Fletton Primary School three days a week. It's early morning and he's got to ensure the school is ready for the day, but has kindly taken time out to talk to me about his colleague, Josh Pike, a teacher I hold in particularly high regard, having seen him teach a number of times.

Neal made some notes the night before and he now takes me through the characteristics demonstrated by Josh that make him a truly great teacher. The first is dedication to maximising the children's learning. 'Josh has such high expectations. He believes every pupil can achieve great things.' Having seen him teach on previous visits, I know that Josh's preparation and planning are spot on.

Josh uses data forensically. 'Josh plans what he does in the next lesson – even what his next steps will be *mid*-lesson – according to what he gleans about what the pupils have understood – to ensure he is taking all of them with him. He spots misconceptions and addresses them in the moment.' It's true. In adaptive teaching terms, I'm not sure I have ever seen a teacher as adroit as Josh. He will never be guilty of the crime of collecting assessment information but doing nothing with it. He knows what is going on in the minds of the pupils both in the literal and metaphorical 'corners of the classroom'.

Josh talks enthusiastically about his work all the time. 'He is working on his craft relentlessly', says Neal. 'He has led mathematics brilliantly. Best results ever this summer. Once he begins speaking about teaching and learning, he's hard to stop!' I know this also to be true.

Lastly, Neal says that Josh cares deeply for the children and their life chances. When you see him in action, this point is so obviously on the money. 'He cares about the work and it kind of rubs off on them. He cares so they do too.' Seeing Old Fletton's pupils launched into a promising future when they leave the school gates is Josh's driving force.

Neal elaborates. He feels Josh's dedication to improving his practice derives from his footballing background. He played premiership football as a teenager and represented his country. He was born in Port Talbot. Having played sport in an elite environment, Neal feels that Josh is used to responding to feedback. 'He is a great example of the importance of the teacher's demeanor in the classroom. He is such an enthusiast, the pupils feel obliged to work hard, for fear of letting him down', says Neal.

The day needs to get underway. It's time to go and watch Josh teach.

———————————

Teaching

We arrive at Josh's classroom and Neal bids farewell. Josh is chatting to the pupils as they arrive. I listen to one half of a conversation. 'How's that ankle of yours? … You spent the evening in A&E and got home at 2:45 in the morning … but you're still here today! That's amazing!' The pupil is still here today because Josh has created something that is worth coming in for. His organisation is second to none. He ensures they all have mini-whiteboards, pens and cloths. The pupils move around, preparing themselves under his direction. There's a starter task on the board. Everyone knows what they're up to. Josh takes the register. The politeness is striking.

'Good morning, Kian.'

'Good morning.'

Today they have their second lesson on worded problems. There are five adults in the room. Josh and I, two teaching assistants and Simone, Josh's co-teacher of the other Year 6 class who hasn't taught this maths lesson before and is watching how Josh does it.

He begins by praising them. They have completed a diagnostic test on ratio and have done well enough. He ensures that those who struggled don't feel down about it. 'We're only in November and you've done amazingly well considering we've got until May to get this nailed. Some of you might have felt frustrated that you couldn't do the pre-assessment as well as you wanted to, but there's no worries. Some of you found the algebra hard. My job is to teach how to solve algebra questions in a way that you'll understand. We're going to build your resilience, with some deeper, harder thinking. Everyone will get to the independent questions today. And then you'll feel much more confident.' His tone is upbeat, enthusiastic, confident and reassuring.

What I hadn't realised, because it is so understated, is that Josh has already re-arranged the seating so that the pupils are in three groups –

targeted, backwards fading,[1] independent – depending upon how they did in the pre-assessment. When I saw him teach this lesson a year ago to last year's Year 6, it worked a treat.

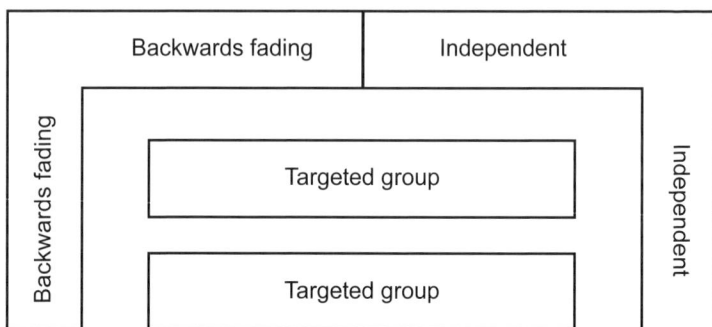

```
+----------------------------------------------------------------+
|                                |                               |
|        Backwards fading        |         Independent           |
|                                |                               |
|  B  +------------------------------------------------------+ I |
|  a  |                                                      | n |
|  c  |             +----------------------------+           | d |
|  k  |             |       Targeted group       |           | e |
|  w  |             +----------------------------+           | p |
|  a  |                                                      | e |
|  r  |           +------------------------------+           | n |
|  d  |           |        Targeted group        |           | d |
|  s  |           +------------------------------+           | e |
|     |                                                      | n |
|  f  +------------------------------------------------------+ t |
|  a  |                                                      |   |
+----------------------------------------------------------------+
```

He begins with the whole class and models the most basic ratio problem, using the whole-part bar method.

$$70 + 30 = 100$$

He has asked the pupils to complete the question using the bar model on their mini-whiteboards. He is sure to make them turn their boards over so that no one can copy and then he is regimented in his 3-2-1-show routine. He asks one of the pupils to explain what she was thinking to get her answer. She replies with utter confidence, including the line, 'they were proportionate to each other 7:3'.

Josh beams, 'I couldn't have explained it better myself.' The pupils have amazing oral fluency. They have the specialist vocabulary and then they have the confidence to speak out loud and clear as they articulate their thinking. 'Soon you'll have all the tools in your toolkit to solve problems when they get harder.' He varies the next problem:

$$60 + \underline{\hspace{1cm}} = 100$$

---

1   'Backwards fading' in maths refers to a teaching method where the students are initially provided with a fully solved problem, then, moving backwards from the final step of the solution, each stage is removed, one at a time, eventually requiring the students to fill in the missing parts themselves, thus moving from a completely guided example to independent problem solving; it's a way to scaffold learning by gradually decreasing support as students gain confidence.

It is solved correctly by the majority. A couple of pupils in the front row are not quite so sure. He reviews the process of solving a ratio problem using a worded question about hats and scarves at different prices and how much change the customer would receive from a £20 note. Old school stuff, taught with real rigour. He reminds them that the toolkit is from Year 4. He moves to the flip chart and talks through his thinking, asking question after question. His clarity of explanation is exceptional. He highlights to them that decimal places are notated by a full stop not a comma. I love that level of pedantry. At this point, he gives everyone a booklet of ratio problems to solve, which are gradated in difficulty. He indicates where each group should begin and then proceeds to work with the pupils in the two rows immediately in front of him, which is comprised of his targeted group. The independents and the backward faders crack on in perfect silence.

Josh is one of the best builders of situational assessment I have ever seen. His radar is permanently switched on. He analyses the level of understanding across the room, pupil by pupil. A pupil's body language is enough for Josh to tell whether they are understanding what is going on conceptually or whether they need a little help. He introduces a rule: 'Do I have a total? If Yes, it's usually subtract; if No, it's likely to be add.' He stretches their thinking. He bounces questioning around the front two rows. 'I think this is an excellent answer. Have a think about why I might think that, Eliza.'

As the targeted group attempt a question on their own, he checks in on the backward faders. It's working. A boy asks about a question he is unsure of. It turns out he is on the right track. 'Shall I just crack on Sir?' Josh reassures him he can. Many of them are onto the independent questions. He demonstrates genuine delight. He is excited by their precision.

With the targeted group we have completely worked examples with expert thinking made visible and then recorded by the pupils. At one point he surveys his bellwether pupils, the ones who may struggle most; if they can solve a problem, he can assume that everyone else in the class will be able to. He looks at their answers and quickly circulates the targeted group. He questions them … why? why? why? He is happy. No point in deconstructing that answer – it would waste time because they have all got it right – and so he moves on to the next variation, which is a more challenging problem. He checks the other two groups again. They are fine. He briefly mentors Simone. His energy levels are high. He is as present as he can possibly be.

With 10 minutes of the lesson left, we have 15 pupils working under their own steam on independent tasks, there are 13 working on backwards fading tasks within the targeted group, overseen by the teaching assistants, and two pupils with Josh. He says to them, 'Show me a bar model with £15,000. Where will I put this in my bar model?'

'In the part', comes the reply.

'Go on', Josh says, 'you do know the method.'

By the end of the lesson, every single pupil has moved on. The two he was working with at the end of the lesson haven't quite reached the independent task, but they have made significant progress. It is in the moment, adaptive teaching made real.

When I watch the literacy lesson after the break, the same features of his teaching are apparent. He immediately moves them round the room. They are trained to be self-starters. Some crack on, some are in his small group – these are slightly different characters from the maths-targeted group. The pupils' behaviour means he can teach like this. They are exemplary scholars. The independence and industry levels are remarkable. Josh finishes by praising them and reminding them how much progress they have made. His enthusiasm for the work is as bright as it was when I first entered the room two hours earlier. He reminds me of a car battery that is charged up when the vehicle is in motion. The more he moves around the room, helping his pupils, the more energetic he grows.

———————————

What the pupils think

I have ten Year 6 pupils in front of me and they want to make Mr Pike proud. When I ask them to discuss what makes him a truly great teacher their chatter is impressive. This is a school where pupils have superb oracy skills.

Lilly and Alana think he makes things fun. They loved the day off-timetable when they wrote about mythical creatures, with the help of images that they were able to create using AI. Tyler, on the other hand, appreciates how much he learns and how he is allowed to spend time in the middle area getting extra help from Mr Pike. Lilly agrees, 'I like the way Mr Pike breaks down maths problems into smaller chunks and makes it easier to learn.' They had a rap, apparently, about long division, which they loved!

What comes through so strongly is that they know how much Josh wants them to do well. 'We like the little groups', says one of them. I pursue that further.

'How do you feel about swapping seats all the time? Pupils usually want to sit in the same place next to their friends', I say. The response is universal.

'It's good', pipes up one of them. 'We know why he's doing it. Like with the word problems today. I can do them now. He broke it down for us with the bar models and I properly understand the questions.' I express mock surprise. To a pupil they reassure me that it works. 'We know he just wants the best for us, for all of us to do well. The only time he gets mad is if we don't try. Which hardly ever happens because we do.' I leave it, satisfied that from a social point of view, Josh's approach is welcomed, not imposed. Their understanding of his motives is impressive.

It's not all work though. 'We have lots of fun. He asks us about what we do out of school and really takes an interest in us', says Kian. 'I love Mr Pike because he helps me with mapping out my timeline on my writing, and then I can ask him about the football. He always asks about how the Posh got on (The Posh is the nickname for Peterborough United FC). He finds time to find out about us.' This seems important to these young people.

I finish by asking them for a single word to describe Mr Pike: spectacular, amazing, fair, caring, kind, funny, considerate and calm. Knowing Josh as I do, it's hard to argue against their choices. 'Spectacular' made me chuckle.

The school leadership's view, part 2

Sarah Levy is the head teacher at Old Fletton. She has the ability to fix your eye and hold your gaze while destroying your argument, smiling all the while. It is quite unnerving.

We meet briefly during her busy day to talk about Josh. The evening before, Sarah tells me, she had sat down and thought about her colleague and why he might be considered a truly great teacher. 'He rolls the "dice" every day', she says. 'He is Dedicated; he has Impact; he Cares about the children; he is Energetic and Engaging Every day. And I use the acrostic, because he rolls the *dice*, he takes chances. Not off-the-wall wackiness. No, I mean he sets challenging tasks. He is alive to opportunities. He's not constrained by a bought-in scheme. He has a grasp of the broader picture and knows the part he is playing in our pupils' bigger life journey.' I nod along, interjecting merely to say that what she says chimes precisely with what the pupils had told me about Josh.

To teach as impactfully as Josh would be almost impossible without knowing the evidence about what might work best when it comes to teaching in a way that maximises learning. Sarah tells me that 'Josh knows all the Hattie research, he is open to learning all the time. I think it might be something to do with his sporting background. But he brings his own approach to the work. He rejected Shanghai maths. He takes an approach to teaching maths that brings everyone along with him. It's a form of mastery maths, for sure, but he genuinely makes it happen in his unique way. The children feel his investment in them. And we've invested in him. I coached him for 18 months. We both learned and laughed a lot!' I just listen. Everything she says confirms what I have seen, heard and got to know about Josh Pike.

As we reflect, I have the *temerity* to mention the importance of value-added data! I point out that since Josh has led mathematics at Old Fletton, the pupils' progress and attainment measures have improved significantly. In summer 2024 Old Fletton's expected progress figure for mathematics was over 80%, their best in a number of years. We end up arguing about whether pupil progress data are a good indicator of teacher quality. With the deepest irony, I find myself defending Rob Coe's quest to find a single, numeric pupil progress data point! Sarah outright refuses to consider it for a moment. From her point of view, the data are utterly irrelevant when it comes to talking about truly great teachers. She is sure Josh Pike fits the bill, however.

I suggest that Rob Coe's search for a single, numeric pupil progress data point and my contention that great results are a by-product of all the things that Sarah has just said of Josh, are just two sides of the same coin. Sarah looks at me intensely. I begin mumbling. She cut in: 'It's the *dice*! You're not always going to get a double-six, but truly great teachers roll the dice every day. And that is what Josh does … Those measures are limitations. People are treating teaching and learning like it's a science. It's an art. There might be effective ways of teaching that have an evidence-base behind them, but it's still an art.' I try to explain a bit further, and in my notebook is a rubbish attempt at drawing scatter graphs of value-added measures of teacher performance. But her stare defeats me.

The thing is, the proof of the proverbial pudding is in the eating. Sarah's school is a restless school. She is a woman after my own heart in that she is permanently discontented with standards. I found Old Fletton a wonderful place to teach and learn. Ironically, I only met her and Josh and the rest of the Old Fletton team because I was helping them with the *WalkThrus* programme, which is based on Barak Rosenshine's research paper, *The Principles of Instruction!*[2] I think, on reflection, that her argument is my argument, in that the humanity of the teaching process is unquantifiable. There is no number to measure how well a teacher like Josh connects with children so that they make tremendous progress, irrespective of the data targets, and maximise their life chances. It reminded me of a line from a long-forgotten blog post by Tom Bennett, where he wrote, 'You know what my expectation of my children is? An A. For everyone. That's the target I set myself, and if I don't get it, well, I try again next year. I don't cry into my coffee, I just try again.'[3] At Old Fletton, teachers like Josh just roll the dice again and again and again. Every. Single. Day.

IRL: Josh Pike

John Tomsett (JT): How did you get into teaching?

Josh Pike (JP): I came from a sporting background. Growing up I don't ever remember thinking, 'I'd like to be a teacher', or anything like that. It was always football, football, football. Then having got released from doing it full-time things started to change, and I hit that, 'What next?' moment. Is it university and then find a career, or is it continue to chase the footballing dream? I was 19 at that time. I decided to go to university. But I wondered how I could still stay in football. I thought I might do my coaching badges so I stayed involved in some way. I still didn't have teaching necessarily in mind.

---

2   B. Rosenshine, Principles of instruction: research-based strategies that all teachers should know, *American Educator*, 38(1) (2012): 12–19, 39. Available at: https://www.aft.org/sites/default/files/periodicals/Rosenshine.pdf.

3   T. Bennett, This engine runs on hope: why schools need to defy the destiny of data, *Tom Bennett's School Report* [blog] (24 November 2012). Available at: https://behaviourguru.blogspot.com/2012/11/this-engine-runs-on-hope-why-schools.html.

At university I studied sports coaching. I did a BSc in sports coaching. In the second year of the sports coaching degree, we had an internship with students delivering PE lessons in primary schools. Then, in the summer holidays back home, I delivered half-term football camps. I went around the primary schools and started to get a feel for working with the children. I think what stood out to me was the progress that they were making, even though it's in a fun environment and in a sporting world. I could see the children developing and getting better and better each week.

JT: **Did you find that satisfying?**

JP: For sure. I felt like I had a purpose at that point, which I hadn't necessarily had all the way through football because it was always, 'You need to become better at this', or 'You're not in the squad, you're not this.' It was at times a very negative experience, because you were always trying to get into that first team and I was never a first-choice first-team player at Swansea. With coaching I felt like I had a purpose. I could see the children developing so much in such a short space of time. I then thought, 'Actually, this could be something that I would quite like to do.' Then, amongst all of that I was getting feedback from my tutors on my course, and from the teachers at the primary schools that I was working in, saying, 'You need to think about teaching.'

So then, during my second year of university, I said to myself, 'OK, I'm going into teaching. I want to do this full-time. This is my career.' I went back and did my maths and English knowledge skills tests and so on. The thing is, I was taken out of school quite early on in Year 10 and Year 11 because I was playing for the Wales under-16s at the time, so I was going around the world. We had schoolwork to do in the evenings. We had an education officer with us on those trips, but I wasn't the kind of student that was an A-star, high-flyer. But I'm a very driven person. I'm somebody who's always looking at the next step.

I'm very competitive – with myself, not necessarily the outside world. I'm obsessed with being better myself, as cliched as that sounds, and that's in anything I do. That could even be washing the dishes. Whether that's come from a sporting background or something else, I don't know, but that's been me from a young age. I've always wanted to get better. I've always been open to feedback.

JT: **How long have you been teaching?**

JP: I'm in my eighth year of teaching, I believe! I had three years at university, and I came to Old Fletton Primary School in 2016. I did my postgraduate diploma in education (PGCE) training here via Teach East. They were the only initial teacher training (ITT) provider who would accept me as I don't have A levels. I've got general certificates of education (GCSEs), a Business and Technology Education Council (BTEC) qualification and I've got a degree. I got a first-class degree, and it's only Teach East that gave me what I'd probably call a lifeline and said, 'Yes, absolutely. Come on the course.' You know Port Talbot. That was my childhood, growing up in what was a deprived area. Mum and dad have always worked, they're working-class. Having been taken out of school so early, my biggest message is that there are other avenues into teaching, not just the typical GCSE, A level, university, PGCE. It's been hard work, of course it has.

JT: **You've got a deep investment in teaching, haven't you? You made that incredibly intentional decision to do this, and your drive to be as good as you can be comes from that competitive stance.**

JP: Yes, 100%. I'm a very reflective person. Lesson to lesson, even mid-lesson.

JT: **You can see that. You're reflecting and tweaking what you do all the time.**

JP: Yes, and that's a big part of who I am as a person in terms of that drive to be better. I knew that I had the ability to build positive relationships with the children, to be enthusiastic about what I do because I love having an impact on them. That said, I remember sitting outside the Old Fletton school gates on interview day and saying, 'I don't want to do this. I don't want to go in. I'm not doing it, I'm going to go and chase football again.' I had that doubt in myself, even though I knew it was what I really wanted. I still doubted myself, and I think that stemmed from not being good enough in the footballing world. Anyway, I came in and it happened that Sarah was working with Teach East at the time and she interviewed me. I found out later that Sarah said that since she hosted the interviews, she got to pick which students she wanted here. She said I was to come here on placement, so I came here on placement, and I haven't looked back.

I try not to be affected by the outside noise. I try not to be affected by anybody else. I do have some elements of self-doubt, but I try to keep positive and ask, 'What's the next thing that I need to do to make myself better than I was yesterday?'

JT: **Just thinking about the work we've done here, watching you teach, I've not seen a better exemplification of core techniques. Your use of mini-whiteboards was exemplary. Think-Pair-Share and cold-call were spot on. The Signal-Pause-Insist routine was textbook. Your attention to detail is impressive.**

JP: Thank you. We have been working on developing these core techniques as a whole school. We have been inviting Neal in for coaching sessions and that has really helped develop my teaching practice. Coming from a sporting background, I was always given feedback. Your coach is always on the pitch alongside you and if you're playing left back he'll say, 'Right, I need you to make an underlapping run, or an overlap.' You always get that live feedback, and I think I thrive off that, whether it's from Neal in a coaching session, or my teaching assistant, or whether it's from a pupil, whether it's from the boss. It doesn't matter who it is. I look for that contribution, because then I can act on it quickly. That's part of the reflective phase, where I take what I've learned one day and I think, 'That worked well. I could tweak it by doing this'. I'm then ready for the next day.

JT: **I think you're the best adaptive teacher I've ever seen, bar none. I love the flexible seating. I asked your pupils how they felt about moving seats so often. Most children want to sit next to their mates and hate being moved, but your pupils absolutely get it. 'If we're struggling a bit we have a bit more time with Mr Pike, or we go out into the middle area and he'll come and help us.' I loved that moment today when the girl ended up with 7,000 as the answer, and you had your radar on and you just moved her – there was no stigma to it – to the end of the row, and you could just work with her and another pupil who needed most help. You'd gone from a class of 30 to a class of 13 to a class of two, where everybody else is liberated to get on with their own work … and they certainly did!**

JP: Yes, and they were all working at the same level by the end of the lesson. They were all on the same task, and I think that's important.

JT: **You're diagnostic. Sometimes you use mini-whiteboards to see what's going on, but other times you don't need to because you've been around the room and you know exactly who's doing what.**

JP: It's about the positive relationships we build with the children. If the children can trust that I am trying to get the best from them, and I can create an environment where they don't feel threatened, where mistakes are OK, it is easy to move the children around and give the feedback required for them to make progress.

JT: **That's how they feel.**

JP: That's how I want them to feel. That's taken a lot of work, because it is quite a threatening thing, standing up and coming to the front to work with me, but I think that's come from the trust that I build between me and the children. It's not to exclude them from their peers at all. It's just, 'Right, quick five minutes. I know what the gap is because I've done my assessment for learning, therefore you can come with me.' I think it's them feeling and knowing that they're not different from their peers. They're going to be doing the same work as their peers, right there, live in the lesson. It's about them knowing that these five minutes are gold and are going to enable them to be where they want to be.'

JT: **Live, in-the-moment feedback is absolute gold.**

JP: Of course it is, and I think giving live feedback and being present for all those children and available to give them attention there and then is the most important thing, I would argue.

JT: **I've certainly seen that in maths. How does that work in other subjects?**

JP: I talk a lot about Christine Counsell's hinterland.[4] That's something I've been working on over the last couple of years, particularly in subjects like history and RE and geography. I think pre-teaching for some learners is crucial, because that allows them to learn the subject-specific vocabulary. Let's say we're looking at the ancient city of Babylon, for example, and we're looking at the gates of Ishtar, and the prophets … I could stand there at the front of the room and lead off, 'Right, these

---

4 C. Counsell, Senior curriculum leadership 1: the indirect manifestation of knowledge: (A) curriculum as narrative, *The Dignity of the Thing* [blog] (7 April 2018). Available at: https://thedignityofthethingblog.wordpress.com/2018/04/07/senior-curriculum-leadership-1-the-indirect-manifestation-of-knowledge-a-curriculum-as-narrative/.

are the facts, these are the facts, these are the facts.' I work so hard on trying to make that become a story, so they're getting the core knowledge from the narrative, and the hinterland as well to a certain degree. I think that's particularly helped my lower-attaining children retain the knowledge, and their understanding is enhanced by the narrative, as opposed to just looking at a smart board. Whatever I'm teaching, one thing that I try to do is pre-assess the vocabulary, so children who need extra help with the vocabulary are able to access the learning in the first instance. After that it's how I tell that story and the next thing I'll think about is the activities that follow. Again, it's about knowing my children. It's knowing who needs what. It might be that all the children are going to label parts of a mountain. All of my children at the end of that lesson are going to be able to label the features of a mountain. Within that framework, one child might need the key vocabulary next to them, or they might need a cloze activity, whereas somebody else might go straight to the independent task of, 'Here's a blank mountain. You draw it, you annotate it according to what you've just been taught.' Importantly, it's still about knowing the children, knowing how they struggle, and knowing what they need to be able to access the work.

JT: **In the moment.**

JP: Absolutely, and it's also important that the children know that the expectation is that they get to the independent work. You're not just going to be pre-taught the vocabulary and that's fine. You're also going to hear the story, the same as everybody else. Yes, you might have a word bank. Yes, you might have a cloze activity. Yes, you might have another scaffold, but ultimately, all of those things are what are needed for you to be able to access the same learning as everyone else.

JP: **You do that in every subject.**

JT: I try to, as much as humanly possible.

JP: So, does your planning take a lot of time?

JP: Back in the day I would think, 'The planning has to look pretty. The planning has to be organised in this certain way.' Because I felt it needed to be perfection in that regard.

JT: Almost obsessive.

JP: Absolutely, I've come to learn through my time here, that, yes, the lesson needs to be engaging, but the number-one resource in the classroom is me, and the more I've come to realise that my being present, knowing my children, having the relationships, that's more important than any fancy font or any word art. For me, when I'm planning, I don't necessarily put the time into making it look pretty. I think, 'What is the core knowledge that the children need to know? How am I going to embed that core knowledge?' It might be through a narrative, or through breaking a maths journey down into small, sequential steps, and then knowing what my children need to be able to learn. I decide what I want them to learn and how best to teach them. Finally, I'll check they've got it. The planning, I promise, takes no longer. The best resource in the classroom is myself, and the moment I learned that and invested in myself, the more the pupils learned.

I spoke to teachers in quite some depth over the last few years about planning, and around how we can make maths more enjoyable for the children, and break the stigma of 'maths being hard', because maths isn't hard. It's beautiful actually, if you get your plans right. If you know your children, you get the planning right and you teach it in the best possible way, there's nothing else that can beat that. Where I see lessons at their best is where thought has gone into the fine details at the planning stage. We came away from the bought-in White Rose mathematics scheme six years ago, and then we looked at the Shanghai model of maths mastery, but we resisted it because I said, 'The more we use bought-in schemes for maths, the more the teachers are relying on turning up and clicking a button.' I want maths to be far more than that. We made a massive change and said, 'We will plan our maths from scratch.' Absolutely use White Rose as representations, as raw materials, use your classroom sequence if you need to, use the National Centre for Excellence in the Teaching of Mathematics (NCETM) guidance. Use the resources that are out there. They are paid professionals that create these resources. What I don't want you to do is go away and just pick up a smart board and deliver the scheme for the sake of delivering it. I believe so strongly in attention to detail within the planning stage and the thinking behind it, 'What's the core knowledge? How are you going to deliver it? How are you going to check for understanding and then adapt across the whole class?' The more we can get teachers thinking about that, the better. I think that's why we've seen a huge rise in our mathematics SATs scores. In 2024 our Year 6 pupils attained the best expected progress rate in a number of years.

JT: **The results are great, but they are a by-product of what you've created here Josh. Teaching's more than just those numbers.**

JP: Yes. The outcomes are one very important measure that we are judged by, but it's not what makes a great school. As clichéd as it sounds, I really do care so much about the kids and their futures.

JT: **I know, and they know you do.**

JP: For me it's about, 'How can I set them up for life?' We know in Fletton, as morbid as it may sound, because of our socio-economic context, life expectancy has been as much as nine years less than the national average. We have a high number of disadvantaged children here. For me, yes, SATs are a measure; however, I like to think beyond that. I am always thinking, 'How am I going to equip them for life outside of a test paper?' For me it's about trying to provide a level of competency in life, to have independence, and to motivate them to have high aspirations for themselves and try to instil in them the motivation that I have towards self-improvement.

JT: **What really impressed me today was their levels of oracy.**

JP: Yes, absolutely. I've worked a lot on metacognition, and I try to make my thought processes so explicit in everything I do, and I think that has really benefitted the children. It has helped them, for certain.

JT: **Explain things. Model your thinking. Check for understanding. Repeat. That's it. There's not much more to it. We overcomplicate this stuff, and you typified everything that's clear and effective about the learning process.**

JP: I talk a lot to staff in school about cognitive load and ask, 'How do we lower the cognitive load so the children understand the process?'

JT: **That's the low floor so everyone can access the work.**

JP: Exactly. The low floor was today. If you think about 70 plus 30 is 100 and 60 add something is 100. That's, what, Year 2? You'd expect our Year 2 children to be able to do that, but it was crucial for them to understand the bar model to be able to be successful in today's lesson. The maths in the early stage didn't matter, I needed the children to understand the concept, the fundamentals, the why, before moving them on to the harder questions. It is about a well-sequenced curriculum.

JT: **I loved it when you quizzed your three bellwether pupils and moved stuff on because they understood, rather than labouring through the answer, because**

you were completely all over where they were and how to challenge them.

JP: It's knowing when to move on. I think you get the feel for where they are in the lesson. Because you've planned in so much detail you know what each child needs to be able to do at each point in the lesson, but I've already prepared for the misconceptions. I'm already thinking, 'What could go wrong?' Well, today I knew that one of the children would have done addition and addition, instead of addition and then subtraction. So, I'm thinking, 'Well, if I know she's going to break down on the second step, what am I going to do?' I'd already planned for some of my pupils not to be able to go from the worked examples to the backwards fading, so when you see the two children moving to the front of the class, that was almost pre-planned. I knew that might happen, so when it did happen, I was able to go, 'Come to the front of the class.'

JT: **I was discussing this yesterday with a secondary food teacher. We've got to find a way of making schools attractive places to return to every day if we're going to solve the attendance problem in schools.**

JP: Exactly. 100%. I think it's striking the balance between having some fun – relating to the children and taking an interest in what they do at the weekend – and then the learning. I know in the maths lesson the core knowledge is *this*, therefore in that hour this is what we're going to be learning. I might go off-piste. But typically it's structured around the core knowledge I want them to know. I've planned for misconceptions and we won't stop until they have all learnt what I want them to learn. However, at breaktime they know they can turn to me and say, 'Coventry lost last night, Mr Pike.' I think striking that balance makes them want to come back to my history session after break.

JT: Absolutely. It is easy to dismiss how important that is. Thanks Josh.

Testimonials

Josh doesn't keep thank you cards! But, a parent who works at the school was keen to speak to me. Stacey Campbell has been at Old Fletton in one role or another, for over a decade. Her two boys were both taught by Josh. They are now at secondary school. 'Mr Pike was the difference. One of my sons was a terrible worrier. But it was Mr Pike – with his fun, his stories, his interest in football and F1, and his acting it out in history lessons – that changed all that. The boys loved finding Mr Pike's profile on FIFA! My son stopped worrying almost overnight. From being on the verge of school-refusing, he was keen to go in the mornings. He began speaking in class.'

'He still had the odd worry, but nothing like before. Those worries were draining for all of us and then, suddenly, they stopped and it was such a relief. He made such a difference. As a family, we can't speak too highly of him.'

So, what can we learn from Josh Pike?

There is one major take-away from this profile of Josh Pike, and it's this: if you want to exemplify in-the-moment adaptive teaching, then look no further than his classroom. He has the best checking-for-understanding radar I have ever come across. He not only knows who understands what and when, he also does something targeted and personalised with that information.

Until I saw Josh teach, I'm not sure I was completely clear what the difference was between adaptive teaching and differentiation. Now I know. It is about the ambition for every pupil to reach the most challenging work, and the ability to provide targeted support for them to get there. It's not about aiming low, middle and high, according to prior attainment. It's about seeing what they can understand of what they have been taught – irrespective of anyone's attempt to guess their potential and stick a number on it – and tweaking the teaching, lesson-by-lesson, and mid-lesson, to keep them engaged and making progress.

Another thing that really struck me was Josh's lightbulb moment, when he realised that the most important resource in the room is him. The importance of saving yourself for the classroom and exerting your energy when you are in front of the class is a lesson worth noting.

Finally, a thread that comes through these profiles, and is evident in this one, is the importance of connecting with all pupils. Josh is not laddish in any respect. But he does know how to connect with his pupils and to tap into their interests, particularly through sport. It's not boorish and it's not exclusive to boys, the girls like football too, and if they don't, Josh endeavours to show an interest in any aspect of their life – their pets, their upcoming dance competition, their favourite books to read and even the art that they've created on a bit of scrap paper over the weekend. But these idiosyncrasies are central to his pupils' world, and, crucially, central to Josh's world. When the recording finished, we spent 20 minutes discussing our mutual love of Manchester United and our despair at their current plight. Sport, for anyone, provides a way to make human connections and to feel a sense of belonging. Spending time in Josh's orbit is life enhancing. If he supported Liverpool, however …

———————————————

Josh Pike's pupils' progress and achievement data

Josh's pupil progress data tracks last year's Year 6 cohort from pre-COVID, so we can see the progress that has been made over time. Although he only taught them as a class for the whole of Year 6, as maths lead, he spent a lot of intervention time with this cohort over the previous four years, whilst coaching teachers on mathematics pedagogy across the school.

Mathematics age-related expectations (ARE) Data for Year 6 2024 leavers, 2019–24		
Year Group	**Year**	**Percentage of pupils at ARE in mathematics (end of year)**
Year 6	2023–24	80%
Year 5	2022–23	70%
Year 4	2021–22	58%
Year 3	2020–21	45%
Year 2	2019–20	60%

A Truly Great Primary Teacher: Nicola Curran

Nicola Curran is a P6 teacher at Moyle Primary School, Larne.

I'm off to Northern Ireland. The past few weeks have been notable for the overcast weather in the UK. Sunshine has not been counted in days, nor hours, but *minutes*, so rarely has the cloud broken. Some 20,000 feet above the Irish sea, however, the sun is beaming down, ever present.

It's a good reminder as we land at Belfast's George Best airport, amidst the mizzling gloom. True to his word, Gareth Hamilton, the wise, avuncular principal of Moyle Primary School, Larne, is waiting for me in the car park. As we drive up to the school, we chat about the American election, his time working in South Carolina when he was younger and Manchester football. I forgive him for supporting City.

I am struck, as we come over the hill, to see how industrial the Larne landscape appears. There are more factory chimneys than I expected. As the cloud sits heavily above it, the beach, stretching down towards the capital, looks foreboding. I remind myself that the sun is always shining, just not here, just not now.

When we sit down to talk about Nicola Curran, Gareth explains that she teaches a P6 class, aka Year 5 in England. 'Nicola began as a learning assistant and developed from there into a teacher. Her expertise is in literacy, especially storytelling. We've spent a fortune on books for her – you'll see when you get into her classroom!' He goes on, 'She is brilliant with young boys who become so enthused in her class, especially when she is reading aloud. And one of her greatest strengths is breaking down key concepts to help pupils understand them.' I nod away, scribbling notes.

We are joined by Marian Mann, deputy principal. She shares Gareth's office, as space is tight at the popular school. Marian knows a lot about Nicola. 'This will sound gushy', says Marian, 'but she is inspirational. She is a fantastic storyteller. The stories come to life. When she is reading, she has the class eating out of her hand.' She mentions Nicola's ability to manage the boys so adeptly. 'One lad, who can be very difficult, has transformed into *Perfect Peter* in a matter of weeks! Nicola is the teacher the troubled boys feel connected to. She tunes in to their strengths and interests.' Gareth and I listen on as Marian extols the many virtues of her colleague. 'One of the parents said to me after parents' evening, "Miss Curran's *got* my boy". She has a rare knack of being able to get down to their level and see the world through their eyes. She has a child-like aura. She's astute, she cares deeply for them, and there is always a work-based buzz in the room.'

Gareth comments on how 'Nicola can run the room despite the disparate activities going on around her. She loves being in the middle of the hubbub.' I finish my scribbles and look at my watch. We are already behind schedule. 'Come on', I say, 'she'll be teaching now. I don't want to miss anything. Let's go and find her.'

Teaching

As we walk into the room, I'm barked at. Loudly. Nessa, the school dog, surrounded by Nicola and 25 adoring children, has spotted an Englishman and doesn't like what she sees. Nicola shushes the dog and introduces me to the children. They are beautifully polite in saying, 'Hello'. The room is light and airy, as the sun begins to break through in this corner of the province. Nessa is half black lab, half poodle. As she passes me on her way out, I manage not to spook her again.

It's carpet time. I've arrived just as the pupils are finishing sharing their news. Miss had seen the new Paddington movie with her nephew, Noah. They had long, jelly snakes in the cinema as a treat. The 4DX effects made it seem that the water was coming out of the screen and all over them. They actually got wet! The pupils attend to every word. We are about to prepare for the PE lesson when Linden pipes up. 'Has Mr Tomsett any news for us?' It is delightful. As I regale them with details of my travels – in the previous week I had been in Jersey, Scotland, England, Wales and, now, Northern Ireland – we track my progress on the whiteboard, where Nicola projects a map of the UK. Another learning moment grasped securely. And then it is question time:

- What type of transportation do you like best?

- Where did you grow up?

- Did you have fun where you grew up?

- What do you catch when you go fishing?

It is joyous. Here I am, made to feel a welcome guest by people I have only just met, in a wondrous classroom (Gareth was right about the books), in what feels like another country, when 90 minutes earlier I was in the bowels of Leeds-Bradford airport in the pouring rain. Clichéd, I know, but I already feel at home.

'Eyes on me, 1-2-3', and Nicola has complete attention. We are off to do PE. I look around the room as they get organised. The displays are beautifully curated. I notice, above everything else, quotations from *Alice In Wonderland*. 'Anything can happen … through the *Looking Glass*' apparently.

As we leave, Nicola hands me a plan for the day and simultaneously crouches down to help a child tie the laces on her trainers. 'We've got the inhalers, check! We've got the medical bag, check!' Pupils have responsibilities. The set up on the playground is highly efficient. Nicola is hugely ambitious. They begin with the 'daily mile', comprised of four circuits of the playground. I think it's probably 350 yards, tops! As the pupils encircle Nicola, she is in her element. I stand sheltered from the wind and feel the apricity of the early winter sun on my back. Nicola explains what is happening. There are four exercises, all based around developing hockey skills. Nicola is in her PE kit. She looks like a life-long sportswoman, athletic and light on her feet. She demonstrates techniques. She insists on following the rules of each exercise. She expects everyone to give the session 100% effort. And then they're off.

It would be easy to write that all the pupils are on task all the time. No one would know if that were true or not. But, the truth is, for 25 minutes – which flashed by – I don't see a single pupil off-task. One boy holds the hockey stick the wrong way and jabs it into his stomach. There are tears. He has a sit down for a minute. Apart from that there is no break in the activities, and in the middle of it all, directing operations serenely, is Nicola Curran. It is a magnificent spectacle.

Back in class, they recover from their exertions on the carpet. A P7 boy pops in to see Nicola. Tomorrow, Saturday, is the 11-plus exam at the local grammar school. He looks tense. Nicola is reassuring, 'You can only do your best. I taught you last year and I know you will smash it. I am already more proud of you than I can say.' His grimace morphs slowly into a grin.

I watch an hour of mathematics, characterised by the same levels of rigour and industry I saw on the playground. What strikes me is the emphasis upon self-regulation, and the way that mathematical thinking is made visible through the use of simple heuristics. She is encouraging but gives nothing away. 'Let's not use the word "worried" Liam. I'm not worried about you getting it "right". I'm more interested in you trying to figure it out. I like that much better. Dig a little deeper for me.' She is keen on developing their vocabulary. I like the way she reminds them of the word 'product' *after* they have done the maths, so that they understand the concept of 'product' and can associate it with the word.

She works them hard. It's been: literacy, news time; PE; mathematics … and now it is developing your *schema* to improve your inference skills. I have only ever come across the word 'schema' when reading books on cognitive science. It describes patterns of thinking and behaviour that people use to interpret the world. I've never seen the word introduced to pupils, primary or secondary. Gareth is spot on – Nicola breaks down the concept into easily digestible chunks, so that everyone understands.

The lesson smacks of ambition. To help the children understand how you develop your inference skills by adding new knowledge to your schema, Nicola uses this A4 template: (see page 58)

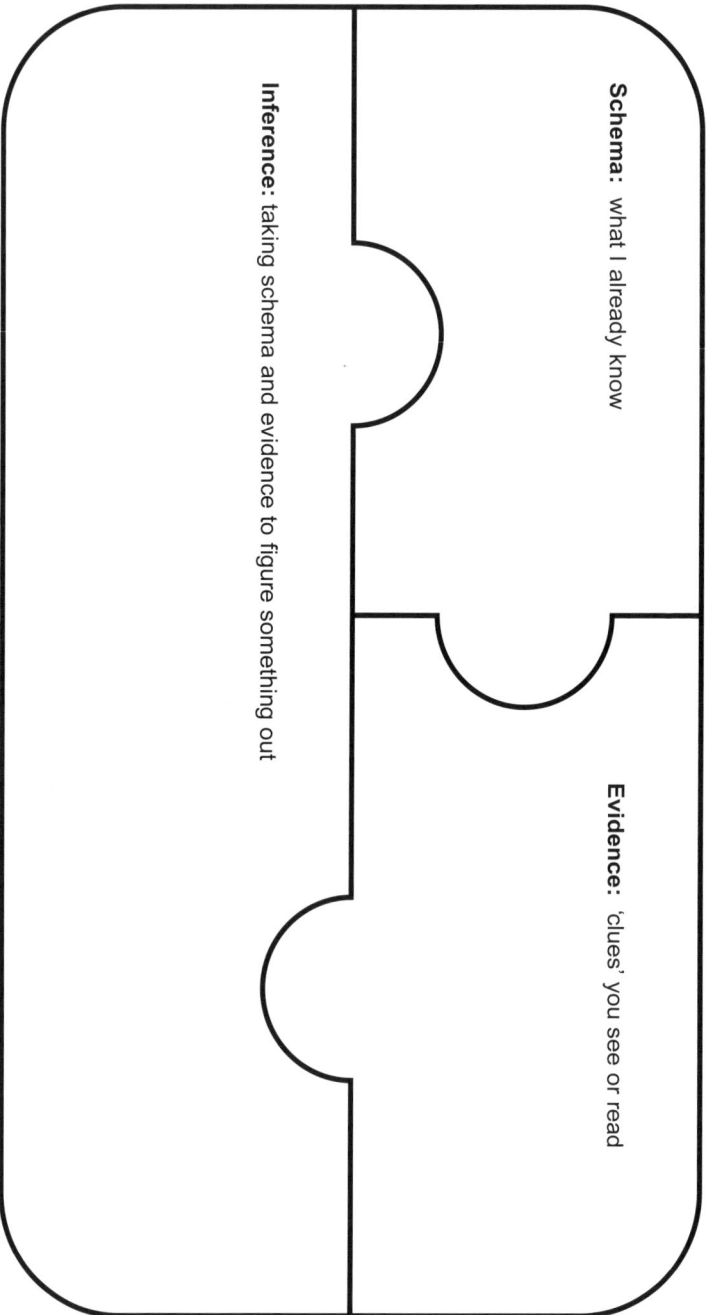

Schema: what I already know

Inference: taking schema and evidence to figure something out

Evidence: 'clues' you see or read

She puts up an image of what looks like a dead leopard. She asks the pupils to work in pairs to discuss what they can see and adds their responses to the Evidence jigsaw piece. She then asks them what they know already about leopards and then lists their replies in the Schema jigsaw piece. They then have to add the evidence of what they observed in the photograph to their schema to provide an Interpretation of the photo of what looks like a dead leopard, which they write in the Inference jigsaw piece.

The children get excited. At one point she says, 'Hold your thought. We live in a world where patience is a virtue.' Theories fly around. Everyone is enjoying themselves. Especially Nicola. Someone notices that the 'leopard' is on a tarmac road. That's odd. Nicola reveals that the image comes from a local paper. Odder still.

Once she exhausts the pupils' responses, and the class is about to burst with anticipation, she reveals, in good storytelling style, the tale behind the picture. 'Well, it happened here, in Northern Ireland. A mum was pushing a pram while she was taking her older son to school. She was in her pyjamas. She got hot, took off her leopard patterned dressing gown and did not realise she had dropped it. Someone reported that they'd seen a dead leopard, so the Police closed the road off, sent for an armed response unit, called in the big cat experts … only to find what looked like a leopard's tail was the dressing gown belt!' Uproar! Laughter all round. Nicola deconstructs what has just happened to their schema and how difficult inference skills are to develop without knowledge of the facts. As the sun streams through the windows, it is time for a well-deserved lunch.

What the pupils think

Having eaten, I sit in a small sensory room with two lots of pupil volunteers, one after the other. I want to know what makes Miss Curran a truly great teacher. 'She teaches really well', says one pupil. 'She makes it easy to understand. She uses words that are easy to understand.' They talk about learning the mean, median and mode. I test them. They know their stuff!

Another one says, 'She's kind of childish, but not too childish.' I know what she means. There is something about Nicola that connects with these young people; something innocent and gentle. When I watched her teach, I'm not sure I had ever seen such a psychologically safe environment in which to learn.

She is fair, according to one of the bigger boys. 'Last year we kept getting mad at each other, but we don't anymore because of Miss and how she helps us make friends.'

'And she never gets mad herself. Well, a little bit if you're not trying hard at your work', says one of the girls. 'But that's fair, because she tries so hard, we have to too.'

One boy hasn't spoken yet. I ask him what he thinks of Miss Curran. 'I love it when she does all the voices reading *Matilda*.' Consensual muttering fills the small space. 'And that other book, *There's Wolves in the Walls*. That's *great*! We don't talk when she is reading because it is THAT good!'

Before they get too fidgety, I send them back to class and the second group file in. 'She's fair and nice. She has made my sums better. She'll come over to you and help you if you get stuck', says another paid-up member of the Nicola Curran fan club. She finishes with a wonderful line: 'We do hard sums but easy methods.' I love the way the pupil doesn't realise the genius of that statement.

Her friend takes over, 'She encourages us to give it a go. Like with the bus stop method. It looked hard but we can all do it now. And the multiplying board really helps.' This one is on a roll … 'and if you are getting bullied, she will help you. Just tell Miss Curran.' They have a clear view of Nicola's moral compass. They go on to tell me how she understands people if they are upset. She likes fairness. And she likes the truth. Being honest is very important to Miss Curran. 'Honesty is her policy', says one of the boys. And then, out of nowhere, another boy says, 'It's rare to get such a brilliant teacher like her.' They all agree.

They make a few more observations: she always looks out for them in PE; they like how she explains the plan for the day, so they know what they are doing at all times; and active spelling is fun. With both groups I finish with the single word descriptor question: kind, excellent, funny ('crazy' – in a good way), magical, extraordinary, clever, nice and fabulous. Magical stands out. There is a sense of something very special in the room when Nicola teaches. I send them on their way and set up my microphone – I intend to find out a bit more about the *magical* Miss Curran …

———————

IRL: Nicola Curran

John Tomsett (JT): Tell me why you became a teacher.

Nicola Curran (NC): I loved primary school, hated secondary school. Just didn't quite fit in. I was quiet, I was shy … *keep your head down, move on.* It was the 1990s and things were very different then to how they are now. I always remembered loving my primary school, so when I was at Antrim Tech and it came to work experience I chose to go back there. I was with a P2 teacher in Ballyclare Primary School whom I knew of but was never taught by. She was great. When you're around children it's magic and I just fitted right in. I went back again and got a job working as a classroom assistant there for four years. I was with P1s, which would be Reception in England. I loved being a classroom assistant.

Then I thought, 'I wonder if I could teach?' If it hadn't been for a very encouraging lady in P1, Miss Wilson, who said, 'Yes, Nicola, go on, go on and do it', I'm not sure I would have. So, I went to Bristol and was there for four years doing my degree. Then I came back home. It's very different teaching over there compared to here. They were a little bit more clinical, more driven by the academic work alone, rather than celebrating the child.

It's not just a job that you walk away from at the end of the day and don't think about until the next morning. It's about the environment you create. I'm here for most of my life. I have loved my job from the minute I went into my first classroom.

JT: **I can tell. So, you became a teacher then. How long ago was that?**

NC: That would have been about, 19, 20 years ago, now.

JT: **Where was your first post?**

NC: I was in Greystone Primary School and I went in as a withdrawal teacher, working with small groups of children withdrawn from class for extra help. Jobs in Northern Ireland were exceptionally scarce, you couldn't get one, but luckily I did. In the end it led to me teaching P7 (Years 6 and 7 in England). A teacher went off for an operation and I was right in the middle of the transfer process between primary and secondary, so I was thrown in at the deep end. It was more than the deep end because I had been Foundation Stage trained and, initially, I was in early years. For three years that was my main focus. Then suddenly I was in P7! A fish out of water! Ironically, apart from maybe one year, that's where I have been ever since. Now, I can't imagine being anywhere else.

JT: **Did you then move here?**

NC: No, I worked for nearly five years in Corran Integrated. It was wonderful. I gained so much experience there. I went there initially to teach P7, and then I had a tricky P6 group. It wasn't easy, but we got along grand. Then I was asked to stay with them into P7 because they were quite settled, so it was a roll-on year. That's the first I've ever done. Teaching the same class for two years is not easy because when you've done your year, you are in a routine, but you've used up all your tricks. They know you; they know how to read to you. It worked with us, but I could see how easily it couldn't have, so I had to keep on my toes. I had to keep it fresh.

JT: **You're brilliant at behaviour. That class today is tricky.**

NC: You've got to earn children's respect. A lot of work has gone into it; they do not give it to you. They know when to have fun with me and when to let go. They know whenever I mean business.

JT: **You make it look easy, but I can see that you're working so hard all the time. Going back to your teaching history, so you moved to here?**

NC: Yes, then I fell on my feet. I came here and Peter Garrett was the principal at the time. They needed a P4 teacher. I was eight years with P4 here, and this is my seventh with P6.

JT: **I'm really interested in your philosophy about teaching.**

NC: I think it's about trying to give them the skills for, while still protecting them from, the world they're going into.

JT: **Tell me a bit more about that.**

NC: The world our children live in now is so fast, and I don't know what they're going home to. Sometimes I can only provide them a safe space in the time that they are here. It's a privilege to be in a position where you're trying to get them to learn, teach them about manners, teach them about social interaction and get them to enjoy learning. Things don't come easily to a lot of people; you have to work at some things, you have to try new things, you have to build resilience in them and you have to make repeated attempts.

They know to share, they know to say the right things, but following through with it and understanding it is another matter. It's because they're not exploring that anywhere outside of a classroom anymore. They're not doing what I did when I was a child. They are building on a computer a vision of how they want the world.

JT: **Roaming away from home at the weekend for children is almost unheard of now.**

NC: We've bred fear by osmosis, the children don't want to go beyond the strict boundaries of their house. They haven't got that instinct to explore, 'What's around this corner, what's going on round here?' They have little curiosity.

In a class I had last year there were a couple of boys who would go hunting and build dens and were very outdoorsy. They made bows and arrows – we did have to confiscate a bow and arrow when they brought one into school. I called them Mowgli or Peter Pan because that's what they were like. It's not a case of sitting there just doing the academic work; they *do* have to learn those tables and they *have* to get their handwriting done. But I want them to develop skills, so that when they're faced with challenges they can move forward. That they can look in another direction; right, that's not working, so how's it going to look if I do it this way? Rather than in the society that we're building now when you're helpless, like deer in the headlights. They don't know what to do.

JT: **I noticed how metacognitive you are about the way you get them to learn and the resilience you give them. You give them opportunities to think about the process that they go through to solve a problem. If**

they can't go one way, they're coming to a dead end, they've got other options.

NC: Yes, there's another way to go, and if it's not working then try something else. If not, then ask for help. Do not do it alone, do not worry alone, do not panic alone. No number, and it usually is a number, is worth anybody's tears. I want children to be in my class without being unhappy and without being stuck.

JT: **You want to liberate pupils.**

NC: Yes, because they're in your care for so long, because you have such an impact, you have nearly a year in these children's lives where you can make a difference. If a child can think back a year on and smile and say, 'Oh, do you remember, she did such and such.' If you can provide memories for a child that makes them smile when they talk about being at school, well …

JT: **Yes, but it's more than that, isn't it? You want them to smile and be academically advanced.**

NC: Of course you do, and to believe in what they can do. You want to support pupils wherever their starting points. Pupils know that they're doing work that's different to this person or that person, but you don't pigeonhole them. They know if they want specific help who to go to amongst their peers. If they're doing numeracy, they'll say, 'Can I go with Mary?' Or if they're doing writing, 'Can I go with Julie?' I build the academic progress up. For instance, after they've completed the numeracy problems today – the bronze and silver – they've got gold and platinum to face next week. Again, that's a different challenge for them, so we're going to have to bring different skills. For some, I just have to get them secure and confident when they see some variation to the problems, whereas others can manage well and are robust.

JT: **You know them really well, don't you? You know where to pitch it with every single child.**

NC: You have to in order for them to learn and you want them to love learning. You want them to be excited about learning.

JT: **They are, extraordinarily so.**

NC: Silly tricks, I mean, that one with the leopard, I made it up!

JT: **Now, let's talk about that because I've never heard anybody outside researchED conferences talk about 'schema' in the way you did in the lesson, so that the pupils will understand what it means. It's really hard to teach inference, almost impossible to teach inference, because if you don't know something, you don't know something, you can't infer anything about it. I was really impressed with what you did.**

NC: I stumbled across that jigsaw that you saw there. I thought, 'I wonder if I can put all of that together in a context for teaching inference.' They make judgements all the time, 'There it is, that's what that is.' No, it's not, there's a story behind that. The first point is, don't look *at* the picture, look at what's *in* the picture. What do you know about whales, for instance? Right, they're in water. Right, water. What do you know about water? Well, I know about this and it can be this deep and it be a lake and it can be a moat. There are blue whales, there are different species. What countries do you find them in? You fill it up with things they know, because they've already got a lot of it. Then, we talk about detective skills and if you decide something, you have to prove it. And then you add what they take from the evidence to what they already know.

JT: **Have you read anything by Sarah Cottinghatt?**

NC: No.

JT: **David Ausubel wrote about assimilation and schema.[1] How you assimilate new knowledge to what you already know.**

NC: Yes, they attach it to prior knowledge, and they build on it.

JT: **Yes, they build on it and extend their schema. Honestly, I reckon 0.001% of teachers understand what that's about. It's just extraordinary to come to a classroom today and find you having devised a piece of work that was so explicit in that regard and so engaging. There was 100% attention and you made it so funny and so interesting. You are doing exactly what Sarah Cottinghatt wrote about in her book on David Ausubel's assimilation and schema. Amazing!**

NC: Yes, you have to look past what you see. If you look past what you see, look what's there, it could be magic.

JT: **Really interesting to see you use that vocabulary. You're also tremendous on the language of maths and the subject specific vocabulary.**

NC: Thank you. Key vocabulary was something in our school development plan about four or five years ago. Particularly with word problems. Again, when children see a word problem, they can get stuck. The challenge is to associate the words with your digits. There's your 24 times 3. That's easy, they can do that, no problem, but the language of the problem takes some unpicking. With my lower prior attainers, they had different subtraction questions written in six different ways, so that they could see 'take away' and 'minus' and 'from' all mean the same thing. The vocabulary wall is so helpful for doing that. When the new boy who had just joined us got confused, I took him to the wall and said, 'Well, look here, that word's the same as that one.' Straight away he knew what to do. Rather than come to me every time,

---

1   S. Cottinghatt, *Ausubel's Meaningful Learning in Action* (Woodbridge: John Catt Educational, 2023).

saying, 'I don't know what to do here', I showed him the vocabulary wall so he would need my help no longer. He now knows exactly what to do and moves on and I'm forgotten about. Phew! They don't need me anymore!

JT: **Which is exactly where you want to get to, isn't it? Otherwise, you learn helplessness; that's what you're avoiding. And they really don't want to let you down.**

NC: I think every adult has to work at that. I trust them and they have to trust me, and I've had to work at earning that. That does not come easily and that does not come for free. That has come through building a relationship. I have to be that safe place. I am firm but fair and that's what I've always told the children. 'The reason I'm telling you "No" is not to spoil your fun, I'm telling you "No" because I know this is going to happen.'

JT: **One pupil said you explain everything. You win the cognitive argument about why they're doing what they're doing.**

NC: I have a nephew who's very curious and he will be at loggerheads with my sister a lot of the time. They're very alike, but he'll always question why he has to do something if he doesn't want to do it. She'll say, 'Because I said so, I'm your Mum!'

JT: **You can't say that anymore to children.**

NC: [*Laughs*] As his mother, she can!

JT: **I mean, they don't take it anymore.**

NC: No, I've taught them to be curious, to question why? You just can't accept things … I don't blame them, because when someone tells me 'No', I want to know why. Honesty is also big too. I'm honest with them and if you're honest with me I'll …

JT: **'Honesty is her policy', they said.**

NC: Is that what they said? [*Laughs*] If you're honest with me, I'll move heaven and earth to help you. I might not like what you did, but I'll help you. If you tell me untruths, if I think you're growing a tail, then it's my trust you're losing. I'll still help you, but you're losing the trust. I tell them that they'd do the same with me. If you thought I wasn't being honest with you, you've no reason to trust me. I don't make empty promises. You have to be honest with children and that is the core of developing relationships, I think. They'll test your honesty to see whether you're true.

JT: **And your repute as a storyteller.**

NC: [*Laughs*] Well, yes! I love stories. I recently became literary coordinator as well. I have a passion for literacy. I love it, I love words. Growing up, the library, for me, was magic. That was my internet. You can fall into words and the sky is your imagination, the creativity, it's just magic. I don't want anything else; I just want to be in the classroom. I have no aspirations to do anything other than what I'm doing at the minute. The literacy position came up and I feel passionately about our school as well and what drives people. I hope to inspire a little bit.

JT: **I hear you're brilliant at voices.**

NC: I like to do character impressions because a child will listen more. When you read a story and you add the voices, they listen more intently, rather than just having the words wash over them. They become *involved* in the story. If I can do weird voices for a character, to grab their attention.

JT: **They were impersonating your impersonations.**

NC: Really?!

JT: **Yes, they were all doing the voice!**

NC: They're getting something from it. They're listening to the story. That's our (pointing across the classroom to a notice-board covered in post-it notes) interactive *Matilda* board. When there's questions – what do you think of the character, how does it influence *Matilda*? – they've got post-it notes and they can just put their ideas up on the board when they fancy. So, 'Can you think of a simile to describe the Wormwood family?' They make ones up and add them. We're doing Jumpstart! Grammar at the minute, and we blend the two things, the grammar and the fiction text. So, they add new words and they make up rules for spelling patterns. They came up with an acrostic for spelling 'because' – 'Betty eats cakes and uses soft eggs' – to help to remind them of because. You know, they've got ideas. It's the same as our wee invention idea.

JT: **I love the invention wall. (A noticeboard where they can add ideas for new inventions whenever they like, again using post-it notes.)**

NC: Well, that was last week. I asked, 'What do you think is the best invention and why?' That was the idea. A couple of nights ago, I was thinking about their world and I thought, 'What do they think Wi-Fi looks like?'

JT: **It's a great question.**

NC: I questioned a couple of them earlier on. It's something nearly invisible. Does it whisper across, does it crawl across, what way does it move?

JT: **You could show them the massive server farms.**

NC: Yes, and it would blow their minds. 'What? There's a bigger world out there?'

JT: **There's a 4,350-mile-long cable owned by Google that connects the USA and UK that goes under the Atlantic.**

NC: Yes. And Boris Johnson wanted to build a bridge from the tip of Larne to Scotland and the children talked about something like that. They said, 'It can't be in the Irish Sea, it's one of the most dangerous in the world because of the currents, because of the way it moves, think when you go swimming.' There's also this trench that goes so deep down, so we went and looked at Beaufort's Dyke, just because that was their interest at the time.

They had questioned it, so we investigated the trench. They come up with ideas, and I think, 'Oh yes, let's have a go and run with it.'

JT: **It strikes me, you've got to make places, like your classroom, where it's great to come.**

NC: Thank you.

JT: **There's the main solution to attendance issues – make it attractive to come to school.**

NC: Yes, and a safe space for them to come and be free to learn and not be scared to learn or intimidated.

JT: **When do you go off-piste then?**

NC: Well, nine times out of ten they've come up with something. Recently, one of them asked, 'Where do rainbows land and what does it look like when it's in water?' We went and learned that it's a 'moonbow' at night. You know, I'm learning.

JT: **A moonbow?**

NC: It's a moonbow when it glows at night. What was it that Pip found out? If we all look at the same rainbow, everybody sees it differently to somebody else, regardless of you being in the same space. Everybody's perspective of it is different.

We were learning about north, south, east and west. For some reason, it was in the morning and every time I stand there, the sun shines through and I can't see, so that's why there's a white piece of paper on the back window, to stop the sun coming in and blinding me. We were talking about this and I said, 'Right, well, think of your house. Where does the sun come up in the morning? Where does it go down in the evening?' They thought and had a wee look, 'Well, I think the direction is here, here and here.' I said, 'Well, is the mobile in the same direction as your house? Have a wee look.' We had a debate about which way their houses faced in relation to this classroom, and then we got the mini-compass out and they stood in the direction where they thought the sun rose. They argued about where they thought it was! I think this was back in September-time, when the sun had started to change. It was a lovely red morning. The views are incredible in the morning-time when you've got the sun rising. It turns blood red, it's beautiful. We were able to see, 'Yes that's where it comes from, that's the direction. Now, try at home and see where it comes in from in your house.' It took a few days, but it was just five minutes every time, just dribble, dribble, dribble, dribble. We do silly stuff in here.

JT: It's great, honestly. One of them said, 'She's kind of childish, but not too childish.'

NC: That's nice. Peter Pan. That wouldn't surprise me. I'd say a Peter Pan kind of personality helps.

JT: Tell me about that, what do you mean by that?

NC: Life is hard. Being an adult is hard. You have to face, what I call 'adult' problems an awful lot. Sometimes I don't feel I'm old enough to handle them, even though I'm middle-aged! So, if you can be in a place where you don't have the worry about being an adult, it's still a safe place, still a responsible, safe place. If you have a kind of a Peter Pan complex while you're looking at the schoolwork, you're more likely to bring them along with you, than if you're creating a teacher and pupils' situation. I think if you asked them, they'd say it's 'us', it's not Miss Curran on her own; we're a unit. That's the culture I try to create.

JT: That's so interesting, that you're a unit.

NC: Yes, we're a family. We work together. It's not them against me. Although, they know I'm the boss, they know what I say goes. Yes, there's a wee bit of Peter Pan in everybody, because life's hard. You forget what it was like as a kid. You think you had no worries, but you did. And these children have worries, and some of them have more worries than I'll ever even begin to fathom.

JT: **The other one they came up with, they thought you were** *clever.*

NC: [*Laughs*] My dad would get a real kick out of that, so would my brother!

JT: **Tell your dad and your brother, they think you're clever and** *magical.* **Isn't that lovely?**

NC: Yes, that's very, very nice.

JT: **It's been just extraordinary to be in your orbit. Truly.**

NC: [*Laughs*] Well, thank you. When they are, say 50, and they look back, I hope I'll have given all the children I've taught some sort of happy memories … What else can you do?

JT: **Thank you so much. It's been joyful.**

Testimonials

'Miss Curran was an amazing teacher to my son. He was extremely shy, but she saw past his awkwardness and encouraged and developed him into a confident and capable young man. She saw him as a person, not just another pupil in her class. She has made a life-long impact on my son and I'll never forget her commitment, dedication and beautiful soul.'

'Nicola is, without a doubt, the best teacher I've ever known. She has such a lovely way with the children and they totally respect her! My son was taught by her in P6 and as we near the end of Year P7, he still visits her almost every day. She had such a positive impact on not only his school day, but his personal struggles with ADHD.'

'Miss Curran goes far and beyond for each pupil, including my own daughter who she teaches. Her kind heart and patience are absolutely fantastic and, first and foremost, everything she does is in the child's best interest. She is very approachable and understanding about parents' concerns. She is an absolute credit to Moyle Primary School and I hope she is there for many years to come.'

'As a colleague, I feel Nicola is a talented and creative teacher who captures her children's imagination through her love of books. She strives for success and treats every child she teaches like a star about to shine.'

'I just wanted to say you have been the best teacher ever and I am going to miss you very, very, very much. I used to be a bit dumber than the rest of the class but since I've been in P6, I'm getting smarter. I just wanted to thank you for being the best teacher!'

'The secret is to surround yourself with people who make your heart smile – then, and only then, will you find Wonderland. Thank you, Miss Curran, for being such a brilliant teacher.'

'We will never forget you. You will be sitting in our hearts. You're the most kind, funny, loveable teacher ever!'

'Dear Miss Curran

I love you so much and sadly I have to go but thank you for all you've done for me. I'm really going to miss you.

PS This card was made with love, and Emily's pen ☺.

PPS I will come and visit.

PPS Hopefully you will get my brother in P6.'

So, what can we learn from Nicola Curran?

I'm never knowingly sycophantic, and I refuse to gush. But, I have to admit, I am not sure I have seen a teacher quite so connected to the pupils she teaches as Nicola Curran is to Moyle Primary's current P6 class. I don't think I have ever visited a classroom so suffused with laughter and love. Now, I know that is all a bit gushy, but it is true. And this is true, too: I have never seen a teacher break down the skills of inference so brilliantly and provide for their pupils such an effective heuristic for tackling comprehension tasks.

Who knew that providing an entirely psychologically safe space to learn, in an enjoyable, collaborative atmosphere, where the content of the lesson is taught with expert clarity – and that content is rich, challenging and ambitious – and where storytelling is at the heart of everything, would result in high levels of learning? Really? *Really*?

Michael Young, co-author of the seminal text, *Knowledge and the Future School*,[2] said in an interview in 2022 that 'if you haven't encouraged students to engage in the process of acquiring knowledge, which is a very difficult process, then all you get is memorisation and reproduction in tests'. Young went on to say, 'I think this is why a lot of kids actually lose the desire to know during their time at school, whereas if we somehow found a way of enabling kids to discover that desire, which is inherent in all of them, schooling would be quite different. It would be a lovely thing to be a teacher, and not a struggle for much of the time. That's been quite a revealing thought to me.'[3]

I was reminded of Michael Young's reflections when I was watching Nicola teach. The way she has cajoled every single child in that class to be a committed, self-starting learner, is extraordinary. In the world of the knowledge-rich curriculum, we have to be careful we don't just

2   M. Young, D. Lambert, C. Roberts and M. Roberts, *Knowledge and the Future School: Curriculum and Social Justice* (London: Bloomsbury Publishing, 2014).

3   G. Duoblys, Michael Young: What we've got wrong about knowledge and curriculum, *TES* (21 September 2022). Available at: https://www.tes.com/magazine/teaching-learning/general/michael-young-powerful-knowledge-curriculum.

'give' children knowledge. If you haven't connected with them, whatever you're 'giving' them, they have the choice to reject and that is what's happening in too many classrooms in our country: 'Here's the *Knowledge Organiser*. Here is your *Do Now* task. Here's the glue stick to stick them into your exercise books. There. You have the knowledge.' Teaching has been reduced to pupils spending five hours a day on low-level administrative tasks. Well, that's not (good) enough, I'm afraid. We have to encourage pupils 'to engage in the process of acquiring knowledge'. In other words, we all need to be a bit more Nicola Curran.

Nicola Curran's pupils' progress and achievement data

In 2023, Nicola was nominated Teacher of the Year by N.I. Families First.

Nicola's class 2023–24

In 2022–23, as Primary 5 pupils, their data was:

- Progress Test in English (PTE) class average: 95.3
- Progress Test in Maths (PTM): class average 98.0

In 2023–24, as Primary 6 under Nicola's tuition, their data was:

- Progress Test in English (PTE) class average: 95.6 (+0.3)
- Progress Test in Maths (PTM) class average: 101.2 (+3.2)

A Truly Great Primary Teacher:
Faariah Jamil

Faariah Jamil is a Year 6 teacher at Thorpe Primary School, Peterborough.

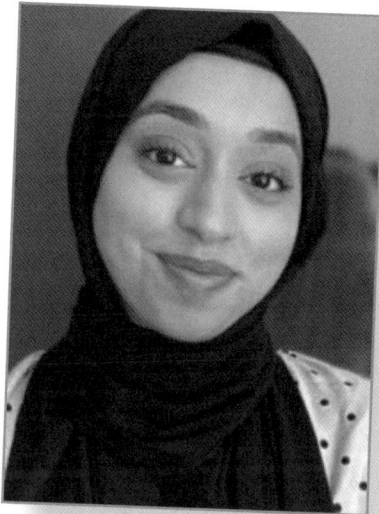

The school leadership's view

I once saw Faariah Jamil ask a pupil to switch her seat so that the pupil could concentrate better. The instruction was delivered with so little fuss, you could have been forgiven for not noticing. She made the request with the deep reassurance of a teacher at the top of her game, someone with years of experience. Without objection, the pupil did as requested. It was classroom management at its finest.

So, when I was thinking about teachers whom I might feature in this book, I remembered that moment. The thing is, when Faariah so impressed me, she was in her second year as an early careers teacher (ECT). This morning, on my return to Thorpe – which is part of the Peterborough Keys MAT – she has been a fully qualified teacher for fewer than a dozen weeks! 'It doesn't matter', says Emma Anderson, Thorpe's impressive head teacher. 'I sat down last night and made a list of things that make Faariah truly great, and they all happen to begin with the letter C! The first one is 'commitment'. She works *so* hard at her teaching. She sees teaching as such an opportunity to make a difference to her pupils. Her commitment to the job is so genuine.'

'It's hard to be as good as her if you don't', I say.

Emma goes on, 'Faariah's second "C" is "calm"', something I concur with, since I have seen Faariah teach a number of times before.

'She has a presence that is quite extraordinary', I say.

'It's true. She's unflappable. It's as though nothing can knock her off kilter.'

Emma nods. 'Who she is, is what makes her a great teacher. She has a softer side, so her calmness is rooted in a love of her job and of the children. There is something about the way she treats them that is pretty special. They feel completely safe.' Emma continues. 'My next "C" is "caring" because she not only cares for the children, she cares about doing a tremendous job. She wants to be the best she can possibly be. Teaching is her thing and she knows what a responsibility she has accepted pursuing this career.' Apparently, Faariah works hard on her practice, on how to teach effectively and on how children learn. She thinks about how to teach in a way that maximises learning. None of this is a surprise. I ask Emma a little more about Faariah's presence.

'You can teach pedagogic strategies – you can improve those technical elements of pedagogy – but presence is much harder to grasp', she says. Whilst we can learn strategies and develop 'presence' through training, we know that some people come to the job with a presence in the room that appears so very natural.'

'She's so calm and respectful', I say.

'And the thing with Faariah is that calm, level-headedness, and that respect, rubs off on the children. They copy her behaviours. And she means it. She's not going through the motions. She is genuine. Her high expectations of them are never lost amongst the niceness. The other "C" is "considered". Her deliberateness is key. Her explanations are so clear.' I nod. Mimicking teacher behaviours is emerging as a key feature of truly great teachers.

We run out of time. As we walk to Faariah's room, Emma talks about her young colleague's ambition, how she is taking on leading a subject, and pursuing a research project. I suddenly have a moment: how I remember those early days of teaching, when you have the energy and enthusiasm to take it *all* on! Emma opens the classroom door and there is the youthful Faariah, calmly running her classroom!

Teaching

I make my way stealthily to the far corner of the class. Year 6 is in the middle of Destination Reader (DR). At Thorpe they split the classes up for DR; with well-trained teaching assistants, it provides smaller classes and targeted support. Faariah's class is reading *Wolf Brother* by Michelle Paver. The pupils are reading aloud. Faariah bounces responsibility for reading around the room. The pupils accept the challenge with relish; Faariah encourages them at every turn. 'Lovely, good girl – fabulous expression in your voice.' She takes hands up for who reads next. The oracy levels in this class are so high. They are all following the words. The school's values adorn the walls: 'Ready Respectful Safe'.

Faariah takes over reading, modelling with expert intonation. The class is transfixed. Every teacher I have seen read aloud so far has exhibited perfect prosody. Faariah is no exception. And then Irkan reads and he replicates Faariah's expertise: 'I love the expression in your voice, Irkan', she says. I reflect upon the importance of narrative in engaging children in the world of scholarship. Stories draw them in. They are round the metaphorical campfire, absorbed by the tales being told.

When words arise that are unfamiliar, Faariah deftly uses the board to clarify their meaning. 'What can you use to find out meanings?' she asks. She doesn't intend to give anything away.

'Word stems?' says one.

'The clarifying toolkit?' says another. This is a list of steps the pupils can take to determine the meaning of a word:

- Read the sentence before and after

- What is the root word?

- Prefix or suffix?

- Proper noun?

- Use illustrations

- Swap for a synonym

- Make links

- Picture the scene

- What is the word class?

'Good, what else can we use, Nathan?' she asks. He struggles. He properly struggles. But she doesn't give in, nor does she corner him. No, she leads him to the right answer. You can almost see his brains bubbling out of his ears as she presses him to think, and he gets there. Faariah says, 'Well done for persevering, Nathan.' And then, to the whole class, 'That's why we don't shout out when people are stuck, because often we just need the time to think.' Such control. Such meta-awareness of what she is doing, and how she wants the pupils to behave.

They work in pairs to define a list of words: deserted, perplexed, bedraggled, hindquarters, mounds, heaved and wolverine. There's no need to work in silence when you have this level of engagement and commitment. She gives them three minutes to find a minimum of three definitions. She's so precise. The precision doesn't straight-jacket teachers, it enables them to use time to its full effectiveness.

I am sitting in bright sunshine. There's a mini-football pitch directly outside. The goals have nets. One lad is mouthing the spellings slowly and precisely. Two boys at the back have finished. One is putting his woolly gloves on. Faariah takes them without conflict. He can have them back at break. The other catches my eye and gives me smile and a little wave.

At the end of three minutes, it's '3-2-1'. And boom! Blimey! Absolute silence. 'I would suggest writing down the definitions. The boys at the front have worked hard and have their definitions. They are just using a dictionary to check them before they write them down.' She narrates the lesson, so that everyone knows what's going on. 'We are cold calling today, so no hands up.' Isabella tells the class that 'deserted' means 'empty or abandoned'. 'What about "perplexed"?' says Faariah. It wasn't in the dictionary, apparently. 'Well', she continues, 'here it is in context: *I saw James with his gloves on and I was perplexed as to why he might be wearing them in a nice, warm classroom.*' James smiles. It is a lovely moment.

DR is over. It is time for the class to return to its full complement of pupils. She narrates exactly what they are going to do. She asks one of them to repeat her instructions: '1. put away DR into cupboard; 2. go to our home seats; and 3. sit ready for science', he says. Faariah then repeats it, in a tone of voice that is calm, warm and resonant. They have three minutes. There is a timer on the board. *Oh. My. Word.* They just get on with it! The class goes into full operation. The clock ticks. It is so lovely and safe and organised. I love it. She is just *there*. Faariah presides over the operation. She has the authority of a president, without being an emperor.

As she counts down the last few seconds, they run to get in place. The next bit impresses me. There are empty places, awaiting the pupils who have been doing DR elsewhere. Most pupils pick up pencils just for themselves. Faariah says, 'Let's see who has collected pencils for the others who have been elsewhere doing DR.' She gives out reward points for those who have shown consideration for their peers. 'If you get something for yourself, the rule is you get it for someone else as well.' By this time the returnees are sitting in their seats; she gives time for the ever-presents to get a pencil for the newly arrived pupils and to explain to them what they are doing next. The moral message matters. She gives them 90 seconds.

We're onto evolution. The key question is: 'Can I identify whether genetic variation or environmental variation has occurred?' As they finally settle and the odd pencil and exercise book are provided, she narrates what is happening. 'Show me that you're listening', she says, and every single pupil sits upright and alert. The subject-specific terminology is challenging: organism, species, sexual reproduction, variation, genome, environmental and genetic. They have to determine whether differences in animals are genetic or environmental.

To push their thinking further, she presents them with a Venn diagram and they have to determine whether certain variations are inherited, environmental or both? The list of variations are:

- Ear-lobe shape
- Piercings
- Eye colour
- Tattoo
- Hair colour
- Height
- Scars
- Weight

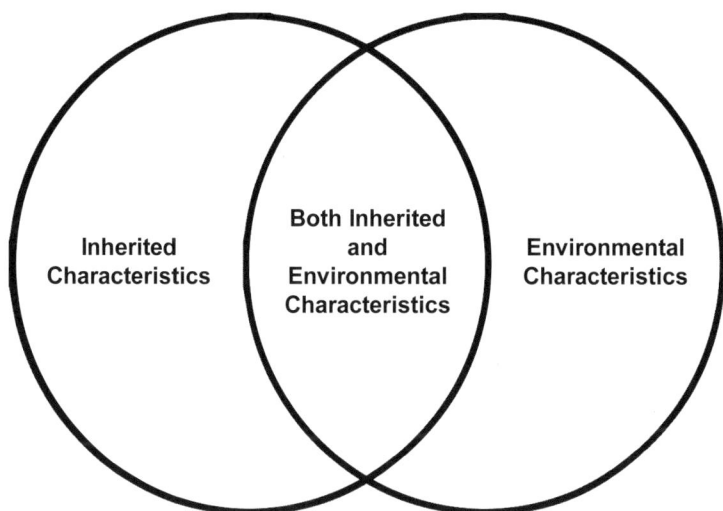

Faariah runs the room in perfect order. She gives them 15 minutes – it's the time suggested by the bought-in scheme of learning – but she soon realises that they need just five minutes. Her situational assessment skills are well-honed. She truncates the exercise and brings them back together to discuss responses. She is happy to go off-piste. We get into an interesting discussion about ears and how ear-stretching (I later find out that it's called 'gauging', which sounds a terrible thing) is environmental and, perhaps, therefore, one could argue that ears can vary due to both inherited and environmental characteristics. It is such fun.

The final phase of the morning – I arrived at 9 am and we finished at 11 am, without a break – sees the pupils complete grammar tasks on main clauses. At the change-over, again Faariah narrates the instructions, they repeat them to her, they enact the instructions and she presides over the room. It's classroom-management perfection.

We're working on clauses – main, subordinate and relative. They are pretty expert at this stuff. They approach nearly two hours of learning without a break. With a few minutes to go, Faariah says, 'We're doing a really good job, but we need to keep going.' She is the team leader.

She asks one of the pupils to analyse this sentence: 'With a big grin the boy tried out his brand-new bike.' 'What part makes sense on its own?'

'The main clause', the girl replies.

'OK. Where is the main clause in this sentence?' No answer. The girl appears stumped. Still no answer. Faariah says, 'OK, listen, I'll read it out …' In a moment of meta-control of her teaching, she says, 'No … no, I won't. That'll tell you the answer.' Instead, she takes the pupil through the process again, recounting the learning that she has already grasped and then she asks, 'Where's the verb?' The girl thinks, and then identifies the verb and then, with a gentle push from Faariah, the main clause herself. It was artful teaching. Faariah takes the opportunity to explain to the class why she was doing what she was doing. 'And that is why we ask questions.' There's an impromptu round of applause.

As they pack away, a number of them surround me. I am interrogated and the only way I can escape from the Peterborough Inquisition is to promise that I will mention them all in the book.

What the pupils think

Straight off the back of two hours' studying, six pupils are gathered in the library to tell me about Miss Jamil. Two were taught by her in Year 4, three in Year 5, and one currently in Year 6. Some of them have been taught by Faariah across more than one year. They are very eager to explain what they like about her.

'She's very positive and she really wants you to understand. She's really not boring', says one of the girls. 'She taught me in Year 4 and into Year 5. I knew her teaching methods. Her rules. If you talk over her, you have three chances and then she takes action.' She tells me that she likes how Faariah has control of the class and how everyone behaves. 'She makes sure everyone understands it and she goes over it again if you don't.' I turn to a boy immediately on my left, who is keen to say something. He speaks very formally.

'Miss Jamil tells us what we are going to do and then checks we know it.' I ask him why that might be a good thing.

'Well', he continues, 'at uni and if you have a job you will be able to look back at what she has taught you.' I tell him how I can see that's a positive thing. He carries on, and his confidence is growing. 'When we found out that I was going to carry on with Miss Jamil from Year 5 into Year 6, my dad was really relieved. My dad is a big fan of Miss Jamil.'

'Why's that?' I ask.

'Because she's always looking at my mathematics homework and replying to my dad when he asks her questions.'

I ask him, 'Are you good at maths?'

He pauses, and then says, without any change in his expression whatsoever, 'I'm pretty much an expert.' I am both taken aback and amused. It is an awesome response, in the true sense of the word, and tells me a lot about the impact of Faariah's teaching.

They tell me that Miss Jamil clarifies things for them. She comes round and helps the table or the individual. They love how much help they get from her. It's a truth universally acknowledged. They also like the challenge. 'They are tough lessons and our brains work really hard. Sometimes I have to breathe and calm down. It can be really hard.'

Faariah is clear and concise, apparently. Importantly to all of them, she is positive and looks for the good rather than the bad in them. 'Miss never shouts. She has a calm tone. She's really well organised and she makes sure where everything is.' That pupils value a well-organised teacher is another noteworthy truism.

The final comment, from one of the boys, was so insightful. 'If you do something wrong, she never shouts. She just asks, "Why you did it?" Shouting doesn't really help anything. I had another teacher who used to shout a lot, and he realised half-way through the year that it didn't do any good. Shouting doesn't make you more focused. *Not* shouting makes you more focused. He realised that. He stopped shouting and for the rest of the year, we all did better. We know Miss doesn't raise her voice. Ever.'

From the mouths of babes . . .

When I ask them for a single word to describe Miss Jamil, they say: funny, optimistic, enthusiastic, positive, calm, selfless and thoughtful. 'Miss is *always* thinking about us.'

———————————

IRL: Faariah Jamil

John Tomsett (JT): What made you go into teaching then?

Faariah Jamil (FJ): From very young, I was exposed to being a teacher and being in a school environment. My mum has been teaching in primary schools since before I was born. I think it's almost 30 years that she has been teaching, including being an assistant head teacher. I was in and out of classrooms a lot, especially during the summer holidays, and without realising it, absorbing a teacher's way of thinking along the way. I was cutting and laminating when I was six years old!

JT: Were you one of those who used to line the dollies up in your room?!

FJ: Well, I didn't line the dollies up, but, as a slightly bossy older sister, I often played the teacher game with my little brother, where I would make him sit down and be the pupil while I wrote on the whiteboard and pretended to be the teacher. I don't know what I used to teach him, but he was forced to sit down and watch. Although, I'd say I didn't want to be a primary school teacher from that age.

I had a range of positive and negative experiences with my own teachers. The positive experiences made me think, 'They've had a huge impact on me and I would like to make a similar impact on the next generation. They're so excited by their subject and they're passing on that excitement and that excitement will then live on in their pupils.'

That idea of passing on your love of learning to future generations stemmed from my history teacher. In secondary school, my history teacher from Year 7 to Year 13 loved his subject *so* much. Stereotypically, history was seen as being quite boring in secondary school, and he completely flipped that. He was *so* engaged; he would come in costume to teach us. He would be role-playing when we entered the classroom and he wouldn't be afraid to make us laugh or make himself look silly to get us engaged. I was impressed by the love he had for history. History and science are two subjects I am passionate about. I'm currently leading science, which I absolutely love. The idea of being able to pass that love for science on – not just the knowledge, but the love of it – is really exciting.

There was my Year 6 teacher as well. She was incredible. I still remember that feeling of being very insecure and not wanting to be different from anyone else when you're going into secondary school. Cleverly, in a way that none of us realised, she made it OK for us to be ourselves and made us proud of who we are. Even though we learned that in Year 6, many, many years ago, that feeling still sticks with me, and becoming a teacher was also about wanting to pass on that positive feeling.

On the flip side, there were some teachers who left a lasting impact on me in a negative way. One teacher sticks in my mind. I was in Year 7. It was a much larger school compared to my primary. It was very clear that she hadn't taken the time to get to know me as an individual. My mum attended parents' evening and she said to my mum the reason why I was not at the expected level or making the expected progress in reading and writing was because I had English as an additional language.

Now, this was bizarre because on the English as an additional language (EAL) spectrum, I was assessed as fluent in both English and a dialect of Punjabi.

JT: **She just didn't know you.**

FJ: Yes, she didn't know me. The reason I didn't make the progress, and my mum made it quite clear, was because I simply wasn't focusing enough and I needed more support. I still remember that feeling of being put into a box and being seen as EAL, not being seen as Faariah. That feeling was hard to understand at 12 years old. My mum was great because she was one of the first women in our family and one of the first women in our community to go into a teaching career, which later developed into a leadership role. She explained, in a very age-appropriate way, that sometimes people put us into boxes, but those boxes don't define us. I still remember in that moment thinking that I didn't ever want to put a child into a certain box. We do need to know that those children with EAL, pupil premium (PP) and SEND labels may have additional needs, but I'm very careful not to put pupils into a box. I remember how suffocating that felt, not being seen as an individual. I experienced first-hand what it was like to not feel good enough, and I knew I never wanted any other child to feel that way. That was a life-changing negative experience. It led to me wanting to be a teacher.

JT: **It was very early on then.**

FJ: Yes, in the middle of secondary school, I'd say I was quite certain. Then, like any journey, it fluctuated again because I got to sixth form and I suffered the bereavement of my grandfather. I was in my late teens then and it sort of re-jigged my perspective on things. I explored optometry very briefly, but it was very boring, in all honesty! On work experience, every day was the same and because I'd had placements in schools prior to that, I could compare the two, and the schools were so much more fun! Every day was truly different, even in that short placement time. There was one video that I watched when I was applying for a BEd and it was a video of a lady called Rita Pierson. That TED talk gave me goosebumps and I got quite emotional after I watched her speak.[1] I think that cemented it. After that point there were no more fluctuations. I was certain that this was the way I wanted to go.

JT: **Was it a BEd? Then you got your first job, here?**

FJ: Yes.

JT: **You've taught Years 4, 5 and 6 since starting here. What are your thoughts when you plan teaching?**

FJ: When I'm teaching it's about whether they understand or not. Is everyone paying attention? At the moment, that's what I'm focusing on, whether everyone is focused and engaged. Whether I've actually given them everything they need to be able to focus.

JT: **You're checking for understanding, rather than just ploughing on.**

FJ: I think if anything, I stop more often than I should, in that, if there's more of them that don't understand than do understand, we'll stop and we'll focus on what they don't get before moving on to the next step, if that makes sense? I'm focusing on whether or not they're understanding and whether we're all together. More generally, in the classroom, it's also about whether they've got everything they need to actually access what we're talking about; whether everyone's working together as a unit. I'm very careful to make sure that children are not on separate tasks according to prior attainment. They're working towards the same goal, but they've got different scaffolds and different ways to get to the same goal. At that moment it's 'do they understand and can they all access it to be able to understand?'

---

1   R. Pierson, Every kid needs a champion, *TED* (3 May 2013). Available at: https://www.youtube.com/watch?v=SFnMTHhKdkw.

JT: **Yes, and they really appreciate that. When it comes to classroom management, I've never seen anybody do what you do, when you articulate the steps they need to take at transition and then they repeat the three or four steps, and then you just stand there and watch it happen!**

FJ: Yes, it's definitely taken a lot of, what I call, *training*. So, in September, I say, you're going to get trained. One of the things that really blows their minds is when I tell them I'm going to train them to know what I'm thinking. I teach them to pick up on social cues. I didn't realise that you have to teach children to pick up on social cues. So, I've tried to get them to be independent problem solvers, by getting them to say what I'm thinking. One of the questions I have begun to ask is, 'Who is doing more of the work, me or the children?' Often, I'm doing way more work than they're doing, and it's not fair to them. They're going to go off to secondary school where they have so many different teachers, and they're going to expect to be told what to do all the time, which isn't the way the world works.

JT: **When I spoke to them earlier, Isaac said, 'She tells us what to do and checks we know.' I said, 'Well, what's good about that?' He replied, 'When we go to university, or we get a job, we'll look back at what Miss has taught us and we'll know how to do stuff.' That's exactly what you're saying.**

FJ: Yes, being new to Year 6, one of the things that I've had to think hard about is how I'm getting them ready for, not just secondary school, but later life as well. I was so naïve about lots of the things that I assumed children would pick up, but that actually need to be explicitly taught. Although it is very hard sometimes to stand back and let them try to figure it out. Or if they come to you with a problem, turning to them and saying, 'How can you problem solve?'

JT: **You're very good at that as well. You give little away. You push it back.**

FJ: It's hard. I have to bite my tongue sometimes, especially with little things, like, 'I haven't got a pencil.' I either give them a blank stare and they know what to do, or I say, 'How can we problem solve?' It is so incredibly difficult when they look back at you and, even though it's 10 seconds of silence, it feels like minutes. It's hard because it's so much easier to just say, 'Here's a pencil.' Or say, 'Oh, OK, go and get one from over there.' I'm hoping it will pay off in the long term.

JT: **It's brilliant, honestly. I would just double down on it. The maturity you have in making sure that they're responsible for themselves, is impressive. Could you tell me about any principles you follow for running DR.**

FJ: DR I really like because I use many of those skills and techniques in the other lessons. The main scaffold you have for DR is that every talk partner pair will have a clarifying toolkit and a bookmark stem. The bookmark stem is split into the skills of clarifying, inferring, evaluating, summarising and making connections. Whenever they verbally form an answer, they use those steps and they're there for them to access. The clarifying toolkit has got lots of different tactics they can use.

JT: **I love the toolkit, it's great.**

FJ: Yes, I like it because I use it in foundation subjects as well for when they're not sure on something. Some elements aren't really relevant, like *picturing the scene*, but many things, like *reading the sentence before and after*, work really well. One of the key focuses with a cohort that is so EAL-heavy is how they articulate verbal answers. They've been doing DR since the beginning of Key Stage 2. A lot of the time when you ask them a question, even in history, they'll think really carefully about how to frame their answer, which really helps with articulating grammatically correct verbal answers as well. I think it's brilliant, and the way you get to explore the text in DR reading specifically, is quite snappy. It's also quite flexible, in that you can decide where you need to clarify more and where you need to explore more. I just think it works really well.

JT: **You're very good on the vocabulary.**

FJ: Yes, that's something that we have to work hard on.

JT: **Tell me about being head of science then. You've got a United Learning scheme of work for science?**

FJ: Yes, we do.

JT: **Tell me about that and how you make that work.**

FJ: I started leading science in my second ECT year. I was leading it alongside another colleague. It wasn't United Learning then, but we were going into the process of United Learning. We are now following the United Learning Scheme, but we're adapting it to match the needs of our cohort.

JT: **How do you do that? This is a crucial issue for me.**

FJ: Yes, so first of all there is scaffolding. I'm trialling it with my year group and then I'm going to have templates for other year groups further down. The United Learning Curriculum offers one worksheet for everybody. I just didn't think that worked, because it's not reasonable to expect everybody to be able to achieve the same goal from that one worksheet without some scaffolding. The first step that I took was making sure there are scaffolds to support or to deepen understanding.

JT: **They told me how much they appreciate the academic stretch that you give them.**

FJ: The second thing was, it's very, very knowledge-heavy, which is great because they need the knowledge, but there aren't many opportunities for practical learning. Again, that's something that I'm working on with Year 6. They're keen to do practical work. The good thing with United Learning is that it has a knowledge organiser, so again, it starts to get them prepared for secondary school, where resources like that are going to be more commonly used. It has a knowledge organiser, so that they know what the knowledge is and they can refer to it. The United Learning scheme doesn't rush into practical work. With science, people fall into the trap of thinking, 'Well, if it's hands-on and practical, of course they're going to learn from it.' But they're just doing stuff. United Learning is really great in that it provides the knowledge before the practical stuff. In my opinion, it doesn't have enough opportunities for practical learning. That's the second thing that I'm working on adapting, trying to include more purposeful, practical work to engage the pupils, practical work for them to actually learn from. For example, in the science lesson I taught today, we learned about the variations. In our next lesson, when we're including a practical element, it will be based on today's learning. It's the learning *and then* the experiment or investigation, which is again, like you said, purposeful, and not just done for the sake of doing something.

JT: **Today they were looking at inheritance and environmental adaptations. What practical work will you go on to do?**

FJ: Bearing in mind the weather, we'll be going to our Forest School area, and we'll be looking for any species we can see. They're going to be noting the different adaptations and the variations and then will be categorising them into environmental or genetic. The challenge will be, of course, that they won't know who the parents are of that offspring. They'll have to try and decide which one of those they think it will be. That, I presume, won't take the whole lesson, but they'll still be able to remember their learning and apply it; it won't be done without a purpose. I think that's a pet peeve of mine when practical work is done but there's no purpose.

JT: **What will the purpose be? To build on what they've learned?**

FJ: Yes, to be able to build on it and to see it for real, to deepen their understanding of it. I know, as a learner, after I've learned something new, revisiting it visually makes it easier for me to remember, because then I retain that picture in my mind.

JT: **Do they do anything in the scheme about possible misconceptions?**

FJ: They do have a teacher slide showing where possible misconceptions could arise. The other great thing is that they have a teacher subject knowledge pack. A number of colleagues have said their science knowledge is a bit thin. The amount they need to know has increased significantly through all year groups. Those subject-knowledge slides help us refresh what we need. Alongside United Learning, we also have annual science days. The whole school studies science for the whole day. It's about ensuring that we're raising aspirations for all children. The day I planned last year was based on careers. Lots of them hadn't heard of many of the careers in science and, unfortunately, lots of our girls still think some aspects of science aren't for them. One of my goals last year was smashing that stereotype. I wanted to steer away from *a doctor in a white coat* as the only science job that you hear of. We explained how a hairdresser is a scientist, because lots of their job involves mixing chemicals and creating substances.

JT: **Yes, you can't get that wrong!**

FJ: Exactly, so we had a hairdresser, personal trainers and nutritionists, and we spent the whole day role-playing those careers for some of the younger children. For some of the older children it was about explaining the steps that you'll need to take to get into certain professions. I planned an investigation for each year group to carry out, related to a specific career. Then – and it's always my favourite part of the science days – in the afternoon, we came together and we celebrated what everyone had done. We focused on *how* they went about their investigation. They had free rein; they had the whole day to think about how they were going to undertake the investigation. Usually, you don't have enough time to plan an experiment, do it and then consider the results, all in one go. Here, at least they get to do that once a year, which is great. You see their independence and them thinking like a scientist, which is what you want with each subject, especially the foundation subjects. You want them to have subject-specific knowledge, but you also want them to see that subject as something that they can do.

JT: **That's amazing. Gosh. Such deep thought about how you plan such learning. And the aspiration for the children. I love that idea of breaking cultural stereotypes.**

FJ: Yes. I had to reflect on how I had quite a privileged childhood and I was always told, by both my parents and grandparents, that I can achieve whatever it is that I put my mind to. Like I said, my mum was the first person to go to university in our family and she graduated with a chemical engineering degree and then went into teaching. But I didn't realise the number of children who wouldn't have even talked about careers or dreams for the future with their families. I think that really opened my eyes. There's a gap that we have a responsibility to bridge, to make sure that they know that there is a future that they can all aspire to. How can I bridge that gap? It's not necessarily the family's fault, sometimes the way that families are structured, careers and aspirations go to the bottom of the list and I don't want that for our young people.

JT: **They are very lucky to have you to teach them! So, that's the science. Then you moved on to the grammar. The language used was impressive. Your situational assessment skills are impressive. You were talking to Imogen and you wanted her to identify the main**

clause? You were about to read out the sentence to help her and you stopped yourself.

FJ: Yes, it was hard to control myself. I still need to hold myself back. I had to think carefully about how I was going to get her there without me helping her too much. Sometimes it needs what I call an awkward silence, but they're not awkward silences, it's giving them that time just to have a think and have a go. Like I said, those 10 seconds that it takes normally, feels like minutes. It's really hard, but I'm working on it.

JT: **I think you said, 'That's why we ask questions because then she can get there herself.' It was such a great moment. What else do you do that you're very conscious and deliberate about?**

FJ: One of the things that I try my best to create is a safe and predictable environment. I didn't like surprises when I was younger and I know how they used to make me feel, and I'm very, very conscious of that. So if there is a new adult in the room, like today, I'll warn them the day before, if I can. If our timetables are going to be switched up, I'll warn them if I can. We always have the same timer and we always have the same packing-up routine. In the morning I'll always be on the door, in the afternoon I'll always be on the door. I like there to be certain routines that are non-negotiables that they know are going to happen every day. They know every day they'll get some time to do some quiet reading. They know every day they'll see me in the morning on the door and in the afternoon when they go home. They know that every time we pack up for a lesson and get started for the next lesson, it will be in the same way. I try not to throw in any surprises.

As I've moved up towards Year 6, I've tried to make sure that they're included in my rationale for decisions. I've found that helps with motivation and with us all being on the same page. When I tried this new thing with cold calling, it was really hard for them to not put up their hands and for them to not whisper the answer to their talk partners. We spoke about it, and I was very open and honest. I said, 'What do you think you're gaining when you whisper the answer?' One of them, really bravely said, 'Well, we just don't want them to feel like they don't know, and we want everyone to feel like they know.' I was very open and honest with them in quite a grown-up way, and I explained that it's not about who knows the answer and who doesn't, it's about making sure *everyone* knows *how* to get to the answer. Now they don't whisper, not because they were told that they'll lose rewards points if they whisper, but because they were told that we don't whisper because we want everyone to get to the right answer.

JT: **It's unhelpful, isn't it? It actually doesn't help them.**

FJ: Yes, exactly, but I found moving from Year 5 to 6, I've tried my best not to say, 'Don't do it because I've told you not to do it.' I explain the rationale behind the rules and the decisions I make. I want to make sure that they feel included, so it's their environment and not just mine. It's *our* environment.

And it's the same with behavioural incidents. We always say, 'You're not in trouble. We want you to understand what's happened as a result of your choices. You made a choice and we want you to know what's happened as a result of your choice. We're educating you on how to not make that same mistake again.' I'm very grateful to have joined a school from the very beginning of my teaching career where everybody has a like-minded teaching philosophy.

JT: **How would you describe that philosophy?**

FJ: Well, I would say at the centre of it, the most important thing is making sure that the children feel safe. I know that sounds as though it's something that's obvious, but it's so integral to everything that we do. Every teacher is on the door every morning, meeting and greeting to make sure that they're welcomed into a safe environment, right from the gate in the morning, so they know they can breathe that sigh of relief they're in school, that they're happy, they're safe. Ready, respectful and safe are our main values and we live by them. I think the respect that we get from the pupils is because we give that same respect back. Manners are always there. We're modelling how we want the children to interact with each other and we are building little people that we're going to send out into society. They learn to be tolerant of different people's beliefs and cultures. That makes me feel great, because all of us are working towards that goal.

JT: **There's a deep humanity in this place. What do you do, then, to ensure high academic ambition for the children?**

FJ: We have very high expectations throughout the school. We do lots of things to celebrate their academic wins. We're starting in writing to have great pieces on the screens around the school, and not just from our more able writers, but our writers who have made lots of progress and those who have put in lots of effort. With reading, we've recently moved from having reading records to having reading challenges. It's similar to a summer reading challenge. They have more fun and engaging ways to read at home. They take a picture of themselves reading in a weird place, for example. Again, we celebrate that with reading certificates and badges. I think we set the bar very high and try to develop their intrinsic motivation.

JT: **What about the popcorn?!**

FJ: Aaah! They told you about the popcorn [*laughing*] …

JT: **Well, thank you so much for meeting with me and letting me watch you teach.**

———————————

Testimonials

Colleagues

'Faariah is a superb teacher. Her classroom is always calm and purposeful, children are happy and confident because they know and understand her expectations. They are also challenged as all children are expected to participate and contribute during whole class teaching.'

'From day one Faariah has shown a desire to become the best teacher possible. She is particularly adept at carefully considering the strategy she is going to use along with the precise words she needs to say to accomplish any task.'

'Faariah has a deep understanding of the diverse needs of the children in her care. She consistently goes above and beyond to ensure that every pupil receives the support and guidance they need to thrive academically, socially and emotionally. One of Faariah's most admirable qualities is her commitment to continual growth and improvement.'

Pupils

'Thank you Miss Jamil, for being a great teacher this year. You have brought me much joy and taught me a lot this year.'

'For the best teacher ever, aka Miss Jamil. I hope you enjoy your summer holidays!'

'You have been a great teacher since I joined Year 4 and I will miss you SOOO much!'

'For all that you have done and for all that you do, I just wanted to say a big, massive THANK YOU!'

So, what can we learn from Faariah Jamil?

Faariah is a British Pakistani and a proud Muslim, which shapes her values and experiences. Her mum is a passionate primary teacher. Her dad and grandparents, who were immigrants, instilled in her a sense of pride in her roots. Her protective siblings ingrained in her self-confidence and the courage to face failure without fear. Education and learning were highly valued in her home.

Her grandparents taught her to be strong, brave and curious, and always to be a pillar of support for others. The line by Rita Pierson, 'Behind every child who believes in themselves is a teacher who believed in them first'[2] resonates greatly with Faariah and she aims to create a safe environment for children, guiding them to become the best versions of themselves and understand how invaluable their unique selves are to our society.

Faariah Jamil is driven. She is a clear example of a teacher who sees her job as more than just securing great academic outcomes for her pupils (which she does secure, of course). Listening to her talk about her formative years, her resolve to break through glass ceilings, her determination to convince her pupils that nothing is beyond them regardless of their starting points, her insistence that she trains them to think for themselves, and her sheer love for the young people she has in her care, are awesome to witness, in the true sense of the word. I have never met a teacher who doesn't profess to have the highest expectations for their pupils, but Faariah does so with the deepest sincerity.

Faariah's strengths are largely rooted in her deliberateness. Many of the truly great teachers featured in this book have great situational assessment skills. They seem to be able to watch themselves teach and alter their teaching depending upon their pupils' behaviours. The way Faariah alters what she does, in the moment, is impressive. As is her ability to encourage the pupils to take responsibility to act for themselves. Many schools aim for their pupils to be more independent, and

2   Pierson, Every kid needs a champion.

yet learned helplessness creeps in. Not so with Faariah. As her charges approach the end of their primary school careers, they are accepting responsibility for making decisions about what to do in whatever situation they find themselves. They are mirroring their teacher's sense of autonomy.

The final thing worthy of note is Faariah's awareness of her status as a role model for her pupils. She is a brilliant young woman. She is eager for promotion, has a deep-seated confidence in her abilities, and is wise enough to know she has a great deal to learn. The way she behaves in front of her pupils, every second of every lesson, matters. They know that and respect her deeply. She can only be the teacher she wants to be because the culture of the school allows her; Emma Anderson is wise enough to know, as Thorpe's head teacher, that she has to enable Faariah to grow. As Holden Caulfield says in *The Catcher in the Rye*, 'The thing with kids is, if they want to grab for the gold ring, you have to let them do it, and not say anything.' As Emma is with Faariah, so, in turn, is Faariah with her pupils.

Faariah Jamil's pupils' progress and achievement data

All the data are from September 2023 to July 2024.

Mathematics

- 96% made good or accelerated progress
- Pupils at expected standard rose by 10%
- Pupils at greater depth (GD) standard rose by 13%
- 94% of pupils with EAL made good or accelerated progress

Writing

- 81% made good or accelerated progress
- Pupils at expected standard rose by 32%
- 83% of pupils with EAL made good or accelerated progress

Reading

- 75% made good or accelerated progress
- Pupils at expected standard rose by 21%
- 89% made good or accelerated progress
- 81% of PP pupils made good or accelerated progress
- 94% of pupils with EAL made good or accelerated progress

A Truly Great Primary Teacher: Dean Salisbury

Dean Salisbury is the deputy head teacher at Sutton Park Primary School, Kidderminster, a Year 6 teacher and the writing lead for the Central Region Schools Trust.

The school leadership's view

Having limped to Kidderminster last night with a flat tyre, I am delighted to have just made it this morning to Sutton Park Primary School, part of the Central Region Schools Trust. I am sitting in the conference room. Dean Salisbury, one of two truly great teachers I am visiting today, pops in to say 'Hello'. I've seen Dean teach before. I remember a deliberate, precise, Year 6 writing lesson. He tells me I will see similar today. The Principal, Lorna Weatherby sweeps by, says 'Hi' and is gone before I know it! Front gate duty calls. Just outside the door, I hear a parent say to her child 'Love you' as she drops them off. It just confirms what I already know: this is a school where love exists.

When Lorna returns, I ask her what I will see when I watch Dean teach. 'It's hard to define. It's more than just pedagogy. It's the small, consistent things he does automatically, on a daily basis. He helps children thrive. There's no dragging them through it. It's a collaborative journey. He gets buy-in and engagement. They really make the effort because they see the value of what Dean does and they know they will get something out of it. His teaching is purposeful, engaging and based on great relationships.'

'He has humanity', I say.

Lorna replies: 'Yes, he has the human element. He's not just a teacher going through the motions, he is genuinely bothered – it's not a fake bolt-on.' She tells me he is the writing lead for the Trust. 'He has great subject knowledge, which is a given, really. He has such good skills, he is able to adapt as the lesson progresses, depending upon who has learnt what.

'Dean has taught Year 6 for a decade, and although the curriculum has changed, he has changed with it and has learnt so much from repeatedly teaching the same concepts. Each year it's a new challenge to adapt for the fresh cohort. He has adapted as the cohorts have become more neuro-diverse. Results in Year 6 have been maintained across different cohorts each year. Whether a pupil has additional needs or is pupil premium, Dean just encourages them to be the best they can be. We are closing the PP gap. With a one form entry, Dean is able to hone his craft each year.'

'It is interesting how the school has allowed Dean to stay with Year 6 for a decade and build his expertise', I say.

'Yes', says Lorna, 'but it only works because Dean is who he is. That wouldn't have happened with anyone. He has a great sense of humour, he cares deeply for them, he is persistent and consistent with his high expectations. He always aims for better than last year, year-in, year-out.

He teaches hard all the time, not just when someone is watching. And he's a role model for the children. He is his best self with them and he promotes that ethos with the children, which is so important in our current society. He wants our young people to be confident in their own worth.'

I haven't had to say much. Lorna knows her deputy very well, it seems. I am keen to see Dean teach again.

———————————

Teaching

I walk with Lorna to Dean's classroom and she departs swiftly.

It's chilly. Having reached 60, I get cold easily. I sit in the middle of the back row. I keep my coat on as the wind drives through the open windows and makes the room a Siberian wasteland. Dean is in a shirt. We are looking at the features of a diary entry. Good old genre writing!

We are waiting for the rest of the class to arrive. The 10 pupils already here are the Sports Crew. They have a responsibility to create games to play on the playground and they look after the younger ones if they're unhappy. At every step, this school thinks about how learning transfers into life.

With a full class, Dean starts the lesson. He is an imposing figure, full of energy and enthusiasm. He is in his element. 'OK, put "Diary" in the middle of your whiteboard.' The girl in front of me has beautiful hand-writing. She finishes the tail of her Y with a flourish. 'You've got a hot writing task coming up. On your whiteboards, I'll give you two minutes to write down all the features of a diary entry. You can work in pairs.' Dean moves people very deliberately so they have talk partners. No leaning across desks, they change tables so that they are fully partnered up. The children get going immediately. Dean explains to me what they are up to. 'We'll go from cold to hot. Pre-teaching around a certain genre. Then features of each genre. End of a sequence. This is diary writing.' He runs the room. He doesn't commit the sin of hijacking a pair's conversation. He just holds an overview of the classroom and listens to what is being said.

I look at the walls. There's BIDMAS. Fractions. The four operations and all their synonyms. There's a writing genre spectrum, from formal to informal: Biography; Science investigation; Instructions; Non-chronological report; Poetry; Persuasive; Newspaper; Story writing and Diary. I'm not sure I agree with the order, to be honest. It would be good to discuss that with Dean, but when he circles round to me again he is talking about the importance of the main character in *Street Child*. He is called Jim Jarvis and has really caught the pupils' imaginations. 'I want them to explore deeper vocab, as well as look at the genre features.'

Despite Dean being dressed for his summer holidays, it's winter. One poorly child is packed up and sent home. I am on the verge of being teeth-chatteringly cold. 'Diaries are full of emotions and feelings. We don't want just a recounting of what happened', says Dean as he begins to take feedback from the pupils. He challenges suggested features that aren't quite hitting the mark. 'Paragraph? Is that diary specific? Doesn't all writing have paragraphs. Is there something you've written that is much more diary-specific? … have a think … Contractions? That's a good one … great! Well done.'

Mrs Campbell, the teaching assistant, writes up the feedback on the flip chart paper while Dean runs the feedback session. They look to be a seasoned double-act. 'Personal thoughts? Good. We're not writing as Jim today … we can be ourselves today! Another idea? … Past tense? Is he completely right? Talk to your partner.' And so it goes on until we have a board full of the features of a diary entry. 'First person. Good. What do we have to do in our writing if we are writing in the first person? Yes! A capital I!!! I'll walk out if I get a small i.' He has 100% attention. He is a 'big' character himself. 'Mrs Campbell, have we missed anything?' Dean asks of his partner in a diary-writing paradigm. He is on top form. 'Remember, we're working towards a hot writing task', replies Mrs Campbell. More like a *cold* task. I'm now officially freezing.

So far, so unremarkable. Thorough, but unremarkable. It's what Dean does next that strikes me as the genius element of his writing process. He reminds them of their visit to a Victorian Village. 'What can you remember about your visit to Blists Hill? Try to think about it in chronological order.' Off again in pairs. A new, chronological list of things they did on the day out and how they felt: excitement and joy; sent to a classroom; Victorian school; we got dressed up; poor person's house; candle shop; sweet shop visit; bank to exchange money; chemist; toilet was in the yard; bakery and lunch. 'You all did these things, but you all had slightly different days', says Dean. This is great fun. It has been hard not to get involved in the lesson. I put my hand up and tell Dean that the council house where I grew up had an outside toilet. He flicks to a slide with one of the pupils in the Victorian loo, 'I bet it wasn't quite like this one!'

'It wasn't a million miles away!' I quip back. It's fun. I also explain how 'chrono' is Greek for time. Chronic illness means one you have had for a long time, not that it is a really bad illness. I then realise I should shut up.

He hands out a sheet with blank thought bubbles on it. 'You have thought bubbles in front of you. I'm going to help you move those exciting events into thoughts. One thought per bubble. This is how we build up our writing.' It is a lovely prop – simple, but highly effective. Dean then plays a five-minute video of the day, featuring all the pupils. 'I just want you to watch the film and think about two things, that will fill your first two thought bubbles. Think about: 1. getting changed and 2. heading down to the school. How did it feel to get dressed up? How did it feel to be marched down to the school? Watch the video. Then we'll watch it again so that you can note down what you were thinking. I'm happy for you to talk it through with your partner. Different thoughts are OK because they are personal.' He plays the video twice. It is wonderful. The importance of high-quality resources. The children are entranced. *Of course* they are! I love the thoroughness of these steps. Dean is getting them thinking hard. They are creating a chronological plan and sequencing their writing, rather than rushing into a hot task (I'd love a hot bath, to be honest), and because the material is so good and so personal, everyone is invested in the content. It means they can spend most of their brain power on the craft of writing.

Dean gives further instructions: ' "I wanted to laugh" might be something you write, but laughter is an action, not a feeling. What *made* you laugh? ... OK. "It was new". What feelings go along with "new" ... "excitement", "nervousness"? ... Bob didn't laugh. Why didn't he laugh? ... "scared". Good. So, when you have written those thought bubbles, we can put those together and move from the thought bubbles to the diary writing. We can slow down.' He asks them to keep working on the vocabulary: 'Seven more minutes.' Timing is such an important thing. It pressures them to keep working and is the same tactic Ted Hughes recommends in his book, *Poetry in the Making*.

Dean keeps the pressure on. He is teaching between the desks. There is genuine engagement in the room. The writing is built up so beautifully and everyone is enjoying themselves. 'We are so much deeper in our thoughts', he says, 'let's gather some feelings and emotions on the board. "Excitement", "nervousness", "we all looked like grandparents".' Dean moves from cold calling to hands up. He narrates what he is doing as he makes situational decisions based on the responses. The final list: excited, happy, nervous, embarrassed, anxious, grateful, frightened, joyful, shocked, sick, disgusted, disappointed, dismayed and confused. 'Right', says Dean, 'I want you to imagine you are lying on your bed at the end of the day and thinking about it ... You can include absolutely anything else that happened. Here's a map to help you, it might jog your memory. But don't be just looking at the map.' He agrees to another showing of the video, with the sound muted. Dean is personable and fun. He is gentle: 'Have a drink ... it's under your desk', he says to a girl who is coughing.

I'm impressed by the thoroughness. The steps and the depth of thinking. The planning of the process to access the pupils' deepest memories.

Ten minutes later he uses the visualiser to showcase some of the work so far:

1   As we walked down the sludgy path we were introduced to the itchy, rough Victorian clothes.

2   I am Harry. I am 11 years old.

3   Today at school we went on a trip to BH. Today we got to do scary things, and we got to go to a school, in the life of a child in the 1900s.

4   Wow! That was such a long day. I'm glad to be home.

Heads back down, beavering away. Mrs Campbell is working with a small group. Dean stops off and tells me his thoughts. 'They find writing as someone else hard enough, but there's an irony in how writing as themselves is, in fact, more challenging. I will mark these overnight. Ready for next lesson. I think I will have to model more precisely. I am not sure they have all got the tone and the structure of a diary entry yet.'

He comes upon Lizzie's piece. 'Wow Lizzie! I knew you were going to enjoy this piece of work, but you've nailed it. This is awesome.' They are all working so hard; there is such commitment. He chooses Frank to read his out loud and it is beautiful.

'Horrific cold stung my face. As I walked down the tight, narrow, corridor my nerves started to kick in and my heart was thumping in my chest. Children were supposed to be seen and not heard.'

Dean offers an immediate critique: 'You have the description and the feelings. From "I don't know where to start" 10 minutes ago, to this – that's amazing!' Frank has grown about three feet in height, and, completely absorbed by what I have been watching, I have forgotten I was so cold!

It's time to pack up: 'Thank you for your efforts. Thank you for your time this morning. If you could help me tidy up . . .' and of course they do. This is *Team Dean*.

———————————

What the pupils think

I return to the conference room where I began the day and am soon joined by six of Dean's pupils. I set them off chatting about why he is a truly great teacher. 'He keeps you involved. We have fun and we learn. And he has lots of energy!' says Sara. It sounds like a recipe for success to me!

One of her friends chips in. 'He is entertaining and expressive. I love it when he puts on voices when he reads aloud. He makes the book come alive, basically. He's like an entertainer. *I can't think of one time when Year 6 has been boring.*' I write that last line down verbatim. Wow!

I press them further about Dean's teaching. 'In lessons he uses a variety of strategies. He shows us different ways of doing things. And he never gives up on you. Mrs Campbell does interventions, which can help improve our skills in lessons, if we don't really get it.'

'What I like is that he is well-organised. When in lessons, he always has everything ready. There's no wasting time. I like teachers being organised, and when teachers aren't it wastes time. It's easier to concentrate when they are organised like Mr Salisbury. And he always makes sure we have a talk partner.' That last comment is so interesting. Too many times I see individuals left to talk to no one during a think-pair-share. It matters to the pupils, hugely.

They are on a roll now. 'There is a good pace to the lessons. He wouldn't move on to subtract fractions before everyone was ready – he looks at tests and then helps people depending on what they are struggling with. It helps that future lessons are planned out. There's no jumping around. He goes at a good pace. It means that we can all focus on one thing. It is challenging but no one is left behind. *Everybody* works as one group. We like it when he helps us at our tables.'

Another one says, 'He starts with cold tasks in maths as well. He then begins with what you don't know. And no one is afraid to put their hand up.' The pupils understand, at quite a sophisticated level, how Dean teaches adaptively, how he assesses where they are in their learning and modifies what he does in class accordingly.

They talk about SATs. 'He is very straight up. He really wants us to pass SATs in May. We need to try really hard … he tries really hard as well. He is successful at helping pupils pass SATs every year. Last year I had friends in Year 6 and they loved it. He was really helpful. He really cares about our education. Everyone respects Mr Salisbury. He wants us to succeed and to work hard.'

We finish off with our single words to describe Dean: inspiring, amazing, humorous, encouraging, super, energised, cares (a lot about our education and how we are doing in our learning – every pupil in every class matters to him) and pride (in us and the school). One of them says, as a parting shot, 'I've never enjoyed school more.' As a testimonial, that is hard to beat.

IRL: Dean Salisbury

John Tomsett (JT): So, what made you teach then?

Dean Salisbury (DS): My passion for sport was where it started. I could see the positive influence it could have on children. My mum was a teaching assistant at the local school, and our house overlooked the playing fields. I went to the same school. I could nip over the fence to go home for school lunch. I loved primary school. Then I went to secondary school, on to college and decided to teach. I didn't know whether I was going to go into secondary PE or primary. I wanted to influence children, provide them with memorable experiences and use sport as a tool to do that. I also had a real passion for working in areas of need. Hence, I've worked here at Sutton Park for 10 years, and previous to that, I worked in Warndon in Worcester for 10 years. Those are the only two schools I've ever worked at, and both are areas of high deprivation, high PP and estate intake. That is where I have always felt at home.

JT: **This school doesn't feel like that at all.**

DS: No. Well, we're sort of up on a hill, out of the way, but in that classroom where you were then, the level of need is quite extensive.

JT: **You'd never know.**

DS: You saw today a number of children who reflect our intake and we are their escape from the challenges of their life. I want to give them memorable experiences, and hope, so they can change the cycle of low ambition, and give them aspirations and a sense of what life could be like for them. As a vice principal and Year 6 teacher, I've got the best of both worlds, in that I have leadership and management responsibilities, so I can make decisions at that level, along with Lorna, but also still have that impact on the ground because I teach four mornings a week. I teach Year 6 maths and English, so SATs are still my responsibility really, along with my team, and then the other areas are covered by a different teacher. It's challenging because you've still got that huge responsibility for SATs, as well as the vice principal role. It does mean that my colleagues are understanding when I ask them to do something, because they know I'm working at the chalk-face too. When I am saying, 'look, I really need you to do this because I'm doing it too', they know I've tested it out already, or they know that I'm not just telling them to do it. Teachers are more likely to adopt pedagogic practices that you promote if they know that you've been doing them yourself. I can say, 'I'm coming in to support you with this, but this works because I've done this, and this didn't work because I did it and it went wrong', and it's meant that I've had a great time working with other staff across the Trust as the writing lead too.

JT: **Tell me about how you teach the writing process.**

DS: I fell into the role of writing lead if I'm honest. It began as a maternity cover. I've always had a passion for making English visual, enthusing the children to want to write. Children like process, so maths can be something that they quite enjoy. Reading is a different challenge, but if you're a good reader, you enjoy it. Out of the three, I find writing has always been the most difficult to enthuse children about. If you find it difficult, it's harder to break down those steps. So, what I always try to do is make it very visual, make it real, and make them want to write. I think that's the key to it.

JT: **But, you wanting them to want to do it doesn't mean they're going to do it.**

DS: No.

JT: **How do you get them to do it?**

DS: I get them to do it by making sure that the choice of text – the driver of the process – is a really high-quality one. All of the sequences of learning that we do are powered by the text. So, *Street Child* by Berlie Doherty ... Obviously, today was a real-life experience, but the previous task was linked to *Street Child*. They're all immersed in it. Whether they've got a reading age of 5 or 17 – which is the range in the room that I'm currently teaching – they're all enthused. We do the shared reading. They've got a real passion for the character Jim, who's fallen on really hard times. Many of them can relate to it, because he's a similar age, and it gives them, then, the passion to write. So, the text as the central driver is key.

JT: **What other texts do you use?**

DS: *Journey to the River Sea* by Eva Ibbotson, which is long but has fantastic openings and descriptive language by a tremendous author. That's a really strong one. We've used *Windrush Child* by Benjamin Zephaniah … It's all about having a character they can relate to, that is what I've found to be paramount, getting the children to be able to imagine themselves in that character's shoes.

JT: **They love you doing the voices. They love you reading.**

DS: Well, again, I think it's that the passion, isn't it? You've got to go all in, and it's draining, and it's shattering, but it's worth it. Things like use of voice are incredibly important, and showing that you are, even on a bad day, absolutely loving the lesson, loving the learning, and I think that relationship with the children then grows. I think humour is crucial.

JT: **They think you're very funny.**

DS: [*Laughs*] I think when used correctly it's a really powerful thing too, and then they want to come in and they want to please and want to write.

JT: **Everybody I've interviewed likes children; I mean *really* likes them. Treats them with deep respect. At the end of the lesson today, you said, 'Thanks for today and thanks for your time. Can anybody help me clear up?' They're all helping you, straight away. It was beautiful.**

DS: You've got to have them on your team. I used to have a poster on my wall, and I've abandoned it over the years because I thought I'd do it a different way, but 'There's no "I" in team.' It's a very simple phrase, but we are all in this together, and I use it in the build-up to SATs. Even prepping for today, I told them you were coming, and I said, 'It's really important that we show ourselves off to be the best that we can be, because when we work together, we're a really high-quality force', and they came with me. It's about teamwork in sport, that's where it comes from, that team ethic in sport that I transfer to the classroom.

JT: **But you can lose the dressing room.**

DS: Absolutely, yes, and at the start of the year I didn't have the dressing room because of what they'd been through with disrupted teaching last year. They lacked a little bit of trust, I suppose. It was a big deal. So, for us to have moved forward so well, very quickly, is great. We were able to have very honest conversations, which I think is important as well – especially in Year 6 – to be able to have a certain level of honesty with them about what makes good learners. I think treating them as young adults, they respect it.

JT: **Tell me a little bit more about the writing process.**

DS: Yes, the text as key driver. Then breaking down the writing into manageable chunks. Looking at a piece of writing and breaking it down into answering a series of questions. What do we want the opening to achieve? What do we want the main part of the writing to move towards? Then, within that, always trying to keep the reader in mind and the impact of the writing on the reader. What do you want that reader to feel? OK, are they going to feel it from how you have written that? No. OK, let's have a look and let's edit. I think what's really important during that sequence is modelling and showing error. Tomorrow, when I write my opening, I'm going to reflect on the fact that their openings weren't strong enough today. I will put one up, but they will see me physically cross things out, they will see me physically improve vocabulary. So again, reinforcing the fact that writing is not something that is perfect first time, and then we start getting children being braver with their choices and editing. That's how we will create the pieces. Small chunks, building it in chunks, and trying to get them naturally keeping the reader in mind as they write.

JT: **Then the technical aspects of it?**

DS: With the fundamentals of writing, obviously, what we try and do is make sure that when we're teaching the spelling, punctuation and grammar (SPaG) elements of writing, we don't teach them discretely. We begin with a cold task, where I get them to write something after some pre-teaching around the genre, a diagnostic piece, really, and then we end with a hot task, where they show me what they can do at the end of the writing process. So, throughout the cold/hot task journey, when we pick up on the elements of style that they need for their writing, whether it's commas to mark clauses and things like that, we teach them as part of the learning journey within the lesson, and they have an immediate chance to practise. So, we have *incidental write*.

JT: **What's an *incidental write*?**

DS: An incidental write is when they're practising the skills, and they do it in a real way. So, we might write a mini-opening to a diary or we might write a setting description, but we just describe a very specific part of the setting. 'Can you now include clauses?' So, we drop the skills in. Another area of writing that I worked on very recently in the Trust was to bring in, at the start of the year, a really useful *Strong Start* sequence of learning from the Curriculum with Unity Schools Partnership (CUSP)[1] materials, which I thought would be really effective. It's a scheme of work that breaks down what a sentence looks like, but it's year-group specific. They only run from Years 1 to 4, but the Year 4 one contains more than enough extension material for the learning in Years 5 and 6. It goes right back to the beginning, and you slowly progress through and build that advanced sentence over time. So, for the first two weeks back in September, the children completed a *Strong Start* grammar sequence of learning for each year group. What it allowed the children to do was get rid of an awful lot of misconceptions

---

1   See: https://www.unity-curriculum.co.uk/.

about what makes a sentence a sentence. Then, when they started their writing, we found they started in a much stronger place, because a lot of the fundamentals of writing had been dealt with.

JT: **When do you teach that? Every year?**

DS: This year was the first year we did it. It will be included in September for the first two weeks, but what teachers have the option to do is, after every term, revisit and drop in a little bit more, so that they can keep plugging those gaps, because until you get that sentence structure really strong, progression can be difficult to achieve. It means that teachers aren't thinking that they've got to get going writing full pieces straight away.

JT: **What made you do it?**

DS: I was in a Year 5 lesson and they were doing a fantastic job of subordinate clauses. Really successful lesson. So, I watched the lesson, just as part of QA. Brilliant! It was whiteboard at the start, peer assessed – everything you want in a lesson happened. I watched the end task, and 80 or 90% of the children were successful at applying that skill to the task, and then I looked in their books. They hadn't used subordinate clauses, and it had been taught before and was being revisited because they still hadn't got it. It was all down to that sentence structure not being secure. The understanding of what a sentence is was not secure. We've realised that we've got to get that right first. Feedback has been really strong as well. Teachers have come back to me across the Trust and said, 'You know what, it really did have impact, it really did.' Yes, it is dry, but it's a subject that needs addressing and I always think that the best teachers can make something dry come alive.

JT: **I like incidental writing, where you're practising a skill, but you're doing it with a purpose. Otherwise, it's just a waste of time.**

DS: Yes, and they don't see the connections, and connecting the learning is key, and that's how we break writing up so that when they come to the lengthier pieces, you'd hope they'll naturally make those connections. The challenge with writing is the number of things that they've got in their heads to do. When you're doing a piece of maths and you're doing long multiplication, you've got four or five steps that you've taught, they know and they will follow. With writing, yes, you're right, we do need paragraphs, capital letters and full stops. All of that has got to be in their head as well as the features of the genre.

We did a similar thing with spelling. The question was, 'Why is our writing attainment across the trust significantly lower than our maths and reading?' So, I went into every school and did interviews with the leaders, interviews with teachers and learning walks. Actually, it was a brilliant experience. There were three things that came through. Handwriting, which we've put on the backburner for the moment because, yes, it's important, but there are fundamentals we need to address first; grammar, where we have targeted the sentence; and spelling. We realised that spelling was being taught by saying, 'Here's ten words of a spelling pattern, go away, learn them, test next week. Brilliant, you got eight out of ten. You're looking all right. Same again. So across 38 weeks, you've covered all your spelling patterns, you've done tests, the children's scores are quite high, they're learning, this is great, they're on board, parents are fantastic and supporting the learning. You look in the books, and, again, that skill's not transferring. So, what we're doing now, is we're teaching rules. We're not sending home ten words. We're teaching a rule and then once that rule is taught, we then give them a set of words that have that rule in, with the odd variation. There's normally two columns that follow the rule and one that's slightly varied. We say, 'We will do a test on those, but they will be from any of those words, because we want you to apply the rule, we don't want you to learn ten words that you'll never use again.' We're trialling that now as well and, again, staff have been very positive, but it's too early to see the effect.

JT: **That's good. The quality of the writing in their books is really high.**

DS: Yes. Data wise here, we've had some really strong writing levels. We were moderated last year by the county and they were really strong, 80%+.

JT: **You could see them** *writing for England* **in there today!**

DS: Yes. It's that passion.

JT: **It's not just the passion, because you were really thorough, the steps were so well thought through. The levels of structure that you gave them almost made it impossible not to be able to write. So that example you read out at the end … 15 minutes earlier he'd said, 'I don't know where to start', then this incredible piece of writing ...**

DS: I have to say, I gambled because I hadn't read it before. I knew he'd struggled to begin, and I knew he had two paragraphs, but Frank is a typical boy writer. He'd been targeted. He arrived around two sub-levels below. I was really pleased with what he read out because he had also, quite naturally, done the descriptive bit as well as the feeling and emotion, which is fantastic.

JT: **The bit about the 'cold on my cheeks'. He's only able to do that because you structured it so brilliantly. It's about giving them what I call a heuristic – a step-by-step process that you've broken down. Such high-quality writing doesn't happen by accident. It happens because you've thought so deeply about what you're doing. I thought it was absolutely tremendous,**

and rare to see that thoroughness. So, is it the same for maths? What's your thoughts about maths teaching?

DS: Well, maths was always my number one subject. I was a stronger mathematician. I did A level maths, and I've always had a passion for number and found maths quite easy. Times tables are key and it's been brilliant that they've brought them into Year 4 as a threshold.

JT: **Do you insist on them knowing their tables?**

DS: We try to insist on them knowing their tables and we've got some great strategies. We work really hard on it. We try and make it enjoyable. There's also a place for learning them by rote. I really do believe that, but when they haven't got that confidence, then it's about finding the other strategies. In the past, I've been lucky enough to work with some great teachers on how to teach mathematics and break down the fundamentals. Some of the areas are really tricky to teach. I used to find teaching fractions quite a challenge. There are things that some children just get and some really don't, and it's how you make it achievable for them all. I find in maths, as well, a bigger challenge is that children can be either very confident or quite anxious, particularly when they get to Years 5 and 6, and they may have had a bad experience around numbers. Again, the philosophy that I have as a teacher within maths is to make it enjoyable; break it down into those steps, give them really clear processes to relate to, so that they feel quite safe, and they start seeing the patterns. The steps they've been given need to be clear and easy to follow. Particularly when we are doing fractions. We go very number heavy in the autumn term. Fractions are part of that, and then they look at dividing a fraction, and then having the ability to break it down via rules. We call it *flip and kiss*.

JT: **Flip and kiss?**

DS: *Flip and kiss* is what we call it, yes, so if they're dividing a fraction by a whole number, the process we teach them is that you turn the right hand one over then multiply them. You see their eyes light up as what looked alien to them on an arithmetic paper suddenly, three steps later, becomes an absolute doddle. I think that's the key to maths, really; giving them those steps, breaking it down, using the correct terminology and things that they'll remember, and, again, making it fun.

JT: **I'm interested, do you teach them why that works?**

DS: Yes, we do, but for some children … that's not a good idea. Some of the Year 6 that I've got this year looked at the theory behind it first, before we applied the concept. So, they had the mathematical understanding because they were ready. For the others I teach, it is a process. There were areas of maths I found hard, but it was quite natural. It's quite funny ending up being a writing lead for the Trust because I've had to learn that. When the new curriculum came and they upped the vocabulary within the SPaG element, getting a handle on that and then being able to help others has definitely been something I've had to learn on the job. I would have thought that I'd have been far more likely to be a maths lead, but writing and I seem to have gelled.

JT: **It's really impressive. What do you think makes you such a great teacher?**

DS: It's difficult. I've always thought that if you start believing that you're good, you're going to slip up. I think that what I would like to believe is that pupils want to be in my class. They feel safe, they're having fun and then you've got a chance that they'll learn. When they're on board with you and they really want to please themselves, through you as a model.

It's pupil relationships. It's wanting to value each pupil. In many ways you can't teach that, that respect for each individual. I always think that's number one, making them feel valued, making them want to be in your classroom, getting to know them, having a laugh with them, and then also being consistent; once you've got that, and you've got that presence within the room, you can do great learning. I think it's that respect, isn't it? If you haven't that two-way respect, then you're in trouble.

JT: **What advice would you give to youngsters coming into the profession?**

DS: I think you've got to come into the profession with your eyes wide open, that this is a really challenging profession. You've got to really want to have an impact on the children, and when you've got those two things and you're prepared to put the hard yards in, then everyone will benefit, and it can be a really incredibly rewarding career. I think if you've got that passion, then it's right for you. If you haven't, then it can be really tricky. I think for me, a new teacher coming in has got to really want to have that impact, and when you're in with the class, just get to know them, value them, make them feel wanted, because a lot of our children have got a lot of challenges outside of school, and your classroom has got to be filled with respect.

JT: **Well, your children absolutely know how much you want for them. It's so clear.**

DS: Well, thank you. It means a lot.

JT: **Thank you. It's been great.**

Testimonials

'Dean is an amazing Year 6 teacher – the SATs results over the last few years are testimony to his expertise. The excitement when pupils receive their results, at the end of the year, is pure delight. He is a teacher that makes a difference. A teacher who will provide fond memories for his pupils when they look back.'

'Dean Salisbury is an inspirational teacher. I have had the pleasure of working alongside him for four years now and it is clear he has a special ability to maintain the perfect balance of firm but fair with all the children he teaches. I am yet to see a single child leave Year 6 saying anything other than what a brilliant year they had, and how many special memories they made, having had Dean as their teacher.'

'Dean is a great teacher who inspires not just through knowledge, but through connection – building bridges of trust with children and fostering collaboration with colleagues.'

'Thank you so much for all the support, encouragement and experiences you have given our daughter this year. We are beyond proud of her achievements and the wonderful young lady you have helped her become.'

'We are very pleased with our daughter's report. She has really enjoyed Year 6 and gained so much confidence, and she has especially enjoyed being part of the Sports Crew. She has been happy throughout the years at Sutton Park, and is ready to start her new adventure.'

So, what can we learn from Dean Salisbury?

The extraordinary aspect of writing that Dean focused upon was stimulating the pupils' imaginations. He delayed the writing of the 'hot' task and cajoled the pupils into spending a significant amount of time accessing the memories of the day at the Victorian village. The other noteworthy aspect of his practice has been his ensuring that every pupil in the school securely understands the features of a sentence. Those two things combined appear to have resulted in the development of some great writers at Sutton Park, evidenced by both what I saw in their books and during the lesson, and the year-on-year SATs outcomes. I have never seen such attention paid to helping a pupil to see in their mind's eye exactly what happened on that trip. The video was a stroke of genius! And when it comes to sentence construction, there is no one I know who has a better understanding than Daisy Christodoulou. Her work has identified, amongst other things, that ensuring Year 6 pupils know the parts of a sentence – and especially exactly what a verb is – is the key to creating more assured writers. At Sutton Park, exemplary writing is engendered through the extra effort put into stimulating memory and going back to the fundamental unit of writing: the sentence.

The other aspect of Dean's story that struck me was the tangible benefits of keeping a teacher in one place for a long time so that they perfect their craft. The depth of experience gained from being the Year 6 teacher for a decade is paying huge dividends at Sutton Park. Developing expertise doesn't happen quickly. Deep immersion over time in what it is that you want to perfect, guided by expert training and enabled by an openness and determination to improve, is the only way. Dean's attitude to his own professional learning is refreshing. Out of his safest space – which is mathematics – he teaches English to Year 6, having spent a great deal of time learning how to develop a process for writing himself. Two decades into his career, he is, admirably, a model learner to his charges and his colleagues, and since he became vice principal of the school, he has played a major part in the school being graded 'Outstanding' by Ofsted.

Dean Salisbury's pupils' progress and achievement data

Below is a table showing the percentage of pupils reaching age-related expectations (ARE) by the end of Year 6 at Sutton Park, all taught by Dean Salisbury.

Year	Reading	Writing	Maths	Combined
2021	90%	87%	97%	83%
2022	86%	90%	90%	83%
2023	86%	86%	86%	76%
2024	87%	83%	90%	83%

A Truly Great Early Years Teacher: Helen Digger

Helen Digger leads the Early Years Unit comprising both the Nursery and Reception classes, at Sutton Park Primary School, Kidderminster. She also supports some early years staff across the Central Region Schools Trust.

Teaching

Having spent the morning with Dean Salisbury, I have 30 minutes to myself. I waste little time nowadays and I am busy writing as Helen Digger enters the conference room where I'm based. We're off to find her class at the end of lunch. We chat as we walk to the bottom of the slope. The lunchtime supervisors are escorting the class. The children are holding hands in pairs. Oscar is particularly kind in helping one of the girls. Helen introduces me as, 'my friend John'. I'm greeted by a tsunami of mini-waves. I am of great interest! If I'm asked, 'What do you do?' once, I'm asked a dozen times. We chat as we walk back up and Helen unlocks our way into the classroom.

The teaching assistant, Jo, offers me an adult seat, but I sit on a doll's-house-sized chair. The children appear completely organised. They hang up coats and sort out their jumpers. Some wander over and interrogate me further, when suddenly Helen says '5 … 4 … 3 … 2 … 1… Show me your good sitting.' They scramble to sit down. The topic for the afternoon's carpet time is Hannukah. There is an image of a hanukkiah on the screen. One of the children is sitting on Jo's lap. The rest, all 30 of them, are facing Helen. I'd like to say they were paying her their full attention, but I am a distinct distraction. I have never felt more interesting!

Helen narrates the day to the children, what they've done, what they're doing now and what they'll do later. This is so important for such young children; it reassures them and helps build a safe environment. We are now on carpet time. Afterwards they will have choosing time. Oscar immediately talks about preparing for the tests in Year 6. One of the Year 6s I met this morning told me he had a brother in early years. SATs have cast their dark shadow across that household, for sure. Blimey!

'Good afternoon, Riley', says Helen. 'Good afternoon, Mrs Digger', says Riley. That exchange replicates 30 times as the children sit perfectly still, bar the odd glance at grandad, the grey-haired interloper. I learn that two children are absent. When full, this class is even bigger than it looks! Helen finishes the register and introduces Hannukah with some zest. She has such remarkable energy. I type into my laptop: 'How does she do it?'

I look around this beautiful room. It's so *warm*. There is an impressive Jack and the Beanstalk display. The phonics wall is both aesthetically pleasing and clearly practical. There is nothing out of place – all the displays are pristine, which is no mean feat in an early years foundation stage (EYFS) classroom. Helen puts her hand up and the children mimic her – a clearly understood signal to gain their full attention. I have rarely seen such order in a mainstream secondary class, let alone an EYFS classroom on this dark, cold December afternoon. It's time to *Wake and Shake*. Adriana is chosen, via the lollipop name jar, to choose this afternoon's YouTube music video for the *Wake and Shake*. I'm not quite sure of the criteria behind her choice, but the children are soon dancing to a song from a children's show … *in French*! There is lots of jumping up around. 'Can you feel the magic in the air?' shouts DJ Digger. I'd join in but I can't get up.

Helen is *so* animated. Jo is dancing with a small group attracted to her like a magnet. The music fades and they sit down, shaken and awakened. There is an image of a nine-candle candlestick on the screen. They also have a seven-candle version. Helen explains that the nine-candle version is a *hanukkiah* used specifically for Hannukah and the seven-candle version is a menorah and is for use throughout the year. Hannukah 'is also called The Festival of Lights', she says and goes on to give the background to the festival. She asks them a question about stained glass and discovers that not everyone has been to a church, let alone a synagogue. 'I assumed you'd have all been to a church!' This cultural gap is just one of the challenges of teaching EYFS in modern Britain, in a white, working-class catchment area. Take nothing for granted.

We see a picture of the inside of a wonderful synagogue. 'Let's say the word "synagogue" … altogether now, "SYN-A-GOG-UE".' Helen, energy levels remaining at 11, produces three props: a Torah scroll, a skull cap, and the Rabbi's white robe, or kittel. She picks Oscar who – with Jo's aid – holds out the Torah scroll at the front of the class. Oscar is keen. Unlike Helen's next choice, who agrees to come to the front of the class and then point-blank refuses to don the skull cap. 'Well, I wouldn't want to force you, lovely', she says, and the boy sits back down. She also gets a first-time-refuser for wearing the kittel as the Rabbi. Eventually we have a team of three. And they are splendid! Helen explains why they wear the skull cap to synagogue, how the Torah contains the first five books of the Hebrew Bible, and how the whiteness of the kittel represents goodness. Helen's 'little helpers' are happiness personified, and their peers clap them off the stage.

Carpet time has taken 25 minutes and attention levels are still remarkably high. Helen explains that they can now choose what to do. I look around. The activities for enhanced and continuous provision are laid out, ready. In terms of the former, they can choose from: playing outside with the building bricks to build a synagogue, to develop their gross motor skills; doing an observational drawing of the menorah candles, with seven candles lit every week for the Jewish faith; and colouring in the hanukkiah candle, which has nine candles and is used to celebrate Hanukkah, to develop their fine motor skills. For the latter, they can choose from any elements of the continuous provision resources that are available to them all day, every day.

The week's learning is encapsulated in this weekly communication to parents that Helen hands me (see page 131).

It strikes me as I listen to Helen explain the learning opportunities, just how incredibly lucky these children are to have such a well-organised, educational afternoon ahead of them. Teaching in early years requires the most skillful pedagogy imaginable. In no other year group does the teacher have less autonomy. Where four-year-old children want to go and what they choose to do is relatively unpredictable and ungovernable. Adaptive teaching is the new big thing, but early years teachers have been adapting their teaching for decades. If an early years child doesn't want to do something, it is hard to persuade them otherwise.

What people working in EYFS do so brilliantly is spot the moment learning can happen and then pounce! Watching Helen, I recalled being in an early years lesson a few years ago when a boy refused, point blank, to engage in the phonics session. The sound for the day was the hard 'c' (/k/) as in 'car'. Ten minutes after the boy had gone awol from formal phonics instruction, he was zooming around the classroom with his toy car, making engine noises. The teaching assistant engaged in conversation without hesitation. 'What's that?'

'My car.'

Celebrations

2.12.24. "My Week at School."

Sutton Park Primary School

THE Story of HANUKKAH

Communication, Language and Literacy	Maths	Understanding the World
During our Literacy, we will be writing about 'The story of Hanukkah'. We will share 'The story of Hanukkah' written by David A. Adler. We will continue to practise writing our letter sounds in the order that we can hear them.	In our Maths sessions, we are learning to add numbers together. We will start with the pairs of numbers that make 5. We will add objects together and explore the many ways to make 5.	This week we will learn about the religion of Judaism. We will explore how and why they celebrate Hanukkah. We will learn the importance of the Menorah candle and why people of the Jewish faith use it to celebrate.

Personal, Social and Emotional Development	Read, Write inc - Phonics	Physical Development	Creative Development
Unique is the value of the week this week. We will discuss what it means to be unique and how it is OK to be different.	This half term we will be splitting our class into four different groups based on their most recent assessment of phonic ability. Your child will be bringing home letter sounds to practise at home so please check their book bag regularly.	We have been enjoying our dance sessions; this week we will explore the Hora, the Jewish wedding dance. We will hold hands in a circle and try to follow the steps in time to the music – watch out for the video of this on Seesaw!	This week our creativity will involve the autumn leaves we can find during our Forest School session. We will create a whole class picture using autumn leaves.

'Can you say the word "car" again for me?'

'Car.'

'Can you say "/k/-/ɑr/"?'

' "/k/-/ɑr/".'

'That's great. "/k/-/ɑr/". And again?'

' "/k/-/ɑr/".'

'Well done – that's great.'

And off he went, saying '/k/-/ɑr/' aloud to himself. Artful, deliberate and genius pedagogy.

The skilled early years practitioner will have a repertoire of questions on the tip of their tongue to elicit verbal responses from their pupils the very moment the learning opportunity arises. Indeed, communication skills are the foundation of successful early years and Helen facilitates the children's talking endlessly throughout carpet time.

What the children think

As the pupils choose what they are going to do next in the learning sequence, Helen sweeps Mary, Oscar, Billy and Hayley away into a side room to speak to me. Emily decides that it all looks a bit too interesting to ignore and, completely uninvited, comes along too.[1]

Now, I have found the discussions with pupils hugely illuminating in the course of researching this book. They have not only confirmed what I have seen and heard about their teachers, they have also provided fresh insights that have helped deepen my understanding of

---

1 Not, of course, their real names.

what constitutes a truly great teacher. This afternoon, however, talking to four-year-olds, feels like it is going to be a little different.

We sit round a tiny table on the smallest chairs in the school. My knees crack. I may never rise from this seat again. I begin explaining what we are doing when Emily, eyes looking to the ceiling and her index finger pointing at her temple, says, 'I must remember to pick up my party invitation and take it home today. Yes … I must remember that.'

I start again. 'So, I am writing a book about *your* teacher, Mrs Digger!' Whenever I have said that in the past, the pupils have been wide-eyed with excitement. Some have even insisted on being named in the book. There is not a flicker from the five in front of me today. I thought the boys – and of course some of the girls – might like Mrs Digger, if only for her surname. Undeterred, I continue in full-on, hyper-enthused children's entertainer mode. 'So, why do you think Mrs Digger is such a brilliant teacher?' The girls just stare at me. Oscar and Billy carry on colouring in their menorah. They don't even look up. 'Have a think. What do you like about Mrs Digger? Mary, what's good about Mrs Digger?'

'We do singing before we go home … and Nursery come into our class …' She smiles at me. I smile back.

'Thank you Mary, that's great', I say. 'What about you, Oscar?' He is doing a great job of colouring in a candle with a purple crayon. He has impressive fine motor skills.

'She does phonics with me', he says. 'I like phonics. It's easy. "Fred in your head" is tricky.'

Before I can thank him, Emily butts in. 'No it's not. "Fred in your head" is easy for me … I must remember my party invitation …'

'Mrs Digger lets me make party invitations', says Hayley. I have no idea if this is true, or whether we are playing a game of word association.

'We've done all these letters', says Hayley.

I smile and say, 'That sounds good.' Silence.

Billy is colouring in. His fine motor skills aren't as good as his co-colourer. He is using a darkish orange crayon. The Hannukah candles look like someone has poured paraffin on them. They are engulfed in flames. I ask him what he likes about Mrs Digger. He looks at me and then says, 'She lets me colour in.'

Hayley says, 'Mrs Digger, lets me make party invitations.'

Oscar says, 'I had two birthdays before I was three.'

Billy says, 'She lets us play.'

Mary says, 'We do PE.'

We're cooking with gas now! 'What else makes Mrs Digger good, then?' I ask.

'Maths. It's a piece of cake for me', says Oscar with an air of nonchalant confidence.

Emily, in a complete reversal of the 'Fred in my head' ability rankings, says, rather dolefully, 'It's hard for me.'

I am then told, in no particular order, that Mrs Digger is a truly great teacher because: she lets them go outside; she tells them nice stories; they read lines in their book; they drink hot chocolate in the Forest School; they dance to the *Wake and Shake* video; and, of course, she lets them make party invitations.

The tsunami of talk subsides. They look at me. Hayley thrusts her arm out, 'I've got a glittery love heart on my arm.' She's not wrong. It's big and purple. She smirks and says, 'Billy had a snake on his, once.' Billy nods in affirmation. In my grumpier moments, I sometimes think I am the only person on the planet without a tattoo. 'And Mrs Digger lets me make party invitations.'

Emily counters immediately: 'I've got my own party invitation.' I hope this party invitation thing doesn't kick off. To divert attention away from the row that's brewing about party-invitation-gate, I ask, 'Is there anything else that makes Mrs Digger a really good teacher?'

Hayley leans forward slightly, stares at me through her glasses, and grins. 'I've just farted', she says. While I'm lost for words, Hayley isn't. 'We do the Red Words as well', she continues, looking over my shoulder at a list of individual words laminated on separate squares of red card, stuck to the window frame: *go, no, the, to, I, we, me, he, she, be.* Impressively, they can all say them out loud. I offer my congratulations, and they beam at me.

The boys finish their colouring, simultaneously, and we are finished, too. They suddenly ignore me completely and begin a game of *who can stretch their arms furthest across the table.* It looks fun. Helen arrives to rescue me. It takes a few seconds to straighten my legs, and by the time I am upright, they've vanished.

Helen and I giggle about my 'qualitative research findings' as we seek somewhere quiet to talk.

IRL: Helen Digger

John Tomsett (JT): What made you go into teaching, Helen?

Helen Digger (HD): I was going to be a midwife. I'd applied to Worcester University, got accepted on the course, and then just had a sudden panic and thought, 'I don't actually think that's what I want to do.' To be honest, I didn't know what I wanted to do. I just knew I wanted to work with children of a young age. Then I thought, 'What about teaching?' So, I went back to college for another year, did an extra year of A levels, and then got a place at Oxford Brookes university. I graduated with a BA (Hons) with qualified teacher status (QTS) and went into teaching.

JT: **Has it always been early years?**

HD: My first ever job as a newly qualified teacher (NQT) was in Reception, on a temporary, one year contract, but then the school was placed in special measures by OFSTED, literally days after I began. I then got another job at a small village school. I have taught up to Year 4, but the huge part of my teaching has been in early years.

JT: **What's the skill of early years teaching?**

HD: I just love how hands-on it is. You try to have a plan, but the children always go off on a tangent, as you found out during your questions! They talk about what they want to talk about. Whether it's *farts*, as they were with you, or it might be that they've got new shoes, or Mummy's been shopping. It's always really random, and it's trying to home in on these conversations, find out what makes them enthusiastic, what makes them want to learn. At the moment, outside its dinosaurs for our boys, and they just want to run. We've created more space and stripped back a little bit to try and encourage them. They want to run because they need to burn off as much energy as they can, outside, where it's safe to do so. We let them build as many wonderful dinosaur kingdoms as they want to. We try to follow their interests, really, but still stay on track with the learning.

JT: **Tell me about the learning.**

HD: There is a long-term plan. We have a two-year cycle, because some of our children in Nursery come to Reception as well. Most of them are in the catchment area, so they stay, which is lovely, because when they start Reception, they already know us because they're in and out all day, every day, from Nursery. They know the staff and they know where everything is. So that side of it works really well. We have to be careful with the topics. We make sure the learning is progressive so that they can still do the same in Nursery as they do in Reception, but we try and rotate the topics so they're not repeating their learning. Apart from this time of year, when you can't say, 'We can't learn about Christmas this year because we did it last year!' Some things have to be repeated. It's just being careful what.

So, we have a long-term plan. For example, at the moment we've got the overarching topic of 'celebrations'. We've had the obvious ones like Remembrance, and Diwali, and at this time of year there is Bonfire Night. It's Hanukkah this week. We're trying to avoid going *Christmas crazy* too soon! But in the last two weeks of term, we've got our Christmas performance coming up, so we will learn about the Christmas story, as we're re-telling it on stage anyway. From this coming Monday we're going with it! We'll be brave enough to put up a tree and Christmas will be *on*!

JT: **So, that's the content. What's your learning priority for the children?**

HD: For us it's communication and language, which is focused upon speaking and listening in the early years curriculum. It's crucial. Then it's literacy, which is reading and writing. We do focus on the reading and writing, but more heavily on the phonics at this time of year, the autumn term.

JT: **Apparently phonics is easy.**

HD: Is that what they said?!

JT: **Oscar finds phonics easy.**

HD: Love it, loving that confidence! Of course it is.

JT: **He said, 'Mrs Digger does phonics with me. I like phonics, but "Fred in Your Head" is tricky.' Emily thinks it's easy, though.**

HD: Yes, she's very confident. That is so encouraging. The thing is in September they didn't find it easy, so they've come a long way … The fact they think it's easy is a win for me, because next week I have to do the final-term assessments to confirm how much progress we've made from September's baseline, which we track. We establish a September baseline, then we assess again in December, and then again at the end of spring term, and then at the end of summer term. We have to try to make sure that we get a certain percentage for Good Level of Development (GLD). Last year we got 71% GLD, which is a little bit above national average, which was good, because they come to us with relatively low levels of development. I think it was something like 20% GLD on entry with last year's cohort.

So, the main focus for us is speech. Because communication and language are massively important in Nursery and Reception. I've got 14 in my class out of 32 that have specific speech and language targets already, at the age of four. There's 47% of pupils in my class with SEND, and all the issues are speech-related. I don't know why, especially. Maybe it's because they're the COVID babies. They were born in the year 2020. But it was the same last year and the year before that. It could be because of modern technology. This affects how we communicate with our children nowadays.

JT: **I think there is research that needs to be done on this, but this is the first generation whose parents have all had mobile phones …**

HD: Yes, and it's quite scary, isn't it? The technology has changed our lives. It helps us find out answers to things – like the difference between a seven-candle and a nine-candle menorah – but we're left with so many questions unanswered.

JT: **So, you're developing oracy skills, then?**

HD: Yes, we're heavily invested in developing their oracy skills. In spring term we focus almost exclusively on traditional tales and re-telling stories, like the *Three Little Pigs*.

JT: **I saw your wonderful Jack and the Beanstalk wall display.**

HD: Yes, *Goldilocks* … all of the ones that we think are part of the common cannon of early literature. They just don't know some of them, so we go back to basics. We do lots of puppetry, lots of storytelling, recording them on microphones, getting them to do the talking before they do the writing …

JT: **Because those stories are timeless aren't they? The problem is, they're not told as a matter of course anymore, culturally.**

HD: If you ask them if they have stories at bedtime, not many of them put their hand up; but if you ask how many of them have got their own tablet, there's a forest of hands go up. I think that is part of their bedtime routine now. There's no judgement there, whatever works for your family, but a lot of them take themselves to bed. So, we tell lots of stories. Hearing stories helps their language and communication, especially if they're hearing new vocabulary. This is also the cohort who would not have seen their parents' mouths move much in their first few weeks and months because we were all wearing masks. There are many reasons why we need to focus on oracy for these cohorts of children. You can't blame it all on technology, can you? Which is why we're throwing so many new words at them all the time.

JT: **In terms of your teaching style then, what are you consciously thinking about in your teaching?**

HD: In terms of content, I'm trying to make it memorable, and trying to make it fun. I want them to enjoy their day, so they come back tomorrow. So, we use lots of props, lots of visual prompts. Getting them up, trying to get them engaged, even though they might not want to, like today when they chose not to be part of the Hannukah role play!

JT: **That was funny. What was good was how they felt safe to say no.**

HD: Yes, that's fine, they don't have to. We did exactly the same for our Christmas performance this year. We gave them all the option to speak on stage, or not. Those that said they would like to be on stage, we gave a little audition, and they had to try and speak in front of the whole class, because we thought if you can't speak in front of the whole class, you're not going to want to do it in front of the whole school and your parents and carers.

JT: **Mary was very good with me just now.**

HD: She's adorable, yes.

JT: **She was very good, and Billy was very good. Oscar and Hayley. They were fab! And Emily too. Blimey, she is amazing!**

HD: I think Emily just came along for the ride! 'I'm coming to talk to you, John!'

JT: **What happened with Emily encapsulated, for me, the challenges that you have in early years. I'm fascinated by early years teaching, because it seems like you have to follow the child and spot the moment where the learning can happen. Tell me about that.**

HD: It's not just carpet time when the learning happens, it's *all* the time. Whatever they're playing with on the carpet is a source of learning. A small group of them were playing farms on the carpet with Jo, my teaching assistant, so she just started telling the story of *The Three Billy Goats Gruff*. They built a bridge, so the next question was, 'How can we make the bridge safe?' They were using a basket, but the basket was wobbly. They're learning all the time, but they don't know it. So, it's knowing your individual children, knowing what they need. There'll be a few children playing that game with Jo that need the vocabulary emphasised, like *pig, cow* and *sheep*, and others will need the challenge to make the bridge secure. It's knowing your children, really, and knowing them well enough to know where they need to take their next step, and in what area.

JT: **Having a radar on for the learning moment … it's such skilful work.**

HD: Yes, and your radar's on all day. Because that could be a moment where I could teach them something. Or you say to yourself, 'I missed that … "Let's write that letter again and just practise it with me"'. You have to tap into their language. When you're teaching, you've got other adults feeding in on the periphery, getting the pupils into the learning as something interests them and then they shoot off at a tangent … and then getting them back into the learning environment. Staff are great at doing that. We had training on our questioning recently and how you foster incidental learning. In those developmental stages, our team focuses upon putting words to what the pupils are doing. It's relentless. Referencing the language to the action is at the heart of our learning philosophy in EYFS.

JT: **Watching you teach is hard, because all the deliberate things you are doing to elicit learning are hard to see. It's much more nuanced than teaching in Year 6, for example.**

HD: It's true. Even doing the register is a learning moment for my class, because they're sitting, they're listening, they're waiting for their turn, they're remembering their sign language.

JT: **You're teaching them sign language?**

HD: As much as we can. Again, it helps their speech, or it helps their self-confidence if they'd rather not talk. I'm not sign trained – we just sort of pick it up as we go along. We do a lot for our Christmas songs and plays. We do a lot of signing as a school. We have a mainstream language unit here at Sutton Park and signing helps us to be inclusive for these children when they join our mainstream classes.

Another thing I do is try to use natural resources. We've tried to strip the whole classroom back and make it calmer, which is why there's so many brown-paper boards, and lots of leaves and trees around. We try to create a calming environment and bring the outside inside. Lots of the outside resources are wooden.

JT: **You've got a Forest School here, where you serve hot chocolate!**

HD: [*Laughs*] We do! I'm the Forest School leader here. I do a Forest School club once a week for anyone who wants to come. And I take Year 1 once a week as well. Nursery, Reception and Year 1 use our Forest School every week.

JT: **Because I found it hard to elicit from the children, without getting embarrassed about it, tell me, what makes you a great teacher?**

HD: I don't believe that I'm better than any of my excellent colleagues. I feel that we are all just trying to do our best in teaching. We all want what's best for the children and to see them make progress and flourish in their own time.

I think I make learning fun and engaging. It's memorable and *they're learning*. They don't know they're learning and I think that's the best bit. Parent communication's quite important for me. The parents know what we're learning about every week. We share the planning on *Seesaw*,[2] where we also share the home learning. We share lots of photographs so they can see what we're learning about. It helps counter that classic parent–child conversation: 'What have you done at school today?' 'Nothing.' At least when they've got photographic evidence they can say, 'Well, I know you've done PE/in the forest, etc.' So, we try and give the parents a weekly snapshot of what they're learning.

---

2   An online learning platform. See: https://seesaw.com/.

JT: **I've seen you do some lovely teaching in there. Do you do any guided learning in the afternoon or is it all continuous provision?**

HD: Jo's doing some guided learning as a follow up to the Hannukah stuff. My TA Heather is doing some handwriting interventions. We try and keep a balance, really, and keep the afternoon more play based. We usually have assembly first thing in the morning, so they've been sitting. Then we do phonics, so they're sitting again. Then throughout the morning it's continuous provision. We call them to do guided adult-led learning, literacy or maths. Then in the afternoon we try to let them just play, and we'll call them to do interventions; we have some with speech targets, or we've got reading groups that need daily reading. We try and read with everyone once a week, anyway, to make sure that they are progressing. It's trying to make sure we're not dropping any plates, and make sure they're all making progress and having fun – and *learning*. I have to make sure all the staff are happy as well. We've got quite a few in my unit, but they all know what they're doing; they're all busy. I don't need to instruct any of them because they've been doing this long enough now. We work well. They work hard.

JT: **Jo's pretty amazing.**

HD: Yes, I'd be lost without her. They're worth their weight in gold, my teaching assistants.

JT: **You couldn't do it without them.**

HD: No, definitely not. Legally I can have the whole class … I can have 30 on my own. How any Reception teacher would survive, I don't know. You've only got to have one have a toilet accident and that's it, you're in the toilets, and you've got to be outside, and you're reading!

JT: **How do you keep the energy up? Watching you is like watching *Play School*, like watching *CBeebies*, but with real children!**

HD: I don't know! It's exhausting. You're 'on' all day long. But I wouldn't do anything else.

JT: **Why not?**

HD: After COVID, I took my reception class to Year 1. We all stayed with our classes because we'd missed so much. I went into Year 1, and then obviously our Nursery teachers went to Reception, because as a job share, we manage the unit. I was still the early years lead, but I wasn't actually *in* the unit, because I was next door in Year 1. Then I stayed with the same class again because when they went up to Year 2, one of the Year 2 staff members was off on long-term leave. So, I went with them for another term, and I had them for nearly two-and-a-half years. They're Year 5 now. They have a special place in my heart, that class. So, I had been out of EYFS, but I couldn't wait to get back in. The first thing I said to leadership was, 'Please can I go back to early years?' Because it's where I'm at home.

JT: **And the energy levels?**

HD: Well, we have lots of biscuits and sweets to keep our sugar levels high! I usually go around with a bag of sweets in the afternoon. Because it's exhausting. But I think I'm quite energetic anyway. I'll go home, I'll run with my husband; we do quite a lot of fitness together. I've got two teenage daughters; they tire me out as well. They're 14 and 17. It's just constantly hectic. But I genuinely love my job. I love that I get the privilege of supporting children and their families in their first days at school and get to watch them grow in confidence and prepare them by learning through play and making that learning fun!

JT: That's a great spot to finish. Thank you so much, Helen. It's been such a great time with you and your children!

The school leadership's view

Lorna Weatherby sits in front of me for the second time in one day, poor woman! Logistics mean that I am meeting Lorna at the end of the day, *after* I have seen Helen teach and spoken to her and her pupils. Lorna clearly enjoys talking about her truly great colleagues, however, and Helen is worth talking about …

Lorna knows my MO, and I don't even need to ask her the first question. 'What makes Helen truly great is her holistic approach to developing the child', she says. 'And what I mean by that is how she is so great at including parents and carers at every stage of their child's movement from Nursery, into Early Years and through to Year 1. She is so gentle and welcoming. But she's assertive too. They respect her. She's not a pushover.' I nod away and type furiously.

'That takes some skill', I comment.

'Yes, she is careful not to alienate them', Lorna replies, 'and lots of parents have had bad experiences at school. Unpicking that to get them speaking to us about what's going well and what's not, is crucial. Making sure the transition from nursery into reception goes smoothly is absolutely key.'

She mentions high expectations and I push her to explain what that means in an early years setting. 'Fundamentally, it's the adults role-modelling to the children what high expectations mean, at every moment. You'll see the conversations between them, the high-quality learning materials, the painstaking planning … they all reinforce our high expectations of the children.' She goes on to tell me about how much the sense of enthusiasm matters and how the caring and nurturing role of the teaching assistant is important in the early weeks of nursery, to support the very young children.

We discuss the role of play in learning in EYFS. 'The role of play is linked to that ever-alert adult. The child initiates the learning through their play and the adult – whether that is me or Jo or whoever – steers the focus of the conversation so that learning is maximised. It's a different craft of teaching. We teach on the carpet as you saw, but then that input will be repeated again in smaller groups in enhanced provision and then there will be related activities in continuous provision. Each child is then assessed against national benchmarks! It is pretty demanding!'

I laugh, and then say, 'Honestly, give me 30 gnarly Year 11s learning *Romeo and Juliet* over 30 law-unto-themselves four-year-olds, any day! I have no idea how Helen does this work, or how she maintains those levels of enthusiasm.'

Lorna nods. 'I know. She is pretty remarkable. She bounces! She's *Play School* performing all day.'

I say to Lorna how much I have learnt to revere early years practitioners and the importance of the EYFS phase. 'If I had my time again and was put in charge of education in this country, I would invest every penny I could muster in early years education. By the time they get to secondary, the die is largely cast. It is easier to ensure high levels of proficient development at four years of age than it is to catch up with that stuff in their teens.'

Lorna feels that for the majority of her colleagues, working at Sutton Park is more than a job. 'Ultimately, Helen has genuine botheredness', says Lorna.

'The Hywel Roberts' thing?'[3]

---

3   H. Roberts, *Botheredness: Stories, Stance and Pedagogy* (Carmarthen: Crown House Publishing, 2023).

'Exactly. It takes a great deal of energy to keep it going every hour, every day, but it matters to Helen. She builds the children's independence, and encourages them to be themselves, to be individuals.' In the light of what I saw and heard of Helen Digger and her pupils, I reckon she's doing a damned good job!

Testimonials

'The very reason my girls would race to school every morning was because you made learning easy for them. You provided an environment where they thrived, a safe and happy place that made them want to learn and made them want to go back and visit you at every opportunity! It is something we will always treasure as a family. Sutton Park is so lucky to have you there as a teacher in their team, and we were so lucky to have you teach our children.'

'Mrs Digger is the best teacher because she is really kind and was always there for me when I was struggling. She taught me for two years and I'd always go to the clubs she helped run, such as Forest Club, because she made it such fun!'

So, what can we learn from Helen Digger?

For anyone unfamiliar with early years, I would recommend spending a day in your local EYFS provision. It's a revelation. It is also sobering for a life-long secondary teacher like me.

I genuinely think there is something uniquely skilful about early years teaching, as it is the purest form of *adaptive* teaching. Watch Helen and her team teach and you soon realise that planning is for the birds! Don't get me wrong, Helen's classroom and the resources she provides are incredibly well-organised, but you have to be prepared for anything to happen, because the direction of the learning is not always in the teacher's gift. The sheer brain activity that goes on in the head of an early years teacher, minute-by-minute is extraordinary!

My own lack of adaptivity was why we ended up where we ended up in my session with the children. Reading back my account of our 'conversations', it strikes me that all I do is ask the same question. I don't adapt because I am intent upon getting an answer to a single question, just like I have done in every other conversation I have had with groups of pupils while researching this book. I hit a brick wall. What I loved about that experience, was just how confident those children were. They were on their own with an adult they had never met, and yet they were incredibly articulate, funny and happy. When they began ignoring me and making up their own game – all they had was a *table* and yet they still conjured up fascinating entertainment – I felt truly humbled. Play-based learning has a bad name in some quarters, but it is impossible to argue with what that approach is producing at this wonderful primary school in Kidderminster. They are testimony to Helen's team and the culture she has deliberately fostered in Sutton Park's EYFS provision.

There were two other things worthy of note. Firstly, Helen's emphasis upon communicating with parents. One in four pupils attract PP funding. Kidderminster contains acute pockets of deprivation that are amongst the 10% most deprived in the UK. Helen's success in attracting parents to the school right at the beginning of the children's school career is key to Sutton Park's success. When I led a cultural review of the school in October 2022, I made this note of the exceptional efforts made to build bridges with the parent body:

> There is overwhelming evidence of exceptional relationships with the parental community and SLT clearly know all pupils/ siblings. The head and deputy were on the gate both before and after school to greet parents and pupils – clearly a daily

occurrence and part of the school culture. A parental café for vulnerable parents has opened and now has 10–20 parents attending. (The teaching assistant who helps manage this – Amy – spoke with warmth and professional integrity regarding their community.)

That Lorna and Helen herself both identify the deliberate steps taken to forge positive relationship with parents illustrates the importance of those bonds to the EYFS provision. The attendance rate when I visited was 94%, not bad for a dark, dank December day in the current school attendance climate.

Last, but not least … reading aloud. My friend and co-collaborator, Mary Myatt, often talks about the findings of the 'Just Read' research from the University of Sussex, which found that just reading complex novels aloud, and at a fast pace over 12 weeks with Year 8 pupils, resulted in 'poorer readers' making a huge 16 months' progress in the time. When the research was extended, they found a similar effect happened in primaries: in one school, 93% of pupils in Year 2 made at least 6 months' progress in 12 weeks.[4] So, I was delighted at the focus on traditional storytelling. It makes sense. Children love narrative and the longevity of those tales is testimony to their value in our children's lives. The fact that Helen has the wisdom to privilege them in her provision comes as no surprise.

Helen Digger's children's progress and achievement data

Helen's latest data show progress from 19% on track to meet age-related expectations as a baseline in September 2023 to 71% met age-related expectations in July 2024.

---

4   M. Myatt, The Teachers' Collection: a story, *Curriculum 101* [blog] (12 October 2024). Available at: https://marymyatt.substack.com/p/the-teachers-collection-a-story.

A Truly Great Primary Teacher: Molly Medhurst

Molly Medhurst is a Year 5 teacher at The Ridgeway Primary School, Reading.

The school leadership's view

Norah Edgar is on edge. But, it has absolutely nothing to do with my visit to The Ridgeway Primary School in Reading. I am here to talk about a young teacher I met last time I visited, Molly Medhurst, and Norah's mind is elsewhere. She is on the verge of becoming a grand-mother for the first time and is, understandably, unbearably excited!

I contacted Norah when I began thinking about finding teachers for this book. Molly is only in her second year of teaching, but when I watched her in the classroom a few months ago, I was impressed. She seemed to have it all, and the pupils were making great progress in their learning. After I had extolled her virtues to anyone who would listen, I was astounded when someone told me how early Molly was in her teaching career.

Molly is local to the area. We are south of Reading. I walked the 2 miles or so from the centre of town to get here this morning, past the university and along leafy avenues bedecked with multi-million-pound houses. Then, as I got within 500 metres of The Ridgeway School, the surroundings suddenly changed and I could have bought multiple houses for one million pounds. 'It's tough round here', says Norah. 'We benefit from the affluence in terms of our links with local businesses and the independent schools, but a fair chunk of our intake come from relatively deprived backgrounds.'

She thinks the fact that Molly grew up here is an asset. 'She gets it. Her grandad is our site manager.'

I interject, 'And the site is immaculate.'

'Quite', continues Norah. 'We need people like Molly to help transform this community. I'm obsessed with teaching and learning. It's what drives me. Why should these children not have the same education that their more affluent peers enjoy at the host of private schools round here? Whitley is on par with areas of Liverpool in terms of socio-economic deprivation.'

I'm sensing that Molly feels that she has a moral obligation to the community. Norah agrees. 'Molly doesn't see the negatives. She doesn't look down on their lifestyle choices and she doesn't damn the children for where they come from. I watch her with them – the way she speaks to them and her body language reflect the respect she has for them. Education is valued in *her* family – like you said, the site is spotless – and she comes from a family that cares about each other and where they're from. I loved her from minute I met her. She's got energy and is keen to do the right thing. She works her socks off! She has resilience and the *Ooomph* that we need to improve the life chances of our children.' Molly is incredibly popular with the children. 'The parents never have a bad word to say about her and are full of praise. The children adore her and recently children in her class asked me to move her to Year 6 next year so that they can continue to have her!'

We discuss how rare it is to find people doing the work Molly is doing and where she is doing it. Coming from a council house background, I was educated into a middle-class milieu and, to a great extent, left my roots behind. Not so Molly, who has returned from higher education to do the work she loves in a place she loves. 'Drama is her subject specialism. I think that helps with the endless performance that is required of a primary teacher', says Norah. 'Teaching's so much more than a job! She has the tenacity to do the right thing and get on with the work. She'll be an asset to any school, but where there are deprived children who really need you, she'll thrive. She has a personality that the children just adore. She can go as far as she likes. We need to keep her positivity. We need to retain Molly and her ilk in teaching because this profession isn't ever going away!'

Teaching

After checking her mobile for any baby news, Norah takes me down to Molly's classroom. I walk in to find the pupils beavering away on fractions. 'Convert $3\frac{2}{3}$ to an improper fraction.' A pupil talks us through the process with total precision. He uses all the subject-specific vocabulary and arrives at $\frac{11}{3}$ with aplomb. He seems to be quiet confidence personified. They then explore the relationship between 5 and 20. 'How do we get from 5 to 20?' asks Molly.

'You times 5 by 4 to get to 20', says a pupil. The whole class rehearses the answer chorally (and loudly!).

'How else might you say that?' Molly replies.

'We can multiply 5 and 4 together and get 20', says another child.

'OK. What's 4 cubed? Have a think. OK,' and she asks a boy for an answer.

'It's 64 Miss.'

'How did you get that answer?' says Molly. I love how she gives nothing away.

'Well, 4 cubed is 4 times 4 times 4 … so, 4 multiplied by 4 is 16.'

'So, you used your square number knowledge …'

'… and then if you times 16 by 4 you get 64.'

'Excellent. Well done.'

'OK, quickly, our Roman numeral for today is CCC.' Whiteboards flash up 300 and are then put to one side. Molly sets some further calculations for the pupils to complete. She teaches between the desks. 'You have a place value chart on the wall to help you.'

It is such a clear room – modern, bright and airy. The sense of focus is tangible. We are subtracting fractions. Molly gives instructions and they are acted upon immediately. A girl comments on the mathematical pattern of the date – 12.12.24 – and Molly replies, 'It's quite a cool date today, isn't it?' and they giggle together. There is a relaxed purposefulness to the room. As she passes, I tell her that we'll just have some fun today and she says, 'Ahh, bless you!'

Molly begins by going over how they add two mixed numbers. She then models the process of subtracting two mixed numbers and then asks the class to explain the steps she took. Hands shoot up. 'Hands down', says Molly, 'but I love that you're so excited.' She selects a boy who gives a word-perfect answer using all the correct terminology: 'numerator', 'denominator', 'equivalent', 'subtract'. She then probes their understanding further. 'What does the denominator represent? … What does the numerator represent? … If you're subtracting will your answer be greater than or less than your original number?'

She then models another example, explains and talks it through and requests choral responses at each step. They are probably the loudest choral responses I have ever heard! There is a boy at the front leaning forward on his desk. Molly just reorganises him as she completes the explanation, without missing a beat. On to a 'we do': $5/6 - 2/3$. 'There are no changes made to the denominator once you have the same denominator', says Molly. They shout it out. And again … 'Fractions must have the same denominator before the fractions can be subtracted.' Finally, you do … $7/8 - 5/16$. She asks one of her bellwether pupils for the answer: '$9/16$, Miss'. She then plays 'I am the teacher'. It's great fun. Ellie comes up to the front and writes out the answer on the board, explaining each step as she goes. It's great fun. Molly is 'Why? Why? Why? Why? Why?' relentlessly pressing Ellie to reveal her process thinking. It is artful teaching and everyone is fully attentive. They complete $8/9 - 1/3$, with a faultlessly disciplined mini-whiteboard reveal, and then they are on to worded problems. Miss Smith and Miss Medhurst both have a chocolate bar each, apparently. Miss Medhurst eats $3/4$ of hers and Miss Smith eats $5/12$. Who has the most chocolate left over? Merely watching Molly teach to observe her classroom management skills would not be that educative for the novice teacher, because she manages behaviour in micro moments. She takes a pen out of a boy's hand whilst still talking to the class and retaining eye contact across the room. A girl's hand is gently put down with Molly's hand as she asks a cold call question. Her voice is calm and authoritative.

She gives the pupils several problems where they have to subtract fractions, with subtle variations. Voices are turned off and they are thinking hard, beavering away. She makes teaching look effortless. She's between the desks. She knows who can do what and where her bellwether pupils are located. I look around the room, because, frankly, for a few minutes, there is not much to see! On a poster, the school's values: Friendship; Respect; Co-operation; Perseverance; Honesty and Kindness. I reflect that those values are being enacted in front of me in this Year 5 mathematics class, where 10-year-olds are being taught so beautifully by a teacher a little more than twice their age.

Molly regains their attention and then begins to test out some basics. It's as though she is going backwards. I am interested in what she's doing. Whilst I was thinking about the school's values, she has been looking over shoulders and seeing what her charges are doing. She attempts to solve $^{15}/_{21} - ^2/_7$. She triples the denominator, but forgets to multiply the numerator: $^{15}/_{21} - ^2/_{21}$. They soon spot her mistake. All good. She then asks them to put $^1/_8$ $^1/_{12}$ $^7/_{12}$ in ascending order and that looks OK too.

Ten or so minutes of the lesson remain. They have been going now for nearly 70 minutes and some of them are visibly flagging. She finishes with what seems to me a completely regressive step. This is interesting … 'I want 100% attention, so you are all listening', says Molly and waits a second or so until all eyes are on her. 'Here are six fractions. I would like you to subtract each fraction from one whole: $^3/_5$ $^4/_7$ $^5/_{12}$ $^2/_9$ $^3/_4$ $^5/_8$. You have five minutes.' I walk around the room and suddenly see some errors. The simple concept that, before they can do the subtraction, the numerator must match the denominator to make a whole was not secure and, while I had been staring at the wall displays, Molly's radar had detected that misunderstanding on her travels. She goes through a series of exercises that disabuse the pupils of that fundamental misconception, and all is well. She sets up a complex worded question, where they have to calculate several different fractions ready for next lesson, and then it is breaktime. As we walk down to the meeting room where I am going to discuss Miss Medhurst with eight of her pupils, we discuss what happened back in the classroom.

'It's a common misconception', says Molly. 'Since they were so fluent at subtracting one fraction from another, it would have been easy to have thought they knew that a whole was when numerator and denominator were equal. But I just had a feeling that they weren't all secure on that, and I was right. But they are now, and we are set up for the next lesson.' Adaptive teaching at its best.

What the pupils think

I have seven very excited Year 5s in front of me, along with a Year 6 whom Molly taught last year. I explain what I am up to. They get even more giddy. A confident bunch, they don't need much time to think about what makes Miss Medhurst a truly great teacher. The first response makes me reflect: 'She makes things simple when they're really hard.' Isn't that what the very best teachers do? Similar critiques have been articulated by pupils about many of the teachers featured in this book. 'She's really good at teaching literacy. Like, when I don't really know what to start with my writing, she has these sentence starters that help me get going. And she's really good at explaining stuff.' There is general approval across the table.

The Year 6 pupil – who is staggeringly mature – picks up the baton. 'She's fun! Miss makes everything seem fun. When she was new, she was a different person in my imagination to the one who turned up in the classroom. *Boom!* She had such a kind face. You could tell just by looking at her, that she was an amazing person. She is so good at understanding what we're going through. She can comfort people and she has the right words at right time. She is more than a teacher, she is a human being as well.' This particular pupil has a great deal to say about Molly; her testimony really is genuinely moving. 'She is so good at teaching English. She helped improve my English through showing me how to do editing, and writing comments to encourage me to go on and improve my work.'

One of the Year 5s chips in, 'When we were reading *Floodland*, Miss was always showing what Alice (the Year 6 girl) had written when she studied it last year.'

Alice continues, 'She is the kindest teacher in the school. Honestly! She's always kind. She rarely raised her voice – maybe two or three times in the whole year. I have 1,000 examples of why she is a great teacher. She always comes to help when we put our hands up. She doesn't tell us the answer. She helps us think of good ideas and then she lets us choose one. She is fair. Everyone gets the same attention. She smiles a lot and gives me a lot of positive energy. Why doesn't she get dimples!? She makes the saddest days the best days when she smiles. She makes our day! Year 5 was a rough time for me and she was there when I needed her.' For this one pupil, Molly has had an impact way beyond anything she might have anticipated. I find what Alice says humbling.

I orchestrate things so that the other Year 5s have a chance to say something, although they are unfailingly smiley as they listen to Alice's account of Molly. The insight the pupils show is educative: 'She doesn't scold us for not knowing. She helps us get through it.' 'She is the type of teacher you want to listen to because of her personality. She has a great voice – it's so loud and clear.' 'We can get stuck. If you're in a little group doing a star question, we get more help – we go on a table and she asks us what we've been doing, and by the end of the lesson we'll all know how to do the thing we were stuck on.'

Although they don't know it, they seem to be describing Molly's approach in a way that sounds like Mastery teaching: 'If we struggle she will make sure we *all* know what we're doing and only when we *all* know what we're doing will she let us proceed, and then in the next lesson she'll do a recap. People used to think I was good at maths, and it was clear that she would speak to those people who needed most help. She doesn't always choose the people who know the answers.' I marvel at their teaching- and learning-related vocabulary, which is truly impressive.

And then, a little magic happened. One of them says, 'There's a spark in her that makes you want to learn something – like history. Divorced, beheaded, died . . . '

'Do you know Henry VIII's wives?' I ask.

One of the girls, called Pearl, replies in the affirmative.

'In the right order?'

'Sure. I know the song. Shall I sing it?' And all the other pupils insist she does. So, Pearl sings the Henry VIII's six wives song – all 37 lines of it

– word perfect, note perfect, and beat perfect. Her friends join in for the chorus:

> *Divorced, beheaded, and died Divorced, beheaded, survived I'm Henry*
> *VIII, I had six sorry wives Some might say I ruined their lives*[1]

Pearl is ridiculously confident. She waits for the beat before she begins the next verse and she moves to the rhythms of the song as she sings. She could be Etta James. It is an extraordinary performance, and we all clap furiously when she finishes. I am in awe of her singing and seven young faces are aglow with pride at what has just happened.

There are a few odd comments before we finish – 'Everyone listens to her … she has an advent calendar and some people get the chocolate.'

Another speaks of Molly's pastoral care: 'I had a friend who was a sweet, passionate girl like me. She left school. I was upset. I thought I'd never hear from her again … I was very upset, so someone told Miss and she gave me some ideas for getting in touch with my old friend and that helped calm me down.'

We run out of time. I ask them for a single word to sum up Miss Medhurst. Alice says, 'I need a dictionary! How can I get the thousands of things she can do into one word?!' But a list of one word descriptions I do get: fantastic, genuine, passionate, compassionate, best, greatest, kind, caring, trustworthy, fun, understanding and amazing. I have to reassure them that what they have said will be in the book. They leave in a frenzy of excitement, as though I'd given them a party packet of Haribo sweets each, rather than just a cookie biscuit.

---

1 *Horrible Histories*, BBC, 23 April 2009.

IRL: Molly Medhurst

John Tomsett (JT): Why did you go into teaching?

Molly Medhurst (MM): I grew up in south Reading, and I went to Geoffrey Field Junior School. I loved it. Everyone there was incredible, and I still remember all of my teachers. They made the experience so special, especially one of my teachers in Year 4, and I just loved it. I had such a great time. They really valued their pupils, they really valued well-being, and I just never forgot that. Then going through into secondary school, I took up mentorship roles. I helped lower-ability pupils with their reading. I was also heavily involved with drama, so I was a mentor in our drama class. I went abroad a couple of times and taught drama over in Alicante and then at a school in Dusseldorf. I was 14 at the time of the first trip, then 17 for the second one. Teaching is just part of my DNA to be honest, from the beginning. I think that incredible experience at primary school mixed with all of the experiences I had in secondary, so that after finishing my drama and theatre studies undergraduate course at Royal Holloway, there was nothing else I wanted to do. Even when I started doing drama, I found myself going for children's theatre. I immersed myself in anything I could that was related to teaching and related to children. Then I did my dissertation on drama and primary school children, and how the two should be linked more in the primary curriculum. There was so much research, especially after COVID, on how drama is beneficial for children. It always kept coming back to education and to working with young people. I did my QTS at the University of Reading, which was fantastic.

JT: This is your second year teaching?

MM: Yes, I'm into my second year now.

JT: **What did you learn in your first year about teaching?**

MM: You're constantly having to adapt. Things get thrown at you, the curriculum changes, your day-to-day changes. What I think I learnt the most was the relationship with the children is number one, always.

JT: **Tell me what you mean by that. Nearly everybody says that. I'm really interested in what that looks like.**

MM: My teachers at school were so fantastic at making me feel valued. My priority is making these children feel valued. Obviously, progress data are important, and making sure they leave school with subject knowledge is important, and being ready to go on to secondary, college, university, whatever, that's really important, but I think if these children can leave at the end of the day and feel they've had a good day and feel happy, that's what I'd want.

JT: **What do you say when people say your job is to educate and challenge academically, because I've just watched you teach hard and press them to understand subtracting fractions?**

MM: Of course, the academic is key, but I don't think I'd be able to teach like that and have such great levels of attention, if I didn't have such positive relationships with those children. Getting to know them on a personal level, treating them like people and building those relationships first is important.

JT: **You do that beautifully.**

MM: Oh, thank you. I don't know everything, I don't know the curriculum inside out, I don't know all about pedagogy because I'm still learning, but I think I really take the time with these children to form those foundational relationships.

JT: **But then your pedagogy is really developed. You're thinking about that all of the time, aren't you?**

MM: Yes. Again, I'm trying, and if ever I have conversations with our deputy and the head teacher, and they've asked me to do something, I'm always willing to take on feedback to develop myself as well as the children. I want these children to have the best-quality teaching possible.

JT: **Let's park the relationships bit, you've secured that. Tell me about the conscious stuff you do in your teaching.**

MM: It's about trying to break it down into small steps. I've got such a wide variety of abilities in the classroom this year, and I had the same last year. I think if you can try to get everyone to one point, pitch everything for those who are lower prior attainers at an aspirational point, but making sure it's been broken down for them, that the steps are precise and the vocabulary being used is clear and specific, then that's a great start.

JT: **Your vocabulary use in the lesson was excellent.**

MM: Developing their oracy skills and getting them talking pushes the children working at a higher level and helps my lower attainers to explain their thinking. They find the explanation a lot easier when I deliberately develop their oracy skills. For example, in maths the higher attainers can write out their sums, but then explaining can be a challenge. That oracy side of things is definitely something I've been trying to work on. Like I say, if I can ensure that everyone is at a certain point, aim to push everyone as far as I can and challenge the GD pupils and the higher attainers, then, fantastic. That's the plan. Pitching it at the top and getting everybody as far up there as possible.

JT: **Tell me about the choral stuff, which I think is just great.**

MM: They're really good at it as well. I think it's really important, like I say, that they are all on the same page. If I can see that they are all joining in, then at least I know that they are able to tell me what they need to do. Again, if they don't know how to find an equivalent fraction, they at least know that they have to get a denominator. It builds a sense of community in the classroom as well, and it puts everyone on the same level. Everyone is able to repeat a sentence, and everyone is able to refer back to that.

JT: **It's really rare that I see people make the effort to encourage pupils to get their tongues around the words.**

MM: Yes, and I try to do that a lot. This morning, we were doing times tables and it's commutative, dividend and quotient, and terms like that, but they can all use them, because I've really tried to take the time to make them understand the meanings of these terms. We'll spend a lot of time talking about the method and talking about the steps you'd take to get there, and then they can plug in what they want to, so they can use the numbers that they feel comfortable with, but then they're all still using the mathematical method.

JT: **What do you do to be so good at teaching maths?**

MM: We've used the *White Rose* scheme as a basis, but then I tweak bits here and there. It takes a lot of work. I found maths tricky at school, but then I also think that's an advantage, because I feel where I struggled so much with maths, I now understand what is difficult about it. When I finished my ECT, my mentor asked, 'What would you want to go on to lead as a subject?' I said, 'Probably something like maths, because I think I understand the misconceptions. I know now, reflecting on doing GCSE maths, what I found hard and how I would have liked someone to explain it.' Looking at the content we're delivering, I'm still having to teach some of it to myself, so I'm still going through the process with them and breaking it down for myself, thinking, 'OK, how would they be able to do that?' I really try to think about how I would have felt being taught that at their age.

These schemes are helpful, but sometimes you look at them and think, 'I just don't understand any of that, I don't get how you've worded it.' I do really try to think from a child's perspective. Again, I think that's why my pupils get the results they do, and that's why they are on my side and respect me as well, I think, because I'm talking to them in the way I would want someone to break it down and explain it to me.

JT: **Behaviourally, they seemed impeccable.**

MM: Again, it's taken a lot of work. I think it's a respect thing. I think it's through treating them like people. I've had a lot of children who say, 'You're not strict. You're not the mean teacher. You're the nice teacher.' I do set boundaries, and they do know my expectations, but I'm not a shouter and I don't think I moan at them constantly. A lot of these kids don't respond to people shouting; I know Norah has explained to you that this is a disadvantaged school, and a lot of these kids are all too used to shouting outside of school. If I was to spend the whole day shouting, that's going to get me nowhere.

JT: **You get impeccable behaviour through just treating them really well.**

MM: I think so. It's about mutual respect and being able to have a laugh with them. It's also about listening to them if they've got an issue. A lot of them come to me with problems, even if it's something as silly as they've had an argument with someone on the playground or someone has told them to shut up. All of these children will confide in me and tell me what's going on, because they trust me, I think. Like I say, I've taken time to get to know them. When they arrive in the morning, I'll always have conversations with them about what they did over the weekend, what they're doing tonight or what they're having for tea. They have those conversations with me as well, so I think they know me on a personal level.

JT: **There was a lovely moment this morning where the girl said, 'Look at the date, Miss. It's 12.12.24', and you didn't say, 'We've got to get on.' You said, 'Yes, so it's a funny day …' and had a chuckle.**

MM: It's those moments where we have a laugh together. They joke around with me. They can tease me sometimes.

JT: **You teach some maths. What do you do for English?**

MM: Literacy involves a lot of 'I do, we do, you do', a lot of modelling, building confidence and taking the time to practise. It's that structured modelling; I'm making sure that they understand what the process is and what I'm asking of them, and then I allow them the time to practise the techniques. It's about trying to really break things down, like stem sentences and word banks, and making them accessible to everyone. Practice, basically, it's a lot of practice. For example, we're doing parenthesis later today, the first half-an-hour is breaking down what that actually means; building different sentences, trial and error, does this work, does this not work? Then we give them the time to do that themselves. Writing is hard, and a lot of these children don't want to put things down on the page because they're scared of getting it wrong, so having that practice time has been beneficial, I think.

JT: **I liked your adaptivity today. When you put up the final task, it felt like it was going backwards, but what you uncovered was a major misconception about what a whole was. It was so perceptive of you.**

MM: Yes, which is why I put it in there, because I knew they would make that error. It does seem basic to say just take these away from the whole. But that misconception was something that's arisen occasionally before, so I thought I would tie in the subtraction – the new learning today – with something that I knew they had found difficult before. In their heads five fifths, seven sevenths, nine ninths, can confuse. You've got to have all the basics right.

JT: **That's the art of great teaching. It's anticipating the misconceptions and knowing what to do when they come up, because you knew that would come up, and you knew to test it out.**

MM: Yes, it's a skill, absolutely.

JT: **You have that skill, maybe because you've been in that position where those misconceptions are flying around you as a pupil. You can almost imagine being those pupils and seeing where the misconceptions are going to come from.**

MM: Yes, that's the thing. With the children of higher ability, the explanation is so important because they can fly through the calculations, and they can answer all of the questions, but ask them to explain it and a lot of them are like deer in the headlights.

JT: **That's what I loved. I loved your process questions, 'Tell me how you got that.' You're making their thinking visible all of the time, and their thinking was really accurate.**

MM: They are an impressive bunch.

JT: **Yes, that was really good. What kinds of SATs are they on track for getting? They seem quite high.**

MM: They are. For maths, I think I've got two working below, one working towards and then everyone else is expected or GD. Then again, writing is a weakness, so I think I've got about eight working towards, and then one below, the rest are expected or

GD. Then reading I've got one below, one at working towards, the rest are expected or GD.

JT: **I love that you know those numbers. You know the pupils. What else do you think, without being all modest about it, makes you a good teacher? I've already found out from the pupils, they've told me what they think!**

MM: Again, I think it's taking the time with them, getting to know them, and being a human being with them. A teacher is never just a teacher. You're a parent sometimes – whether you should be or not – you look after them, you're a therapist and you're a first aider; you're everything. It's a million roles put into one, so I don't see myself as being just a teacher, and I think that makes up a big part of it. This isn't just a job to me. Again, I know there's a big debate about whether it should be or not, but for me it's not, it's so much more than that.

JT: **You give your heart and soul to it, don't you?**

MM: Yes, I've got 25 little people in there who come to me every day and look to me to be an educator, someone that they can come to, a safe person. I think having that knowledge and my understanding of that, I think that makes me a good teacher.

JT: **What have you learnt recently that you use in your work?**

MM: I love Think-Pair-Share, I think it's fantastic, because in maths especially there are mixed ability pairs, and they bounce off each other. Having that thinking time has made so many of them more confident, and I vary the way I do my thinking time. Sometimes, I might get them to do note taking, or sometimes I'll put pictures up, so they have a pictorial reference to help them think about stuff. Other times they've got stem sentences and word banks, which help them form their thinking time, but then when they go to their partners, all of them are now talking to each other. Again, this is a generation who didn't have that social interaction during COVID; they didn't know how to share, they didn't know how to turn take and things like that. All of them now can work together, all of them are sharing ideas with each other and working collaboratively. It's improved the quality of the discussion and feedback, and it's rewarding because you've got some in there who wouldn't dare to say anything to anyone, and they are now giving articulate answers. Whether that's been from their partner or from them, they're still able to explain what they were talking about, and it's built the children's confidence so much. Also, I've been naming one as pupil A and the other as pupil B and getting them to take turns, so they both have to talk, they both have to get involved in conversation. So, that's been a really helpful technique and it's one we've been really hammering home across the school. We also use show-me boards, because some of these pupils are super keen and they just want to blurt out everything, but with the boards they can write it down and show me. It then allows me to pick out good answers, pick out the fantastic examples, and then pick apart ones that might not have necessarily gone to plan, that have certain misconceptions, and they make fantastic talking points, especially in literacy.

If we're talking about speech and they write a speech down, and someone has not included a piece of punctuation before the inverted comma, that's great, that's a talking point, and it completely helps – it changes the way a lesson goes. During guided reading, for example, if we do Think-Pair-Share and we're having a conversation about a character, their feedback and their answers can completely change the way a lesson goes.

JT: **Just a few more things. How much does it matter to you that you're back in Whitley?**

MM: That's a good question. I think at one point I didn't want to be here. But coming back again, it's given me an understanding of the children that are here. Growing up, I probably had similar experience to a lot of these children here, and I think some people talk down Whitley and talk down Reading.

JT: But you don't.

MM: No, and I don't think an area should ever define what you think of a child, because you find this anywhere, you find kids struggling anywhere, and I think a lot of people put labels on these children the minute they come through the door because they know where they've come from. That's completely unfair. I think as well, when I tell the children that I'm from Whitley, so many of them are so excited. One little boy in my class lives five minutes from where I grew up, and that completely blew his mind. He said, 'So you know the shop round the corner, you know there's the fire station round there?' And many of them are impressed I went to university. It's something to aspire to. They know that I've done teaching abroad and they know that I went to university. I think it's nice for them to have that special bond.

JT: Something that's in your moral universe that says to come back here is important.

MM: I think so, yes. I think taking the time with the children, treating them as people, I think that's number one. If you can form those relationships, if you can earn their trust and their respect, then all of the other stuff kind of falls into place. Then you can do the teaching. I think that's where you've got to start. If you don't do that, if you don't give these children the time of day, then why should they give you the time of day? Why should they sit and listen to you talk at them for six hours? That's my number one thing. That's so important.

JT: Molly, thank you so much, it's been a pleasure.

MM: Thank you very much.

———————————

Testimonials

'You have made my child enjoy coming to school again. She has absolutely loved being in your class and you have created a safe environment for her. She is devastated that you will not be with her next year.'

'Thank you so much for your time last week and for sending over all those useful resources for my son. He will have plenty to do during his summer break and to be prepared for French school. Once again thank you for your time and everything you have taught him during his last year at the Ridgeway. Your effort and kind nature haven't gone unnoticed. My son has been incredibly lucky to have you.'

'During her PGCE teacher training, it was clear that she was a natural leader with a spark for inspiring others. Molly embodies the qualities of an amazing teacher: kindness, understanding, positivity, enthusiasm, resilience, dependability, and flexibility. Her patience and willingness to go the extra mile quickly earns her pupils' respect and admiration. With her creativity and passion for drama, she seamlessly blends meaningful experiences and knowledge into her lessons, fostering a love of learning in her classroom. It has been wonderful to see her confidence grow and I genuinely do not think she realises how truly amazing she is in such a fast-paced profession. In our school community, she already has a reputation for being an incredible teacher, marking the beginning of what will undoubtedly be a hugely impactful career that positively touches many lives.'

'The children in Molly's class adore her. Molly has a fantastic relationship with every child she teaches. She puts her heart and soul into teaching and is an inspiration to not only the children but others like me who are just starting their career as a primary school teacher.'

So, what can we learn from Molly Medhurst?

When we first hosted a researchED conference in York in 2014, Tom Bennett got lost on a train and never made it to Huntington School. I delivered the introductory keynote and delegates were tweeting out soundbites from my talk. Tom followed proceedings via Twitter and from somewhere on the train network, he tweeted, 'Apparently @johntomsett just said 'People are what matters.' WHERE'S HIS EVIDENCE? Oh God, I'm having a breakdown #ntenred.' I thought it funny at the time and have always remembered it, and you can hear the legacy of that comment from Tom in my interview with Molly, when I focus upon the academic progress of her pupils, rather than the relationships she has fostered.

And yet … the trusting culture Molly has fostered in her classroom, where people are exactly what matters, should surely be celebrated as a fundamental prerequisite for truly great teaching. Every teacher I have met whilst researching this book has prioritised developing positive classroom relationships with their pupils, before they can think about teaching in a way that results in their pupils making progress in their learning. When you meet the pupils of someone like Molly and listen to them extol their teacher's virtues so warmly, it is impossible to deny the importance of treating children with decency and respect.

Ultimately, I don't think Tom Bennett and I see things differently. We both think that positive teacher–pupil classroom relationships are fundamental to learning. Tom gets twitchy about this stuff when the teacher–pupil classroom relationships are characterised by low academic expectations. To watch Molly Medhurst teach with such deliberate expertise and so clearly enjoying herself, was a joy. She has the ability to cultivate relationships with her pupils which enable them to feel safe, cared for and academically ambitious. The pupils' attitude to learning was unerringly industrious. They were genuinely enjoying themselves as they wrestled with subtracting fractions. If we are going to attract everyone back into schools and resolve the post-COVID decline in school attendance rates, we have to make our classrooms more like Molly's.

Molly Medhurst's pupils' progress and achievement data

Here is a snapshot of the progress for Molly's class last year. It needs to be recognised that The Ridgeway is an improving school, the most improved in Reading.

Subject	Progress made over the year
Reading	5% of pupils made below expected progress
	42% of the pupils make expected progress
	53% of the pupils made more than expected progress
	Over half of the class made accelerated progress over the course of the year.
Writing	21% of pupils made below expected progress
	47% of the pupils make expected progress
	32% of the pupils made more than expected progress
	The pupils made more progress than their peers in writing with a third of the class making accelerated progress of the course of the year.
Maths	53% of the pupils make expected progress
	47% of the pupils made more than expected progress
	The pupils made more progress than their peers in maths with the whole class making at least expected progress and nearly half of the class making accelerated progress.

A Truly Great Special School Teacher: Mary Cawley

Mary Cawley is a Year 9 teacher at Kingsley High School, Harrow.

The school leadership's view

I'm in the depths of a non-descript housing estate in North West London visiting one of my favourite schools on the planet! Kingsley High School is a community special school. It provides a high-quality education for children with visual impairment, hearing impairment, autistic spectrum disorder, multi-sensory impairment, severe learning difficulty, and profound and multiple learning difficulty. It is coeducational with 126 pupils aged 11–19 years but, as a special school, is not deemed to be of any phase of education. When I talk about the school, I find it hard not to enthuse. As Mary Myatt has often said to me, 'John.

Stop your tears. These people are just doing their job.' And one of these people who is *just doing her job* is Mary Cawley, the topic of my conversation with Lee Helyer, the head teacher.

'Mary has been teaching for over 40 years and is our most experienced teacher', says Lee. 'She is unconsciously highly competent, but, as with the humble nature of true experts, she won't know she's being so good. People like Mary are very careful not to feel too good about themselves. Trying to get a sense of their worth is incredibly difficult, and, for me, effecting some sort of tangible, repeatable knowledge transfer from Mary to our less experienced teachers is near impossible as it can be with some experts in their field, though I am sure she does this naturally whilst working with staff and modelling.' We talk about the Marxist view of labour as just another dispensable factor of production, and how it is all too easy to see people reach the end of their career and be dispensed of, and how important it is for leaders to cherish such colleagues, value their vast experience and make the move towards the end of their careers as positive as possible.

Lee is clear-headed about his role: 'There are systems and processes that we follow to make the school run, but Mary will adapt those when necessary to meet the needs of the young people. I just need to get out of the way of people like Mary. When I go to watch her teach, what have I got that I could contribute? Nothing! I just need to give Mary the resources she needs to do her stuff and then just keep out the way, offering development or support where it's wanted or needed.' We laugh in mutual recognition of the limitations of headship. Lee continues: 'Mary's strength is the world she creates in that classroom. The atmosphere she creates is purposeful and meaningful. She supports her colleagues and they work as a well-oiled machine. She has such expertise, she makes it look all so effortless. And these children have complex needs and are so physically active and such individuals who need careful care and specific learning interventions.'

'How many children does she have in her class?' I ask.

'At the most six to eight. I think she has four today, all Year 9s, and she has three colleagues supporting her, so, with you, there'll be more adults than children, but it will still be incredibly busy!' I mask my surprise as Lee rises from his seat and we make our way down to Mary's classroom.

Teaching

We knock on the door. Mary unlocks it and lets us in. We shake hands, and she introduces me to her colleagues, Louise, Monica and Veronica. Mary is one of those people who has smiled all her life, and so, even in repose, she looks happy and content. It is a bright and airy, smallish room, with enough tables for 10 people arranged in a U shape facing a big bright screen. I am introduced to Joshua, Adrian, James and Ahmed. We also shake hands. A couple of pupils are away today.

I sit on the corner desk, between Joshua on my left and Adrian on my right. I have to admit, I feel like an interloper. I am not sure I have felt this nervous for years. I have arrived halfway through a writing lesson. I watch Mary with Adrian. He is writing his name but is intent on missing out the first letter. Mary is incredibly patient. She asks him to hold the pen, and, in turn, she holds his hand and scribes the letters so he can feel the direction the pen moves and the shape the letters make. Despite Mary's best efforts, Adrian seems to have embedded into his muscle memory the elimination of the first letter of his name! Mary grins. It is time for two minutes' rest and snack time. Mary asks Adrian to say 'snack' and he obliges with the most beautiful smile.

The boys eat voraciously. Having had two boys myself, I know how much they need feeding and the dangers of letting them get 'hangry'! Whilst they eat, Louise tells me about them and how they understand the zones of regulation, and how Mary and the team know them all so well and all their idiosyncrasies. They now have such great support from parents when, not long ago, there was none. A newly formed parent teacher association (PTA) is 32 members' strong. I look around the room. The mission statement catches my eye: 'We support learning to enjoy and achieve whilst preparing for adulthood, through a broad and balanced, ambitious curriculum with relevant skills and knowledge for all.' I am reminded of Oliver Caviglioli, previously head of a special school, when he said that there was no point in teaching something if the learning did not transfer into something that helped children prepare for life beyond school. 'No transfer? No point.'[1] It seems to me that Mary and her team take every chance to put the onus upon the boys to do things. The snack has calmed them down and Mary says: 'Can you pack up now, please?' And the boys dutifully tidy away their snack detritus. In that short interaction, learning is happening. It is skilful and deliberate.

Adrian takes my prompt sheets, which Mary has given me for my session with the boys later, and puts them in his resources drawer. He thinks it is very funny and Louise insists he hands them back. They begin a brick game, where they match the bricks by colour as they build. Mary is asking Joshua questions relentlessly. When he sneezes, she teaches him to put his hand over his mouth. When he throws a plastic bag on the floor, she asks him to pick it up, and he does. I notice that everything is narrated for the boys. 'I'm going to ask you to tidy up.' 'I'm going to ask you to put your things away now.' Furthermore, inter-actions are relentlessly agreement-based, with the team asking for the boys' agreement when they decide to do something. For instance, when Joshua gets frustrated and begins hitting out, mainly at himself, Mary says, 'You don't need to hit. I'm going to move away, now. Alright?' They also give the boys a choice, because it empowers and calms them. We play a game of guessing your favourite McDonald's meal. Adrian wants, 'chicken nuggets, chips, ice cream and water'. It is fun. The room is full of smiles.

It's time for an exercise break followed by maths. Ahmed is especially enthused. He has tremendous energy to expend. We exercise our neck and shoulders, we run on the spot, stretch and shake and jump. After

---

1 M. Myatt and J. Tomsett, *SEND Huh: Curriculum Conversations with SEND Leaders* (Woodbridge: John Catt Educational, 2023).

20 jumps we are all exhausted. As the session ends, James approaches Mary looking distressed and he appears capable of losing control. Mary takes his arms, puts them by his side, holds his face and narrates what we are doing next. His ire subsides. The whole team is so very assertive. All the boys are physically strong and strong-willed – Ahmed, especially, is big for his age – but the team are fearless, talk calmly, look into the boys' eyes and hold their arms if necessary. It is all done with assertive love.

We are into our mathematics. Mary has put the scheme of learning on the board, and we follow it pretty much verbatim. Joshua drops his sheet. Instead of picking it up for him, Monica asks him to pick it up and to put it on his pile. Each one of us is given a wooden shape, taken lucky dip style out of a bag. We watch a video and when our shape comes up on screen we have to hold it up. First out is a triangle and Ahmed shouts out in his soft voice, 'Me!' and holds his wooden triangle high in the air. We all applaud, and he looks the epitome of contentedness. It is a lovely moment. He then gets up and takes two lunch plates from Mary's desk – which she was using as circle representations – and puts them on the draining board next to the sink. I sense the importance to Ahmed of things needing to be in the right place, the need for order. That's why I am pleased to be able to watch the lesson. The boys seem to have accepted my presence in the room, despite me being out of the ordinary.

We go through all the basic shapes: square, rectangle, triangle, circle, star and hexagon. We focus on the hexagon. Through skilful teaching, we all establish that a hexagon has six sides. When Joshua gets the number of sides right, he gives Monica a fist pump. Ahmed suddenly decides to lie on the floor in the middle of the room, beneath the big screen. Mary moves him back to his seat, with a lot of kerfuffle. The lesson continues. I watch Mary. She is checking in with her colleagues all the time, confirming what they might do, smiling, orchestrating and adapting. It is the most skilful teaching. I also notice that she is signing when she speaks to the pupils. It is understated, but important. They are largely non-verbal, so the signing helps with communication. Louise helps Joshua – with his permission – and he counts all six sides of the hexagon. Then Mary spells out the word hexagon phonetically, and all the pupils say it aloud. It is a moment of success that we celebrate enthusiastically.

Mary produces a decidedly weighty wood/cardboard tree, with eight squares of velcro in the branches. Adrian is asked to hold the tree. As he stands there, grinning, he realises that it's the perfect object to club Mary with! Veronica plays security guard, whilst Louise gives out Velcro-backed shapes. As each shape's name is called out, the person with the shape comes up to the front and attaches the shape to the tree, via the Velcro. It works a treat, until James places his circle on the tree, but then decides he wants to steam around the room. He wants to watch *The Snowman* video, it's his favourite. Mary interrogates James quietly to see if he needs anything else, but, no, just *The Snowman* video. Mary realises that time is up on the tree-exercise and decides that drawing the shapes is the next activity to embed their learning. They have six shapes on one sheet of paper, and they have to copy them across onto a blank, keeping each of them within one of the six empty boxes.

Triangle

Star

Circle

Rectangle

Square

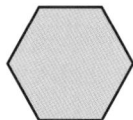

Hexagon

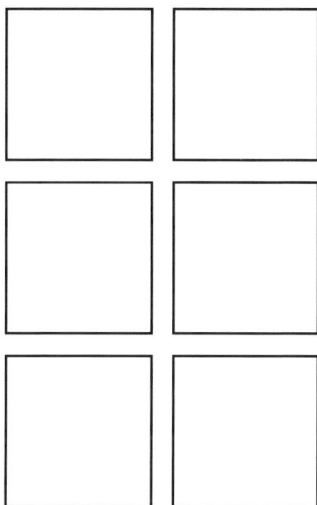

The boys do as they are instructed, and every single one of them is successful. 'That's fabulous', says Mary, 'now write the words underneath the shapes.' Mary sits with Joshua. She understands him so much more clearly than I could ever imagine. James sets off around the room and Monica leads him back to his seat, assertively, talking to him all the time, narrating what is happening, giving him choices. Mary asks Joshua if he would like a book, as he has finished his tasks. But he begins hitting himself, hard, while beginning to yell in despair. Mary says, 'Joshua, you are feeling very angry. What can we do to help? You can show me.' Joshua points outside. They get his coat and he sits outside, exorcising his anger by shouting. Mary says that the book triggered him. It was not one that he was familiar with and he could not read it. They leave the back door unlocked whilst Joshua is out there and James immediately dashes out and away. Veronica sets off to get him and a minute or so later, James is back with us. He wanted to check the bush where they had been blackberry picking a few weeks earlier, to see if there were any berries left.

The final activity of the morning is understanding shadows, which is part of the science curriculum. Each boy is given a torch and we begin to make different shadow shapes on the walls using the torches. Joshua is still in distress outside. He is screaming loudly. The team are all aware of him, but none is distracted from the activity in the room. Veronica is so, so patient with Adrian, who thinks it's fun to keep hold of the torch, even when Veronica has asked him to return it. Ahmed goes into the dark, calm corner where it is great for making shadow shapes. Suddenly Joshua decides he wants to come back in. Mary doesn't hang his coat up for him, but insists he does it himself. Every opportunity to develop the boys' independence is seized upon, even when Joshua has been terribly distressed. Joshua is shown out of the room to hang his coat up, and the door is closed behind him.

Ahmed begins to dysregulate. He lies on the floor again. They encourage him to move, but he immediately returns to where he lay. There is no point trying to persuade him to move. He is given a weighted blanket to *try* to reduce arousal. He then jumps up and heads for the darkened room. He is jumping and shouting. He is probably 5 feet 9 inches tall and weighs about 12 stone. In a moment of behaviour-management magic, seconds later Mary has him tidying up. I could try to explain how she does it, but I don't have the words to describe something so imperceptible, yet so brilliant. Mary is then required to attend to Joshua, to try to interpret what it is he needs to calm him completely.

As the morning's lessons come to an end, and they prepare for my session with them to find out what makes Mrs Cawley such a great teacher, I have a few seconds to think. How does this team anticipate what the boys are going to do next? Where do they get the courage to assert themselves so calmly? Where do they find the energy to do this eight hours a day? How on earth are they so patient? They are terrifically well-trained, for one, and they work in a superbly led school, where Lee acknowledges their expertise and, as he says, gets out of their way. But, without being mawkish, the ultimate answer is, of course, that everything they do for those boys comes from a place of love.

What the students think of Mary Cawley

The room is finally tidy. As you can imagine (and, to be honest, I didn't until we actually began) discussing with the pupils the strengths of their teacher is challenging. Mary, Louise, Veronica and I sit with Joshua, James and Adrian – Ahmed isn't in the room just at this moment – and we use question sheets that have graphic images that the pupils can circle to express what they feel. All three circle the smiley face when asked 'Are your lessons exciting?' Judging by the way they react to Mary's team and the activities provided for them, that is so clearly true.

They universally enjoy food technology. James likes art. Joshua likes writing. Adrian and Joshua like ICT. Indeed, I had noticed that any opportunity to access the iPad is eagerly taken by all of them, especially Ahmed. James and Adrian then decide that to circle every image on their sheet would be a fun thing to do, so their data are slightly unreliable, as they claim to like everything they do in school! We all laugh! It is a lovely moment. Adrian signs his name (*sans* the letter A, obviously …), quite legibly, at the end of his second sheet, along with the time of day, 12:15 pm, which he copies from the large screen. Joshua finishes the session by writing the title of his favourite website which is, fittingly, www.helpkidzlearn.com:

help
kidz
learn

Joshua's writing is testimony to the purposeful culture Mary and her team create. The fact that Joshua, who was so troubled a mere 20 minutes ago, is able to sit quietly, answer all the questions on the sheet (without being tempted to join in the fun of circling every image), and then communicate clearly on paper his favourite website for learning, is nothing short of remarkable. I ask Joshua if I might keep his piece of paper and he passes it to me with a smile.

IRL: Mary Cawley

John Tomsett (JT): How did you get into teaching, then?

Mary Cawley (MC): Well, it was probably my last year at school, in the upper sixth. We were asked what we'd like to do. At that time, my mum used to be involved with the local church. Every now and then, they would give parties for people with learning disabilities, and she would ask, 'Do you want to come along?' I would go along, and it would be really good fun. I didn't have any qualms about it. I wasn't afraid, I just slotted in. So, when I met with our careers teacher at school, I said that I was interested in nursing people with learning difficulties in homes or hospitals, which was an absolutely stupid thing to say, because I hate needles and I hate blood. But she said to me, 'Have you ever thought of teaching?' I hadn't thought of teaching because I was unaware of any special schools at the time.

JT: What year are we talking about?

MC: I think it was 1976. From there, I was asked to look up various places and I really liked Wall Hall teacher training college. They had a specific course for special education. I think it was called the Education and Psychology of Mentally Handicapped Children and Young People. That term was still in use, but it had a horrible undertone.

I attended Wall Hall for three years. It was quite a 'hands on' course. There were just four of us on it. It wasn't a degree course, although we had many links with our fellow students! Our course provided us with various opportunities to learn about many different subjects/areas and relating this to how you would teach those with a learning difficulty. We visited classes in local schools, with a Nursery attached to the college. We visited Harperbury Hospital, which was, at that time, an institution. I remember going into a long dormitory and walking down long corridors, every door was locked behind us.

JT: **They were like mental institutions.**

MC: They were. That's what it was. It was heartbreaking to see how little control of their lives the patients had. The single beds and just a little locker. There were about 20 beds in the long dormitory that we saw. We were told not to leave the group of people who were showing us around. From Wall Hall College, I found my first job as class teacher in a special school in Ilford. It was a lovely school, and the head and deputy head teacher, in fact all the staff, were friendly and welcoming. The head teacher knew I played the piano, and asked if I would like to be in 'charge' of music. I said I would give it a go. It really only involved playing the piano in assembly and organising the Christmas band. I was there for about eight years, and it was a real community.

I learned such a lot and built some wonderful relationships with pupils and staff. I am still friends with the deputy and head teacher from that time, plus some of the teachers, pupils and parents. We write and exchange cards at Christmas. There are even phone calls from some of my ex-pupils from those days. It's lovely that they've kept in touch. I remember meeting one of the boys at a school Christmas fair

I asked him, 'Peter, what do you actually remember about school? Do you remember your school days when we were in the classroom? Do you remember the first time you could write your name?' He said, 'Well, no, I don't. But I remember when Bryan Young got in trouble and when he was taken out.' That was the thing he remembered. Nothing about the academic part. It was just the fun, the fun that he'd had. He'd made it to living on his own in sheltered accommodation, which was wonderful for him. Other ex-pupils also live in sheltered accommodation or family-group homes. It was a real milestone for me to find out how independent they had all become.

I opened a Leavers Unit for 16–19-year-olds as the teacher in charge, roughly four miles away from the main school, in Barkingside. I stayed there for approximately eight years. We had many links to the local community, including pottery classes, weekly work experience on a city farm, horse riding, access to nearby shops, hairdressers, library and swimming pool. There was a wealth of independence skills to gain! It was an amazing time.

I resigned when my son began school. I wanted to be involved more in his life. We had a lovely childminder around the corner from the school where I worked, and I just wanted to take him to school and pick him up. After about 18 months/two years at home, I contacted local authority supply pools, one in Harrow and one in Watford. I put my name forward for special schools. I then wrote to all my local special schools to ask if they were interested in employing a supply teacher. All replied positively. I worked at four different schools. It was a busy but fulfilling time because I learned so much from those different schools. Each school had a different approach to their curriculum and how they approached their students' needs. There was a variety of learning and physical needs, as well as behaviours. It was incredible. When I first worked here (Kingsley) on supply, the school was a very old building. It was called Whittlesea School. I began working here more frequently and eventually took a part-time permanent contract.

JT: **What I really want to pick your brains about today is teaching. How much of what you do is deliberate, and how much of it is deeply unconscious competence, because you've been teaching for 44 years? I'm going**

to try and unpick what you did today. I'm going to try and relate back to you what I think you were doing, some of the principles, and you can then just tell me if I'm right or wrong.

MC: Oh, OK. That's interesting, yes.

JT: **I think you give them as much choice as possible about what they do, about their behaviour, because you always give them an option to do something. What you're working on there is developing their own self-regulation, rather than you telling them what to do.**

MC: Yes, I avoid the 'now do this, now do that' approach. There usually needs to be a negotiation, rather than a demand.

JT: **That seems to me a principle.**

MC: That is. That's right.

JT: **You make the effort to get them to say stuff a lot, as much as you possibly can, and we celebrate when they do.**

MC: Yes, brilliant, but bearing in mind we have many non-verbal students, signing is as important as vocalising, plus the use of symbols, pictures or pointing to an object.

JT: **When Joshua was saying 'triangle' or 'circle'.**

MC: Yes, he was using his voice, which was brilliant to hear, but there are occasions when we may not have understood what he was trying to say, in which case we would ask him to write it down.

JT: **Just pointing, we're just celebrating that cognition. I think you're thinking all the time.**

MC: I think it has to, yes, because if one strategy has not worked, you need to be ready with an alternative. You also need to be aware of pupils that may have reached the end of their ability to focus and need a calming choice of activity or a different task.

JT: **About where they are, and what they're doing. You treat them like adults, really. You treat them very civilly.**

MC: Yes, I think there has to be respect and an awareness of how each pupil communicates. It may be vocally, signing or both, or taking you by the hand to show you a meaningful object. We celebrate everything!

JT: **Yes, so how much of that sounds like some of the conscious principles of what you do?**

MC: Most of the above is conscious, but awareness of behaviours, for example, or needing a different approach with a task, or the need to do something independently, that has reached an unconscious level for us as a team.

JT: **Talk to me about what you do, then. That was an extraordinary lesson I saw today.**

MC: Thank you! During a lesson you are aware of the content; you have briefed your staff team; you have a selection of tasks; you have specific communication boards for those students who need them, particularly featuring what is happening 'now' and what will be happening 'next'; you are aware of the different methods of communicating, and if one method has not worked, you try another; and you are constantly anticipating what a particular student might do or might need, for example, when I asked Joshua if he would like to read because he'd finished a task. Often, he likes reading specific books, 'reading' to himself. He has memorised the words of his favourite books. The book he chose was not the book he usually chooses.

JT: **Is that what triggered him?**

MC: I think that's what triggered him. He opened it and he couldn't read it, and even when I said, 'Can I read it to you?', or 'Do you want to change it?' he couldn't cope with this. That's what I feel upset him. But by then it was too late to do anything. Once he reaches that point he has to 'let go' of his frustration and he then needs to calm down by himself. There is no point interrupting him, for example, saying, 'Okay, Joshua, two more or three more minutes' (at the table) because he is unable to continue for two or three minutes longer, but that's OK. We can manage that.

Yes, you do have to anticipate things. For example, James is finishing his task. He will want to watch *The Snowman* film, so if it's not a designated reward at that time, we can turn the computer off when we have finished using it as a teaching tool. I often turn the computer off totally as it can be a huge distraction. Ahmed and Yana, who was not there today, would have an argument about it, because they would each want their choice of YouTube clips!

It's important to treat our students with respect. They are young adults. They're 12/13 years old. Next year they'll be going into Key Stage 4, which is the next step towards leaving school. I think subconsciously they appreciate being treated like adults. We use symbols and pictures a lot, because we are all busy together and some may be walking around. Often our pupils cannot cope with a voice and the use of pictures and symbols is plain and easy. Often that works with Ahmed. We just show him a picture of the chair and he will go and sit on his chair.

JT: **You're adapting every second of the lesson, depending on what you get from them.**

MC: Yes, on what I've got back. And if I see that somebody does something that isn't quite what I'd asked them to do, but they had extended it by themselves, that's fine. I'm not going to go back and say, 'Oh, gosh, you've done that wrong', because that's great. Also, when they use their initiative, that's a real cause for celebration.

JT: **Did that happen today, do you think?**

MC: Yes, I think it happened with James. He was doing something with the shapes that I hadn't quite asked him to do, and Monica had sat back a little bit. That's the other thing that's very difficult. In the past, with some colleagues I have worked with, because they want our pupils to succeed, they may help too much. I have to say that our staff team do not do this!

JT: **But *you* let them either succeed or fail on their own terms, and through their own decision making.**

MC: Yes, and it has got to be that way, because that's the stage that leads them to to learning to be independent, which is what we're all about, learning to be independent. I didn't show it today, but we have a list of skills that we would use for that particular lesson, and it belongs in our skills workbook. So, for example, today would have been learning how to use a torch, using it properly, not throwing it. I thought Ahmed might throw it any second, so I was nervous about that, because it's not my torch, but he didn't. He was quite interested in what he was doing, so I think all of that comes into play, as well. There are always skills to be worked on to move towards adulthood and independence.

I think the first thing, in September when we have new classes, is making that relationship. That's the first and foremost interaction that you need. I had Joshua, James and Adrian last year, so we already had a relationship, but I didn't with Ahmed, or Ricky or Yana, that's the first thing. Regardless of what you want them to write, what you want them to learn … you've got to have that relationship and spend time forging it.

JT: **How do you get that? Everybody I've interviewed, and I'll have interviewed 19 teachers for this book by the time I do my last one on Wednesday, everybody says that forging relationships is the first thing.**

MC: It is. I'm glad everybody's saying it!

JT: **It's no different. So, how do you get that with these lovely young people?**

MC: With ours, you would spend time with them doing nice things, or finding things that they're interested in, sitting on the floor with them, singing with them, playing a hand game with them, maybe just twice or three times a day, or at the same time the next day. Then, they get to the point where they're ready to sit around a table. James usually has a workstation at the back of the room where he's looking out at us, which keeps him feeling secure and focused. I don't mean secure in terms of him not running away. I mean secure in his head, because it's a safe space, and nobody comes and annoys him there! Lots of the class are still very sensory orientated, so we have a lot of objects that light up, make a noise, feely, touchy.

JT: **The dark room.**

MC: Yes, so Ahmed sometimes will go in there and just lay down and we have a TheraBrush™ that he puts under his head and lies on. Sometimes you have no idea (well, I do know) what they're trying to achieve. They're trying to achieve regulation in their bodies. As you say, looking at Ahmed, it's just constant. That energy flow through him is constant, and I'm amazed he sits at the table for as long as he does.

JT: **He does it beautifully.**

MC: He's talking, and it's lovely to hear his little voice.

JT: **He has got the whispering. He has got the tiniest voice for this big lad.**

MC: I know! It's great and the teacher he had last year, she'd done such brilliant work with him. He has come from a very quiet class where he was able to sit quietly at the table, and so was everybody else. Whereas our class, you know, there's one up, one down. But you give them that time. You build your relationship by being with them. Getting into their world. Finding out about them, finding out what they like, and what they don't like.

JT: **It's about having a bit of imagination, is it?**

MC: Yes, totally. Yes, going for a walk around the school, you find out lots.

JT: **Trying to imagine what the world is like from their point of view.**

MC: Yes. My colleague, Julie, who I share the class with, often says, 'I just wish I could see the world as they see the world', because they see it very differently to us. School is one environment and home is another environment, and they've got to adapt to the school environment, which they have done from when they were small. Obviously from reception to Year 6, they've been at Woodlands School, our partner primary school, and then there's the huge transition when they come here. They've got all of that to cope with – new staff, new pupils, new class, new visual things. It's extremely hard when they first come from primary school. The transition moments are difficult but really important, so we have a lot of space to allow that to happen. The transition time is much longer now than it was, and for those that can read symbols, we give social stories to take home, send pictures of the new staff that they're going to be working with, so they have this information to look at throughout the summer holiday. Anything that will help their next journey.

JT: **Yes, so you're very deliberate about the choices you give them. You've got your radar on all the time, from a health and safety point of view, I guess, because there's a whole load of things they could do to damage themselves, and you. How do you cope with that?**

MC: Well, we have our behaviour strategies, so you wouldn't go towards Ahmed and physically try to move him.

JT: **No, because I was going to ask you about whether you ever get to the point that if Adrian hadn't handed the torch over, would you ever take it off him?**

MC: I wouldn't try to, because Adrian has got such a strong grip. I have in the past, but he doesn't let go, and then it escalates and he thinks it's really, really funny, and the more attention you give him, the more he carries on. He's like a little boy, really, and so I say, 'OK Adrian … when you're ready, you can give me the torch', and then I walk away.

JT: **Yes, so you make it less of a deal.**

MC: Then he'll say, 'Mary.' I'll say, 'Yes, when you're ready. I'm not interested yet.' If it was something dangerous, then I would take it from him, but usually it's a torch, or a pen, or your papers, and then he'll giggle, and smile, and say, 'I've got them.'

JT: **So, you have procedures for every child?**

MC: Yes, so for Joshua, for example, that's the zones of regulation we would use. Ahmed, we try and use pictures or try and use a gentle voice. Once you have recognised that he has got to do his bouncing and jumping or lying down between tasks and then he will come back to the table. You either count down or you use a timer. He loves kinetic sand. I don't know if you saw that.

JT: **He's feeling it, because there was still a sand tray, wasn't there?**

MC: Yes, so that's his station for when he has his 'leisure' time and wants to build, when he wants to use the sand, even when he wants water play. We say, 'Okay, you can use that now. It's time. You choose what you want to do'; symbols would have been placed on his *Now and Next* board to show him what's happening next.

JT: **That's the other thing you do; you narrate all the time. You narrate what's happening in the tiniest**

interactions. 'Now, now, now', and you're also very agreement-based, it seemed to me.

MC: Agreement?

JT: **'Could we do this? Can we do this?'**

MC: Oh, yes.

JT: **You ask them for their agreement to do stuff.**

MC: Yes, not that they always reply.

JT: **No, but they do.**

MC: In their own way, yes. If they choose to do whatever they have chosen to do.

JT: **Yes, they are accepting your invitation.**

MC: Yes, 'Can we do this and that?' Yes, I wasn't totally aware of that.

JT: **There's very little forcing them to do anything.**

MC: I think it has got to come from them. Otherwise, if you're forcing and they don't actually like or they are not interested in what you're doing, it won't work. You can't make it totally exciting all the time, because then that can escalate, as well. Just a bit of difference, like putting things on a pretend tree. Okay, it's not a great activity … The next part of the science lesson was going to be showing the light box, which would have been quite a nice activity. But it was great that they were experimenting in the dark room. I saw Ahmed experimenting just by himself, and he'd got the hang of it, and so he was anticipating what was coming.

JT: **Yes, that was amazing. You get them to speak as much as you possibly can, and, actually, I looked at Joshua and he understands a lot, doesn't he?**

MC: Yes, and then the time that you think he has understood what you've said, he hasn't. I can see his eyes and I think, 'OK, Mary, just water it down a bit again to two or three words.' Sometimes he will just hang on to the last word. He is quite 'on the ball' with his films and his selection of what he wants to use on the computer. I think at home, as well, his iPad is important to him.

JT: **Is there anything else you do, consciously or unconsciously, pedagogically?**

MC: I know I try and encourage our students to speak as much as they can, but if not, we would use symbols, but I also think, probably unconsciously now, you're just aware, totally aware all the time … 'OK, he has finished that. I need to go over there', or 'I can see he has moved his hand. He may be about to get up from his seat.'

JT: **Yes, do you become able to read them?**

MC: Yes, you do, and I don't know if that's just a thing with me or everybody. I don't think everybody can, because sometimes you have agency teaching assistants come in to cover planning, preparation and assessment (PPA) time, and, for example, Ahmed gets up, and they'll say, as soon as he gets up, 'No, sit down, sit down.' We will say, 'He's going for his movement break. It's okay. He knows what he needs to do.' 'Oh, but he needs to sit down at his table.' And we say, 'But he doesn't. He will come back. You're escalating him.' For some people, it has got to be that they sit at their tables all the time, which not many of our pupils can do. They can't focus for very long. They sat for half-an-hour, I think, each time this morning.

JT: **That was pretty impressive.**

MC: Which I was surprised about. It might not have happened if Ricky was there. He would probably have been in his own space. He has his own space to explore things.

JT: **Ahmed, it seems to me, gives you very little facial messaging about what he's thinking, but the others were much more expressive.**

MC: Yes, he does.

JT: **I thought James gives you everything.**

MC: Yes, and then he has got that little smile.

JT: **Yes, this lovely smile, but then he can look really angry.**

MC: Oh, very. It changes.

JT: **Ahmed's is almost quite blank.**

MC: Yes, and he will push you if he doesn't want you standing near him. He might accept what you've said, but he can push you away medium hard, and if you're standing in the way of something that he wants, he may push you. Our behaviour strategies with Ahmed will come into play, though, and all staff will be aware of what might happen.

JT: **You're communicating all the time, so you sign a lot.**

MC: Yes, so that's just another addition, because we're a total communication school.

JT: **Right, tell me about that.**

MC: It's signing, it's speech, it's symbols, it's pictures, it's objects of reference for some of the PMLD class, or even in our class, to explain what you're going to do. I had used different shapes. OK, a plate was one of them, and, of course, for Ahmed that wasn't supposed to be with the shapes. It was supposed to be *there*.

JT: **Yes, he was obsessed with putting those plates on the draining board.**

MC: Because why would I want a plate on my desk?

JT: **Why would I want a plate on the desk? I want a plate on the draining board, because that's where they go.**

MC: Which is where it should be.

JT: Fair enough.

MC: Yes, that was great. He has got that. So, we sign, and it just helps them to focus more on what you're saying, because you're doing something, and sometimes they will sign back. Joshua probably won't, because he's too busy talking.

JT: He's quite verbal, isn't he?

MC: Not always clear though. Which is frustrating then for him, because we haven't understood what he said, which is why we started asking him to write down, which was another wow moment, the first time that he did. I thought, 'He can write what he wants, look!' That was fantastic. We have communication books, and we have separate communication boards, say, in art for colours. 'Can you choose what colour you want and which paint brush? Okay, you go and get it from the cupboard or from where it is over there.' It's another enablement to independence, I think. The relationship between you is crucial, because communication is the be all and end all, the key thing to everything, and all the behaviour is a way of communicating to us.

JT: Yes, because what's happening to them in their head affects what they do, doesn't it?

MC: Yes, absolutely, and also they are looking around them. Ahmed, even though he wants to do what he wants to do, like putting the plate back, he's also attached to the timetable. As soon as we finish something he takes it off the plan for the day.

JT: I felt I massively impinged on their world today.

MC: They accepted it.

JT: They were quite good, weren't they?

MC: Yes.

JT: **I was surprised, because I thought, 'I feel massive in this room in terms of an alien presence.'**

MC: Oh, I think Ahmed is bigger!

JT: **I know! I felt like a big thing in the corner, which is not usually there. But you put visitor up on the plan for the day, so you anticipated me.**

MC: Which brings us back, doesn't it, to the unknown of when you first meet somebody with learning difficulties, and because you don't know them, you don't know what they're going to do, or what they're capable of doing.

JT: **Is there anything else that you and your team do deliberately? You're running that whole group of people, aren't you? You've got four adults in there.**

MC: Yes, you couldn't do it without a team, they're so important. I think we make sure that whatever resources we use are tailor made for them. Deliberately, as well, we ensure that they can use whatever resources we have. It's hard to say deliberate, because I think we just know now. Using our knowledge of them to enable them to enjoy their day is deliberate. It's about fun and it's about providing the right resources for lessons to make it that little bit more exciting or different. Not doing hundreds of worksheets, with lots of writing on them. Just plain, simple stuff, but making it harder each time they go along. I think that physical side of things is deliberate and the building of the relationship is, and remembering what it is they like. You're constantly thinking about the next thing that you can try to enable that person to do his best or her best.

JT: **Would you ever have done anything else?**

MC: No. Honestly. By the end of that first year, we'd been on holiday together, some wonderful trips out, I was caught. By the time we had the post-16 unit, we were in a fantastic place in Barkingside. We managed to teach students to go to a shop and buy a pint of milk using the zebra crossing. We were on tenter-hooks, but they did it.

JT: **It's like when you let your own kid go to the shop for the first time on their own.**

MC: Yes, one of the girls went to the hairdresser, with her mum's permission of course. She came back with this huge perm! All of this was fostering independence. No, I couldn't have seen myself doing anything else.

JT: **Passing on the baton, Mary, to a new generation of young people going into teaching, what advice would you give them?**

MC: I would say go for special, because it's not standing in front of a class of 30. Some of ours have homework, so we do have just a little bit of marking to do, but not all do, because home is home to them and school is school. Why on earth would you be doing what you do at home, some do not understand. So, I would say go for it, because there's such a lack of special needs teachers in mainstream, as well as in special schools.

JT: **What is it that has made you stay at it for 44 years?**

MC: I think the excitement and the surprises. There are always surprises, and always something happens that you never thought would. Like James finding the letter S for snowman and walking around with his snow picture, and us not getting it at all for a long, long time.

JT: **In the end, he communicated.**

MC: In the end, I think he was desperate. He was desperate to communicate this, or Joshua writing what he wanted to know. There are always behavioural challenges, and it's about getting into that person's world to find out what is it that's making him tick? What is it that's causing him this pain? What is it that I can do to help? What can I do to help make that person's life a bit better, a bit easier? It's just so interesting. There's never a dull day. Never a day the same.

JT: The days fly by.

MC: They do! It's just exciting. You meet so many interesting people, as well. Some agency teaching assistants who come in have gone on to want to be teachers, because of what they've seen, which is the best way forward, isn't it? Go for special needs teaching.

JT: Is there anything else you think I ought to know about you before I write this chapter in the book?

MC: Just how much I enjoy it. OK, we get tired, I know, and sometimes we 'moan' because there's another task to do, where we would rather be in class doing what we need to do. I do enjoy being in class and, although our PPA is so important and I *so* appreciate it, being in class is, I think, the absolute. Just being around your little group and your staff, obviously, because I want to recognise them and how much they do.

JT: They're so brilliant, aren't they?

MC: They do so much ... without our class teams, we would not be able to function properly in the classroom, we would not be able to support our pupils and we would not have access to their brilliant ideas

My friends say, 'Oh, when are you going to retire?' I say, 'Well, maybe next year. I'll see how I feel in May', because physically I'm fine. I'm still able to jump around and chase somebody down the corridor, which is necessary sometimes.

JT: Yes, that's just brilliant. Well, thank you so much. It has been a real pleasure.

MC: I've enjoyed it!

Testimonials

'I have had the privilege of working alongside Mary for over a decade. During all these years, I have known Mary as a colleague with strong work ethics. Mary is an incredible professional with excellent communication and listening skills, who collaborates, adapts, and has empathy and patience.

The specific characteristics of her effective teaching include an engaging classroom presence, value in real-world learning, exchange of best practices and a lifelong love of learning. Her strong passion for teaching inspires both students as well as fellow teachers.'

'Mary always displays patience and understanding, and creates a calm happy learning environment. She manages chaotic behaviours extremely well. No matter the incident she has a way of remaining softly spoken and peaceful. I watch in awe, and remember thinking "I want to be like her". Mary is both supportive and encouraging of me. I am now an unqualified teacher, and Mary continues to cheer me on to gain my QTS. She asks my opinion when we share lesson ideas and she happily takes on board my views. This will always surprise me, as she is such an experienced teacher, with a wealth of knowledge. She is a dedicated, understanding, caring, professional, and friendly individual who is always on hand to offer me any support or answer any of my concerns.'

So, what can we learn from Mary Cawley?

It's an easy thing to say about colleagues, but I've never been more genuine when I write that watching Mary teach was truly humbling. That said, trying to surface the expert features of her teaching that have been so entirely embedded in her person, that even she is hardly conscious of them, is pretty difficult. But in the interview I managed to highlight some aspects of her practice that any teacher might learn from:

- Spending time finding out about each child helps establish the foundations for the learning relationship with individual pupils.

- Giving pupils choices at every opportunity is hugely beneficial. It enables them to develop their independence and helps them feel a modicum of autonomy.

- Using an agreement-based way of communicating makes for calmer classrooms.

- Narrating the day, through the *Now and Next* cueing process, provides certainty and a degree of safety for pupils.

- Having your *anticipating-what-might-happen-next* radar on in a very deliberate way is crucial to effective behaviour management.

- Communicating closely with fellow adults in the room, in the moment, and giving them the autonomy to take actions that might prevent behaviour issues escalating, seems to be an obvious learning point from Mary's classroom practice.

Now, there is much more that we might learn from Mary's practice, but these six observations are a decent starting point. That said, if there is one more thing that struck me about how Mary goes about her work, it's this … in her fifth decade of teaching, she is never without a smile!

Mary Cawley's students' progress and achievement data

- 2023–24 SEMH: 54% target achievement (compared with the ASD 47% average target achievement).

- 2023–24 Learners' personal learning plans (PLPs), our main sources of progress targets: 96% achieved or partially achieved (compared with 93% for all ASD, 92% for whole school).

- 2023–24 Community and Independence: 92% targets achieved or partially achieved, in line with general school and Key Stage data, taking into account the complex needs of the learners in the class.

A Truly Great Primary Teacher: Megan Bull

Megan Bull is a Year 2 teacher at Alexandra Park Primary School, Stockport, where she also co-leads mathematics.

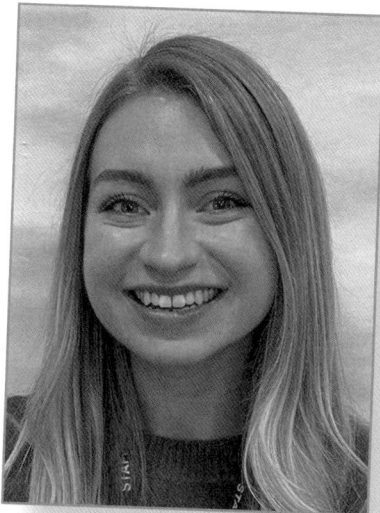

The school leadership's view

Having led Huntington School, one of the first five Research Schools in the country, it feels great to visit Alexandra Park Primary School, one of the latest to be designated a Research School.[1] I am here to meet deputy head teacher Claire Williams to discuss her colleague Megan Bull. It is two days before they break up for Christmas and festivities are in the air!

---

1   See: https://researchschool.org.uk/.

I was invited to Stockport when I met Claire and head teacher Phil Brooke at a conference where I was speaking. I had mentioned my truly great teachers project, and Phil had caught me at the end and suggested that Megan was worth including in the book. At the time I said I couldn't, but then I had a *volte-face* and here I am.

'Megan is one of those teachers that instantly stands out', says Claire. 'The thing that is special about Megan is she's very understated. When you see her teach, she is not all-singing, all-dancing, but she very carefully knows and understands every child and what they need. She's been with us through our school improvement journey, which has focused for the last six years on learning behaviours. All our professional development has been around, "How do we get children to want to be in the classroom, to engage, to listen, to cooperate, to do all of those things that mean we can deliver the curriculum and ignite a passion for learning?"'

I ask Claire about the support Megan's had at Alexandra Park. 'We're really lucky, we've got two forms, so in every year group in our primary school we've got an experienced teacher in the other class, so, although we might have less experienced teachers in one class, we always make sure that we've got somebody who knows the curriculum really well, who knows the systems and the structures of the school, and then it is their job to support that new teacher. She's had that. She's been able to really develop her teaching without having to particularly worry about finding the content for lessons, she has just been able to focus on her core business of the children in front of her.'

I suggest that that allows her to work on the pedagogy, checking for understanding, knowing her pupils and finding out whether they have learnt what she's taught them. 'Yes', says Claire, 'and building those relationships with the children and the parents, and the staff. She's great, she's a really good team player as well, so that she can hone those skills. Because she is so capable, she has very quickly become a maths lead. We've got two maths leads, because we do a lot of outward-facing work through the Research School She's embraced that, she's the sort of teacher where if the conditions are right, she will be high-performing.

I think what also stands out for me is Megan is not working ridiculous hours; she knows how to prioritise her time and understands that if she is well rested and has a life outside of teaching then she is a better teacher for that. She's really high performing, she's an excellent teacher, but not at the expense of her own well-being.'

I ask Claire what she would say the role of leaders is in developing teachers like Megan. 'I think it's our job as leaders to provide the conditions for that teacher to flourish, for that teacher to be their best. Behaviour, for example, is exemplary here. It is our responsibility as school leaders, particularly for teachers at the early stages of their career, to allow them to focus on being good teachers. You need time and you need that cognitive capacity when you're in the classroom to not be dealing with particular behaviours.'

I wonder if there is anything else we need to know before we go off into the whirl of the day. 'One of the things that I think you'll probably see this morning is how we make sure that the teachers know our school values, and, "Care" is the first thing that you work on. Relationships with children and parents, everything else comes after that if you get that right, even if you've got something really tricky or a child that's really struggling. When you've got those relationships, that difficult conversation with a parent is easier, that difficult transition for a child is easier, and I think that's where Megan has really benefitted, as well as being very committed.'

Finally, Claire talks about Megan's professional behaviours. 'She's constantly questioning, always thinking about her practice. She's quite naturally inquisitive and optimistic as well. She loves teaching, she loves the children and she gets the reason why she's in the classroom.' Has she engaged with the Research School work? 'Megan has really benefitted from our Research School status, and is benefitting the school with her contributions. I think it's the really strong focus on classroom practice, those small, incremental gains that you can make in a lesson that actually over the year really add up to some really powerful learning for children. She understands our evidenced informed approach and the valuable contribution she and all the school staff make in bringing their professional expertise and contextual knowledge to inform decisions and strategy.' All this is music to my Research School ears. I suggest we go and see Megan as it's already gone 9 o'clock.

Teaching

Megan's Year 2 pupils fill the small, brightly lit, high-ceilinged Victorian classroom. They are sat in eight groups of twos, threes and fours, all facing Megan in a sort of crescent shape. It is an interesting hybrid of groups and rows. They have their mini-whiteboards out. Megan narrates what she wants them to do. I appear to be very interesting and all 30 heads turn and watch me sit in a chair on the far side of the room. Breakfast is going on, along with *Number of the Day*, which is 58. To the tune of 'If you're happy and you know it', they sing, 'The number of the day is 58, the number of the day is 58, Oh, the number of the day, the number of the day, the number of the day is 58!'

'How many tens?' asks Megan and she gets the correct response. 'How many 1s?' and she gets the correct response. There is informed talk about place value. The attention is absolute. She segues into a part/whole model exercise, using mini-whiteboards as sketchpads. The task requires no explanation from Megan, so well-trained are the pupils. 'How have you partitioned 58?' she asks. And a range of answers are confidently proffered: '51 + 7', '58 + 0', '50 + 8', '40 + 18'. It's really speedy stuff. They count out loud from 48 to 58 to 68 and back to 58. There is a number fluency here that is quite special. More answers are elicited by Megan: '48 + 10', '55 + 3'. 'What about taking away to get to 58?' posits Megan. '78 take away 20', '60 take away 2'. Everyone is having fun. It feels alive in this room.

With the *Number of the Day* done, coming up is, according to Megan, a *Christmassy* English lesson. 'Your *Snuggle* day is tomorrow', says Megan (that's when they can bring in their favourite soft toy or blanket, to *snuggle* up with – it is always worth being reminded just how young these pupils are). 'Today we are going to be writing riddles.' She displays a poster of a dozen different Christmas items.

She then reads this riddle, and the pupils have to guess what it is describing:

I am tall and evergreen

I have twinkly lights all over

You can find me in living rooms all over the land

People love to decorate me

What am I?

Megan's teaching assistant, in true double-act mode, guesses it is a Christmas Tree. Megan regains their attention with a sharp, Signal-Pause-Insist routine, where she acknowledges compliance, pupil name by pupil name. The pupils *so* want to please Megan, that once the non-compliers see she is praising those who are compliant, they think, 'I want some of the praise from Miss, too!' and swiftly comply. Megan has a great, authoritative voice, with enthusiasm riven through her tones. She reads out the next one and preps them to shout the answer.

> I am precious and exciting
> Shiny paper and a big bow
> You find me under the tree
> People love to give and receive me
> What am I?

'After 3 . . . 1, 2, 3 . . .'

'PRESENTS!!!!!'

'That's right', says Megan. She presses one of the girls as to *why* she thinks it is a present: 'It has a big bow, Miss and you find it under the tree.' She presses one of the boys on the same issue. If one was being stereotypical, he looks like he might have behavioural issues. He responds in a scholarly manner, 'Because it says, "Receive me".' He is praised enthusiastically by Megan. It is such fun! They run through a couple more – Snowman and Advent calendar – before we begin to look at the patterns in a set of more formalised riddles in poem form. She judges when to move on superbly well.

She declares they are going to write their own riddle poems. A frisson of excitement spreads across the room. They look at the three short riddle poems and unpick the common features – what repeats, where? They end up with a structure like this:

> I am _____ and _____
> I have _____
> You find me _____
> People _____
> What am I?

She creates a poem, explaining why she chooses which words in precise metacognitive talk. She begins with the reindeer. 'OK, I am . . . what?' And the suggestions pile in fast: 'Furry and ginger', 'magical and special', 'fluffy and brown', 'fluffy soft'. Lots of boys are giving up answers. Megan decides to use 'I am magical and fluffy' and then works through the writing process, methodically. 'Big capital "I" … finger space … "am" … finger space … "m-a-g-i-c-al" … "and" … "f-l-uff" how do I finish this word?'

'With a "Y" Miss.'

'Good. With a "Y" – nice to see you using the letter name.'

'What does the reindeer have?'

'A red, glowy nose, Miss.'

'WELL DONE! An expanded noun phrase with two adjectives. What do I need between my two adjectives?'

'A comma.'

'Correct! Well done.' She is animated without being exaggerated. She doesn't ask them to think about stuff or do a cold call when she doesn't need to. It keeps the momentum of the lesson going. She takes answers from volunteers right across the room. I notice a girl near the front looking a bit stroppy. 'Lisa, thank you', says Megan, before she gains the attention of the class, ready to move on. But Lisa is on the verge of tears. Her face screws up in red fury. It looks like the boy next door is the cause of the upset. Megan gives the class another pair-share task (which, to the trained eye, is obviously not where she intended going next with the lesson), kneels down in front of Lisa and talks things through. Lisa recovers herself. Whilst she isn't all smiles, Lisa has composed herself and we are back on track with the lesson. Megan writes the reindeer poem riddle on the board. As she writes, the pupils speak the words out loud as she does so, without being asked:

> I am magical and fluffy
>
> I have a red, glowy nose
>
> You find me in the snowy sky
>
> People love to feed me carrots and stroke me
>
> What am I?

When Megan asks for answers, she takes Lisa's first and, rightfully, praises her for being correct. It is perfect behaviour management that takes skill, effort and 'botheredness'. It doesn't affect the rhythm of the lesson, whatsoever.

Frankie is yawning – it's the day before the school breakup for Christmas and there are lots of tired people in this room, yet they are still on task. I haven't seen anyone disengaged, even for a moment. 'Mrs Kirby and I are looking out for great collaboration and we will be handing out prizes for the best teamwork we see when you work in pairs, writing your own poems.' So they move into the final stage of the 'I do-We do-You do'. The two girls next to me couldn't be more engrossed. As one writes the other contributes. The latter bends over the table with her head almost on the desk to look at the pencil tip as the words emerge on the page. It is wonderful to watch. She takes over the writing in an amazing collaborative effort.

> I am red and white
>
> I have lovely gifts inside me

They get stuck a little at where you would find a stocking. I suggest 'at the end of my bed'. And there it is. One of the fundamental differences between me as a run-of-the-mill teacher and the brilliant Megan Bull. She makes them think and tells them nothing, while I just tell them a good answer. Is it years of working in secondary, where the pressure to spoon-feed is overwhelming, I wonder? I do wish I could have my time again in the classroom, knowing what I know now about teaching and learning.

The girls' riddle poem ends:

> People love to open me
>
> What am I?

The girls are delighted with their effort. 'We are going to perform them soon', declares Megan. She runs the room. All on task. Lisa is back with us and the boy next to her looks relieved. She spotlights good practice – three of them are practising reading out – and the others begin doing the same. They want to be doing this work with all their souls. They are making word choice decisions. They are writing. That pressure to do something Christmassy at this time of year does not compromise the learning. In many ways, it has enhanced it.

Megan gains complete control of the room again. 'The most important moment in the lesson is coming up. What do the presenters need to be able to do? Discuss in your pairs.' So ensues a constructive discussion about performing.

'Practise so they don't get any words wrong.'

'Stay fully focused because if people are talking they may not be able to hear.'

'The audience need to show respect', says Ryan.

'What does showing respect look like? Who can build on Ryan's answer?' asks Megan.

'By not talking, letting them say their lines, by being quiet.'

Megan puts the 12 pictures back up on the board. 'Let's tidy our tables before we present, so that we are not distracted while people are presenting.' She gives a reason for doing everything she asks of them. She wins the cognitive argument all the time, so that there is no reason not to do what she asks. 'I can see table 8 are going to be a respectful table when people are presenting. I like how Rhiannon has turned her chair to face the speakers.' There is deliberate praise for everything she would like to see emulated across the room, and when she asks who would like to perform their riddle poems, the whole class burst to be first. They stretch their arms so high, that it's like they might even touch that Victorian ceiling. She gives the first pair the choice of presenting from their table or from the front. They choose the latter and for the final ten minutes of the lesson, every single team delivers word-perfect renditions of their riddle poems; every time a poem is finished, Megan orchestrates a 3-2-1… choral response answer from the whole room. It is a joyous event. Megan is still making deliberate learning interventions. She praises how hard they have worked with their partners and identifies a number of meta skills that the pupils are demonstrating. The lesson has flown by. It is breaktime. 'Table 1 and 4 have crossed arms and are facing the front. They look like they are ready to go to break. Which table will line up first?' The tables are simply numbered, so even when they are being dismissed, table by table, they have to do a mathematical calculation. 'Double 4 can go first … 10 take away 9 … 10 take away 8 … double 3 … one less than 8 … double 2 … 4 plus 1 … half of 6.' They line up in silence, coats on, ready to brave the winter weather. Megan stands at the door and sees them out into the corridor in complete order. It is a perfect end to a perfect lesson.

What the pupils think

Over break, I sit outside the room in a small open-plan teaching area with eight empty seats waiting to be filled. It has been a wonderful morning. I am so glad that Phil invited me to meet Megan. In the final moments of my career, all I want to do is hand the baton on. I was the future once; Megan and her ilk are it now. And that's a damned good thing. When it's easy to fall prey to pessimism, watching the likes of Megan in the classroom fills up my reservoirs of hope.

Before I realise it, the eight seats are filled. Two girls sit very close to me, on the other side of our shared table. 'Hi. Are you alright?' I ask.

One of them replies, 'Are *you* alright?' in the tones of the most caring GP. It's as though she's 46 years old, not six. I reassure her that I'm just fine. We establish that I'm called John.

I ask them all to work in pairs for two minutes and talk about why Miss Bull is such a good teacher. As I am so close, I can hear Isla and Heather's conversation. In her broad Mancunian tones, Isla says, 'Because she's lovely and *very* kind. She just loves us. We're spoilt by her. I *love* her.'

I stop eavesdropping. We open up the conversation. 'She sometimes let's us pick what we want to do', Tim says, 'and she's really kind and does kind things for us.' He is wearing a yellow badge. Despite him being just feet away, my failing eyesight means I have to ask him what it says. He replies, 'well-being ambassador'.

Not only am I losing my sight, I must also be going deaf, because I reply, 'What's a yellow bean buster?' They giggle. A lot. I am in danger of losing the class, and there's only eight of them.

I apologise. 'You must be very kind Tim', I say and push the conversation on. Trinity says, 'She tells you what to do all the time. Well not *all* the time.'

And then India reveals an acute observation: 'She tells us what we're going to do, *but she doesn't tell you the answer to things*.' She is so spot on. She knows she will have to think for herself in lessons with Miss Bull. Exactly what I'd observed. India continues, 'She's kind and when you're stuck she helps you lots. One time I got stuck on 57 add 45 and she helped me.'

Oscar pipes up, prompted by India's comments. 'My writing was really bad and then she helped me and now my writing's really good. She showed it to Mr Brooke.'

'Your handwriting's beautiful, Oscar', interjects Isla. 'We were blown away and we fell off our chairs when he showed us, because Mr Brooke said, "Hold onto your chair cos you're gonna be blown away by Oscar's writing!"'

Isla has a Miss Bull crush. 'I can't really think of any one thing because I've too much to say about her. She's just really lovely. She makes us laugh. She's absolutely lovely. I *love* her so much. I'm glad I'm with her for a *whole* year.'

'John, do you know how to spell my name', interjects Oscar. I reassure him that I do. Timothy starts saying his name phonetically. Frankie asks whether I can spell his name.

One of the girls tries to get us back to Miss Bull. 'I like that she has lots planned for us. Every day we do a lot of work. And the way she teaches us. She tells us what to do. I love the way she makes her own stories and there are really funny characters. A dog with big goat horns. It was really funny. And she played tig with us and it was really fun. She's a brilliant teacher . . .' And it's here I ask why she is such a brilliant teacher. I'd had one moment of enlightenment earlier, about Miss Bull never telling them the answers, and here I get a second. 'Well, she always tells us what to do first, and then we all do it. She helps us learn. Sometimes she writes what we have to write, and draws what we have to draw, and it helps to look at that because it shows what we have to write. Before you do the work on paper, she does it on the screen and then we do it.' So, Miss Bull is great at live modelling and metacognitive talk. Who would've thought?

And maybe it was because they were so delightful that I lost my concentration, and perhaps it was because I was a bit tired, but I clean forgot to ask them for a single word to describe Miss Bull. But looking through the transcript of our conversation, I reckon they might say something like this: kind, lovely, helpful, funny and brilliant.

IRL: Megan Bull

John Tomsett (JT): Why did you go into teaching?

Megan Bull (MB): I have always wanted to work with children. My mum is a teacher, both of her parents were teachers, and she did the opposite of putting me off, really! She loves her job. She's a primary teacher. She still works a couple of days a week and she's just always been really enthused by it, so she was a really good influence. Then when I was about three years old my younger brother was born and he has down syndrome and severe autism and quite a lot of learning disabilities, so it's just been a natural thing to want to work with children, to want to help teach people and look after people. I wanted to be working with children and seeing them day-to-day.

JT: **You did your degree in linguistics. Has that been helpful?**

MB: I think I learnt a lot about the acquisition of language and the barriers that children can have to language acquisition and how it's built really early on. I think that focus on language and oracy is so important, and I think that choosing the right language to use with children and trying to get them to use the right language back is really important in the classroom. Also, understanding how they develop and all of the little key milestones that they need to meet, has really helped with that. I also studied teaching English as a second language, which showed me how to teach children who haven't developed much language, children who don't have a really rich vocabulary, and how to try to model language to them. I learnt a lot of that through my degree.

JT: **Where did you train?**

MB: I trained at Manchester Metropolitan University, I did a PGCE through them. The year in between my undergraduate degree and my PGCE, I worked as a one-to-one teaching assistant in quite a deprived area of Manchester, and I worked with one particular child with quite severe social, emotional and mental health issues. That was really eye-opening.

JT: **What did you learn then?**

MB: Just how important care is. I think it really focused that. If they're not coming into school ready to learn, what can you do? And all of the different things that come before teaching a lesson, that nurturing side of things. It taught me how to adapt lessons for children who aren't ready to access the activities that the rest of the class might be doing.

JT: **This is your fourth year here. What are your core teaching principles?**

MB: I want the children to love learning, and I want them to love being in the classroom and love being in school. I think to do that, especially with the younger ones, it's about making it fun, and showing that *I* love it. I enjoy being in the classroom so much. I enjoy all of the lessons that I've planned, and I look forward to teaching them all. I hope that comes across, and I think that has an influence on the children.

JT: **I didn't realise until I'd done this research quite how important teacher behaviours are. Teacher behaviours and teacher attitudes, the pupils just mimic you all of the time.**

MB: Yes, and don't get me wrong, it's a hard job isn't it? We all know that, but I think the children seeing that you want to be there, and you want to teach them, and you want to help them, they then want to do their part and it's a two-way street. They know how much I enjoy being there and hopefully they know how much I care for them. They then match that, they match the energy, don't they?

JT: **Yes, both ways. If you turn up without any energy, why should they have any?**

MB: Yes, absolutely, exactly. They need to see what we value and what we think is important, and I think they can see that and then they mirror it, which is really good.

JT: **One of them said, 'She never tells us the answers.' And you don't, good teachers don't.**

MB: I think they do so much more thinking than me and it's interesting that they realise that, but I'd say our lessons are even less than fifty-fifty. They're doing so much more than me!

JT: **Tell me how you deliberately make that happen.**

MB: We've talked a lot at this school about not just giving children opportunities to learn, but also *not giving them opportunities to not learn.* Trying to avoid any moment where they cannot learn and putting the onus on them and getting them to do a lot. It's very backwards and forwards – so we'll do a little bit and then they'll do a little bit, and they are so familiar with that across the school, that they know what's coming and they're prepared for it. They go into a lesson ready to be active learners, they're not sitting back and letting it wash over them.

JT: **They like the way you narrate what's going to happen.**

MB: Yes, and I think the consistency in that across subjects and across classes, prepares the children for learning and gives them so many opportunities to pick up knowledge and then apply it. I think that's important.

JT: **They know the modelling helps. They said, 'Miss shows us on the board, then it's easy for us because then we can see what we've got to do.'**

MB: Yes, and sometimes I'll quite explicitly say, 'You're going to have to do this in a minute, so I'm going to show you how to do it, and I'm going to show you what I'm thinking as I'm doing it, so then you can do it independently.' I think that's what we do as we start to implement those activities, but eventually they know when I get a visualiser out or when I'm doing something on the board, there is going to be an expectation that they're going to do it as well. It has become an immediate response: they're so aware of what's coming in the lesson that they can prepare themselves rather than us reminding them all of the time to get ready to do this or that.

JT: **I think, watching you today, only an experienced teacher would see what you're doing.**

MB: Yes. It's really tricky to pinpoint what it is. It's even tricky for myself, when I'm reflecting on things.

JT: **Tell me about Lisa who you helped brilliantly. Tell me what happened in that episode.**

MB: Lisa does have quite big emotions, and she can find it quite difficult to be resilient sometimes, and she's worked really hard on that this year. I think she can struggle to recover if something goes wrong. Her partner had taken something further away than she'd have liked it and she wanted it in the middle. Sometimes she'd be absolutely fine with that, it depends on the day, and it depends on what's come before. I think she does like having control and she does like having ownership of a situation, and, sometimes, depending on which partner she's with, her partner can take over a little bit or she sees it as that …

JT: **What you did was to give the class a task that you hadn't planned. 'Have a think about that for two minutes.' You focused in on her, resolved the issue, and then, when the first chance she had of being successful presented itself, you went to her.**

MB: Yes, and I prepared something that she could say with her so that she could feel like she was back in control of the situation, she was succeeding, and she was achieving in that lesson.

JT: **All that thinking goes on in the moment, doesn't it?**

MB: Yes, and without really realising it. It's kind of like an immediate response and you've unpicked that perfectly. I think it comes with knowing the children really well. I think in that moment, I know she really likes bunnies, so I was talking to her about the reindeer and how soft it would feel, and which one would be softer, her bunnies or the reindeer, and she was straight away back on track.

JT: **Her bunny or the reindeer?**

MB: Yes, because it was something she can access in the moment. It does take time to get to know children, and she is one of the key children with emotions that you do put time into getting to know. I think obviously in primary school it's a bit easier than in secondary because you're with these children all day every day, and they share so much, they share so confidently and so happily. It's just trying to make that connection and adding their specific interests into what you're doing and trying to get them to buy-in to an activity.

JT: **Where do you think they are at the moment, in terms of their language and their writing?**

MB: I think they've come on so much. They were amazing in Year 1, the teaching they get throughout the whole school is of such a high quality. We encourage the children to say everything before they write it. I think that oral rehearsal is so important, especially for children who struggle with the fine motor skills, their handwriting or their spelling. None of that is a barrier for them when they're just talking it through. We try to make sure that they've had every opportunity to prepare what they're going to say and to plan what they're going to write, without any of that cognitive load of holding the pencil, putting the pencil to the page and working out the spelling of things, so that when they begin writing, they've done all of that foundational thinking and they're ready to go. I think they just need to hear so much language and so much high-level vocabulary. They need to hear it first and then be able to reproduce it themselves before we can expect them to write anything on the page.

JT: **When they get to talk something through, they can imagine it, think about it, articulate it and then write about it.**

MB: Yes, and I think it stops that deer in the headlights moment where they've got an empty page, and they don't know what to write. They are so well prepared before the paper even comes out that they love writing, and even the children who struggle with fine motor skills, they're willing to write. They love it when they've done a piece of work, they're always proud of it, and that's a really important thing, I think.

JT: **You also co-lead maths.**

MB: When I first came, I was the modern foreign language (MFL) lead, and I've still got that in the background. I did A level French and Spanish. Maths isn't my background necessarily, but in teaching and working here, a lot of the practices that we run through the whole school come from maths, so when we started working on learning behaviours, we started with a focus on maths and that then spread out through the rest of the curriculum. We've worked with the NCETM a lot, so even in my first year as an ECT, I was involved in a lot of the training, I was doing modelled lessons for people coming in for the NCETM programme.[2] I've just always really liked teaching maths. I really like the structure of the lessons. I really like how you can unpick it and get the children to unpick it too – thinking about that accessibility point, all of the thinking that comes with planning maths. I started being maths lead towards the end of last year, I was initially joint maths lead and now I'm leading Key Stage 1 maths. We have a lot to do as a Research School with NCETM.

JT: **As a Research School you've got access to all of the great thinking.**

MB: Yes, it is amazing. I think being here as a student, I've seen nothing but outstanding teaching, so I've never had to unpick bad habits. I feel like I've never seen poor teaching, because everything that I've learnt has come from somebody in this building. I am a product of all of my colleagues, really, and every time I've popped into a classroom I've picked something up,

---

2   See: www. https://www.ncetm.org.uk/.

and I've just collected loads of little bits. I'm really grateful for having the opportunity to learn from such experienced colleagues. Being a Research School, we're really confident in that every practice that we have in place is going to be effective and has the research behind it. It's kind of a selection of lots of different things. I'm really lucky to have had the CPD that I've had through this school and been able to see such experienced colleagues who are so good at what they do.

JT: **Is there anything else pedagogically that you can tell me about that you do with such deliberateness?**

MB: I think it's not necessarily deliberate anymore, but we've worked a lot on metacognition throughout the school, and that modelling of your thought process (right, I'm going to plan this, and while I'm writing this, I'm thinking about the shape of this letter) and making everything so explicit for the children. That's one of our main focuses, making the children think, and not just when they're asked a question and they're thinking of an answer, but also in everything that they do. Constantly reflecting on what they're doing. Visualisers help. With a visualiser they can see us work through exactly what they're going to see. It's an exact carbon copy of what they're going to do, so it takes away all of that cognitive load of figuring out where they're starting their writing and everything to do with that.

JT: **How have you developed vocabulary?**

MB: We've worked a lot with metacognitive questioning, encouraging the children to think 'How do I know this? What is my first step?' and all of that has come along with vocabulary. We started last year, you might have seen it on the classroom, *Sticky Words*, which is a vocabulary programme that we've been setting up in this school. It was developed by my year-group partner, and I feel really lucky to have been part of the development of the project. We're starting it in January with this cohort. We did it last year with the other Year 2s. We teach them a new word every day. We give them the definition of the word and an icon with the word, and put it into a couple of context sentences, then the next day there'll be some retrieval of words that they've learnt, and then a new word again. It's a constant cycle of retrieving and learning new words. It's always a word that comes up in one of the lessons later that day. Sometimes, they can guess which lesson it's going to be in. Sometimes, they're on a bit of a hunt for that word in a lesson, and I think just that focus on words and their curiosity about words – what they mean and spotting the connections between them – has been really effective in developing their interest in vocabulary. So, it's not just teaching a list of words, and trying to get that into their English writing. It's that curiosity about which words might be connected, and if we know this word, then that's related to that and we know the meaning of that, so we can figure out the meaning of this one. I think getting them enthused and giving them those skills to figure things out for themselves is really important.

JT: **It's interesting you said you're a product of all of the teachers here. What do you think makes you a good teacher?**

MB: I think enthusiasm. I think, and I'd hope you agree, that the children are really enthusiastic in the classroom. They see every lesson as fun.

JT: **They couldn't wait to come up and read their stuff out.**

MB: Yes, and it's so nice to look across the classroom and see children with their hands up who might not be confident in other things, and we think that they might find that really tricky because they struggle to read, but their hands are still going up. I love seeing that. I think that's one of my favourite parts of the job. You can see from my highest achiever to the child who has the most natural barriers to learning, they've both proudly got their hands up. That's my favourite thing. I love that.

JT: **Enthusiasm. What else?**

MB: I think deep thinking. We're really lucky in the fact that across the school we do everything collaboratively. The other Year 2 teacher and I have PPA together and it's not like he plans English and I plan maths, we both plan everything together, so we're having really high-quality, professional conversations about every moment in the lesson. It takes a little bit of time at the beginning, but it just becomes second nature eventually. Thinking hard about every activity that we're going to do. Can the bottom 20% access it? What resources might they need? What scaffolds might they need? How are we going to get the children talking at this point? What do we want them to produce? Is this a small enough step? Do we need to add anything else in? All of those conversations happen all of the time and so naturally in our planning cycle, that I think it's really tricky to sit back and reflect on how we planned the lesson, because it is just second nature now – doing it in a totally collaborative way and having those conversations at a microlevel.

JT: **Then also having the ability, like you did with Lisa to think, 'I'm just going to do this now, I need to go and sort her out.'**

MB: Yes. I think having the knowledge of your class and of your children and having the confidence to do that helps you to be adaptive in the moment.

JT: **You've got enthusiasm, you've got co-planning, which is extraordinary. You have a head teacher who has allowed you to co-plan with your co-teacher, because that allows high-quality teaching and learning to happen.**

MB: Yes, and not even just at the planning stage. Staff meetings see all of us sharing best practice and sharing things that we've tried, things that have gone well, and it's so collaborative. I can't say that word enough. I think when you can get that, everything else comes really naturally. We love teaching the lessons that we've planned because we loved planning them, because we can go back and say, 'That worked', or 'I can't believe that didn't work.' We'll stand on the playground and say, 'How was this person in maths? How did that work? Maybe next time we could do this.' It's a constant – I remember being here as a student, and on the first day I went into the staff room, they all just talked about how the lessons went that morning, but it's so natural and it's so embedded as part of the culture of this school, that it's that constant cycle without having to enforce it, of doing and reflecting, collaborating and planning, and it's just always in the background, the drive to improve. It's all about the culture, absolutely. It's a hard job, there are hard days, but because we are such a good team, everyone just helps each other out, and everyone gets each other.

JT: **There's no fear here, is there?**

MB: No … we've got such an open-door policy that if you want to see something, you'll just send a quick message round, 'Has anybody got any modelling coming up in a lesson? Can I pop in and have a look?' or 'I'm going to try this in my lesson. We've been doing it a couple of weeks and it's gone really well, feel free to come down and have a look.' It's that constant working together, even from Year 6 to early years, everything is team-work, nobody is doing anything by themselves.

JT: **And it's all about teaching and learning. Highly informed, professional practice. You've got enthu-siasm, you've got the co-lesson planning, you've got the whole atmosphere of the school. Anything else?**

MB: Is it *nature* or *nurture*? I think I am *naturally* a teacher, but I think my upbringing and my early experiences – since I was three years old, when my brother was born, we were doing speech therapy and setting SEND targets, without me realising – means that I was also *nurtured* into being a teacher. Being in a school like this has just brought everything together to allow me to thrive in the classroom.

JT: There is something that has been in your fibre. Maybe not in your DNA, but in the culture you grew up in.

MB: Yes. I think having my brother with some disabilities, every single opportunity to learn was taken, and that's just always been in the background. Like, if we're going on a walk, let's count as we walk. I think I put that into my classroom. The transition points and everything is an opportunity to learn, so you're constantly drip-feeding.

JT: Even dismissing them table by table.

MB: I think just trying to find every single opportunity for the children to learn without realising that they're learning. I feel like they do it in a way that they don't feel like they've worked really hard, they've really enjoyed themselves, and yet they're soaking so much up.

JT: You can only teach at the pace you're teaching at if you're really enjoying it, because the energy needed to teach like you teach is massive.

MB: The cognitive load of so much has become automatic for me. It's what I've always done, so I have the extra space to go to someone like Lisa and adapt to events, because the rest is so embedded in what I do, I can deal with extra things that come up.

JT: Your Signal-Pause-Insist is the best I've seen.

MB: I think the consistency of that is key … I will do that all day every day, and they know then exactly what my expectation is. They're very good at picking up habits and routines, and I stick to those, so they know where they stand.

JT: **Thank you so much. It's been great to visit a Research School.**

MB: Yes, absolutely, I am a product of that, so thank you.

JT: **That's great. Thank you so much.**

Testimonials

'Miss Bull has been wonderful with my son since he joined her class three months ago from another school. The change in his confidence is incredible. He used to be very shy, especially when it came to reading, but now he reads to us without hesitation. His writing has improved significantly, and we can actually read it now! He's also developed a keen interest in maths and loves asking us to test his skills. He has become much more resilient and better at handling and understanding his emotions. His previous school mentioned he was very underconfident and needed a lot of one-on-one time. However, with Miss Bull he's become super confident, always participating in class and eager to raise his hand to answer questions. We believe this transformation is all thanks to Miss Bull's welcoming teaching style and her encouragement. She makes the kids feel safe to learn and make mistakes, which was something our son was really worried about before. Thank you to Miss Bull for making our son's transition so seamless.'

'I feel that my little boy improved massively over the course of Year 2 with Miss Bull. This included his reading and writing in particular, and with his confidence in himself. I would like to express my thanks and appreciation to Miss Bull for her continued support. My son himself said, "She is a great teacher" and loved being in her class.'

'My daughter absolutely thrived in Miss Bull's class. She became a brave and confident learner who embedded a deep thirst for knowledge. Miss Bull worked closely with my daughter's previous teacher to nurture her and ensure that she was encouraged at the right pace in her social development and ensured that she was appropriately challenged in her learning to make exceptional progress. Most importantly, my daughter shared that Miss Bull was always happy! She positively enthused and engaged my daughter through her creativity, care and excitement for the lessons that she taught. Miss Bull knew my daughter well and skilfully identified her strengths to enable her to overcome any worries and bloom – ready for her transition into Key Stage 2. We are very grateful to Miss Bull!'

So, what can we learn from Megan Bull?

What I found fascinating about editing the transcript of my conversation with Megan, was just how little editing I had to do! It made me wonder about what helps make teachers truly great. Her focus upon oracy skills and developing the pupils' writing through giving them the chance to discuss what they are going to write before pen even meets paper, has, perhaps, developed her own oracy skills. Maybe her lifelong work of helping her brother has made her a supremely articulate speaker, and this is helping her develop her pupils' verbal fluency.

Megan is yet another teacher whose enthusiasm is infectious. To watch her teach was truly inspiring and, despite being way beyond my sell by date, made my old teaching heart feel young again. She has the same impact upon her pupils. Despite some yawning – one or two looked very tired – there was an unbridled zest for the work, and Megan was as enthused as anyone about what was happening! The enjoyment in that class was tangible. Megan made it look effortless (I know it wasn't), but, in truth, it really didn't look like work to me!

And, finally, there is the school culture. When I was a young teacher and I was head of sixth form, the head of English went away on a course and came back with a quote from Roland S. Barth.[3] He gave me a copy, and said, 'There you go, John, I think it describes the kind of school you might create.'

'I'd like the chance to work in a school characterised by a high level of collegiality, a place teeming with frequent, helpful personal and professional interactions. I'd become excited about life in a school where a climate of risk-taking is deliberately fostered and where a safety net protects those who may risk and stumble. I'd like to go each day to school to be with other adults who genuinely wanted to be there, who really chose to be there because of the importance of their work to others and to themselves. I would not want to leave a school characterised by a profound respect for, and encouragement of, diversity, where important differences among children and adults are celebrated rather than seen as problems to remedy. For 190 days each year, I'd like to attend an institution that accorded a special place to philosophers, and constantly examined and questioned, and frequently replaced embedded practices by asking why questions. I can even reside for a while in a laundry dryer if accompanied by a great deal of humour that helps bond the community by assisting everyone through tough moments. I'd like to work in a school that constantly takes note of the stress and anxiety level on the one hand, and standards on the other, all the while searching for the optimal relationship with low anxiety and high standards.'

That quotation from Barth describes Alexandra Park perfectly. Hats off to Phil Brooke and the team at Alexandra Park. What they have created at this school allows the teachers like Megan to thrive. The best piece of advice I ever had in my career was from Tom Bentley. He used to work for a think-tank called DEMOS.[4] I heard him speak 20-odd years ago. He said, 'Once you know what your core purpose is', and the core purpose at Alexandra Park is to ensure high-quality teaching and learning at every step, 'then you change the structures of your school to accommodate that core purpose, rather than contort your core

---

3   R. S. Barth *Improving Schools from Within: Teachers, Parents, and Principals Can Make the Difference* (San Francisco, CA: Jossey-Bass, 1991).

4   See: https://demos.co.uk/.

purpose around the existing structures'. What you've got in Phil Brooke is a head who understands that. The opportunity for joint working on how to teach the curriculum content, at every micro-step of the lesson, is crucial to the success of Megan Bull and the success of the school as a whole. The place is devoid of fear. The school is suffused in the humanity of the learning process, in the desire to do the very best for the pupils and colleagues. It is underpinned by what the evidence says has the best chance of working. It is a school that grows truly great teachers . . . *truly great teachers like Megan Bull.*

Megan Bull's pupils' progress and achievement data

2023–24 data summary

All children

End of Key Stage 1	% ARE	2023	National	+/-	% GDS	2023	National	+/-
Reading	80	83	72	+8	17	21	20	-3
Writing	83	74	63	+20	15	7	9	+6
Maths	83	74	73	+10	10	19	17	-7

SEND

End of Key Stage 1	% ARE (7 children)	National Average	Difference
Reading	57	36	+21
Writing	57	25	+32
Maths	57	40	+17

All children

End of Key Stage 2	% ARE	2023	National Average	Difference	% GDS	2023	National Average	Difference
Reading	89	93	74	+15	38	49	28	+10
Writing	86	84	72	+14	32	26	13	+19
Maths	92	97	73	+19	35	28	24	+11
Grammar	84	84	72	+12	38	40	32	+6
RWM	81	83	61	+20	18	14	8	+10

Key: grammar, punctuation and spelling (GPS); reading, writing and mathematics (RWM)

Disadvantaged

End of Key Stage 2: Disadvantaged	% ARE	2023	National Average	Difference	% GDS	2023	National Average	Difference
Reading	86	79	62	+24	43	50	18	+25
Writing	93	79	59	+34	36	14	6	+30
Maths	86	86	59	+27	29	50	13	+16
GPS	86	86	59	+27	50	36	20	+30
RWM	86		45	+41	14		3	+11

SEND (excluding education and health care plan (EHCP))

End of Key Stage 2	% ARE	National Average	Difference
Reading	67	48	+19
Writing	58	36	+22
Maths	67	44	+23
GPS	42	39	+3
RWM	50	25	+25

What Might We Learn from these Truly Great Teachers?

This final chapter begins with a huge caveat. I certainly don't consider these nine teacher profiles to be irrefutable research evidence, or what I say in this chapter to be definitive. Despite the caveat, I do think there are things we might learn about teaching from these teachers. All I intend to do in this final chapter is identify the major common features of the teachers' practice and highlight aspects of their work that seem to me to be both extraordinary and useful. Before that, however, it is worth explaining the particular lens through which I have looked at these teachers. For the past decade or so, I have thought about classroom practice within the context of a model for learning and a closely linked model of the curriculum, both of which are detailed below.

A model for learning: Daniel Willingham's Memory Model[1]

I once purchased a vintage leather satchel as a colleague's leaving present. The stitching was rotten, so I ripped it all out. I bought a proper needle and thread for stitching leather, found a YouTube video on the subject and spent three nights repairing the satchel. When I had finished, it was as good as new. But I hadn't learnt how to stitch leather satchels. If I had wanted to repeat the feat, I would have had to revert to watching the video again. My brain had merely enacted the leather stitching technique *temporarily*, through in-the-moment mimicry; it hadn't assimilated it. In essence, then, learning is a *permanent* change to the long-term memory.

Over the last decade, I have come to understand a simple truth about teaching, namely that it is difficult to teach in a way that has the greatest

---

1   D. T. Willingham, A mental model of the learner: teaching the basic science of educational psychology to future teachers, *Mind, Brain, and Education*, 11(4) (2017).

impact upon pupils' learning, if you don't have a model for how pupils learn in the first place. According to Dr Anita Devi, 'You need a model of learning. It gives you the questions to ask when a child is not learning.'[2] And answering those questions is key to progressing pupils' learning.

To gain a fundamental understanding of how pupils learn, Daniel Willingham's memory model is a good 'best bet'. It is clearly not definitive. When it comes to how the brain works, we have a distinctly limited understanding. Willingham's model can only ever be a work in progress. Nevertheless, it has some avid fans: esteemed educators such as Sarah Cottinghatt,[3] Tom Sherrington[4] and Josh Goodrich[5] subscribe to Willingham's thinking about memory and learning.

In essence, Willingham's research suggests that pupils have a working memory and a long-term memory. The longer pupils pay attention to, and struggle cognitively with, what we are teaching them in their working memory, the more chance there is that there will be a change to their long-term memory and learning will happen. We need pupils to regularly retrieve what we have taught them, in order to embed that change in the long-term memory. To learn how to stitch together leather satchels, I would need to repair quite a few, over an extended period of time.

A crucial, additional element to understanding the learning process is recognising the importance of building upon what we already know to extend our learning. It is difficult to understand negative numbers, for instance, if you haven't got a fluent understanding of the basic number system. We extend our understanding by assimilating new learning with the schema that already exist in our long-term memory.

---

2   M. Myatt and J. Tomsett, *SEND Huh: Curriculum Conversations with SEND Leaders* (Woodbridge: John Catt Educational, 2023).

3   S. Cottinghatt, *Ausubel's Meaningful Learning in Action* (Woodbridge: John Catt Educational, 2023).

4   T. Sherrington, *The Learning Rainforest: Great Teaching in Real Classrooms* (Woodbridge: John Catt Educational, 2017).

5   J. Goodrich, *Responsive Coaching: Evidence-informed Instructional Coaching that Works for Every Teacher in Your School* (Woodbridge: John Catt Educational, 2024).

Ultimately, there is no learning without remembering and, as Willingham famously claims, 'memory is the residue of thought'.[6] If we can encourage pupils to attend to, and think hard about, what we are teaching them, the better chance there is of learning happening.

This graphic (see page 236), taken from Josh Goodrich's book on instructional coaching, illustrates Willingham's learning model and the kind of questions we might ask about where teaching might be adjusted to increase pupils' progress in their learning.[7]

A learning model is crucial for teachers to plan their teaching and for them to adapt it if their pupils aren't learning. It is equally important, perhaps, for anyone like me, who watches people teach, to have a model of learning. Josh Goodrich's questions are an helpful *aide memoire* for beginning to evaluate whether the visible teaching you have seen might lead to pupils learning (which is, of course, invisible). Only when you hear or see what pupils produce as a result of the teaching that has happened, can you even begin to gauge whether learning has taken place.

While I saw a very limited sample of teaching, the lesson visits recorded in this book are hugely detailed. I wanted to be able to give a sense of what it was like to be in the lessons, and some indication of whether learning was taking place. At best, perhaps, all we can glean from the lesson visits, using the Willingham memory model, is that there is a decent chance learning was taking place.

---

6 D. T. Willingham, What will improve a student's memory? *American Educator* (Winter 2008–2009): 17–25. Available at: http://www.aft.org/sited/default/files/periodicals/willingham_0.pdf.

7 Goodrich, *Responsive Coaching*.

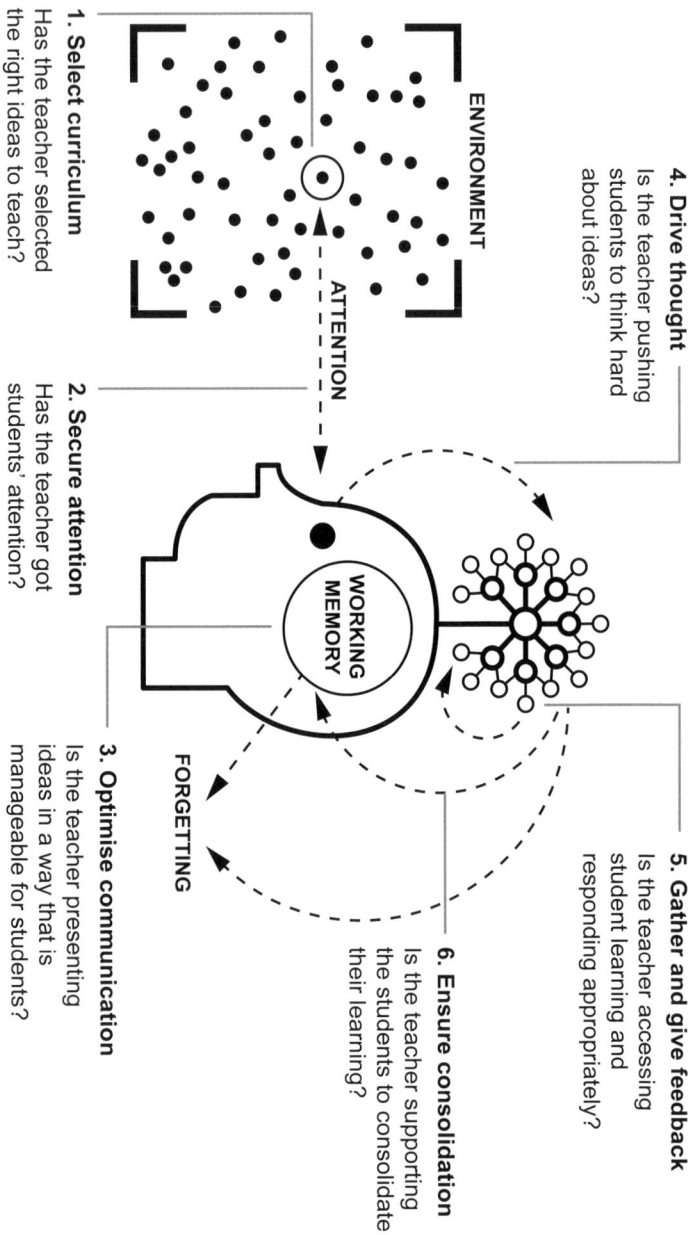

4. Drive thought
Is the teacher pushing
students to think hard
about ideas?

1. Select curriculum
Has the teacher selected
the right ideas to teach?

2. Secure attention
Has the teacher got
students' attention?

3. Optimise communication
Is the teacher presenting
ideas in a way that is
manageable for students?

5. Gather and give feedback
Is the teacher accessing
student learning and
responding appropriately?

6. Ensure consolidation
Is the teacher supporting
the students to consolidate
their learning?

ENVIRONMENT

ATTENTION

WORKING MEMORY

FORGETTING

A model of the curriculum: the curriculum triumvirate

The focus upon developing the curriculum in England has led to some unintended consequences, one of which has been an obsession with content over the two other elements of the curriculum – pedagogy and assessment. The quality of pupils' classroom experiences depends on both *what* is taught and *how* it is taught, all underpinned by short-cycle formative assessment. The three elements of curriculum – content, adaptive pedagogy and assessment – I have dubbed the curriculum triumvirate. When they work together in harmony – when the content is rich and ambitious, the teaching is vibrant and expert, and the teacher's formative assessment ensures no pupil is left behind – they provide all pupils with irresistible learning experiences.

Now, when I watch colleagues teach, I use my knowledge of all three aspects of the curriculum to help me get a sense of whether the pupils are participating in the lesson in a way that is likely to result, at some point, in learning. So, is the content they are being taught rich, challenging and ambitious, pitched at the Goldilocks level of academic demand – that is, not too hard that they have no hook to begin engaging with the content at all, but not too easy that they can complete what is asked of them without having to think – where it challenges them to wrestle with the content and builds on what they have learnt before? Is the way the content is being taught clearly explained, in a way that makes it irresistibly interesting to the pupils? Is there sufficient time allowed for checking conclusively whether all the pupils have at least begun to grasp what has been taught? The relationship between the curriculum triumvirate is dynamic.

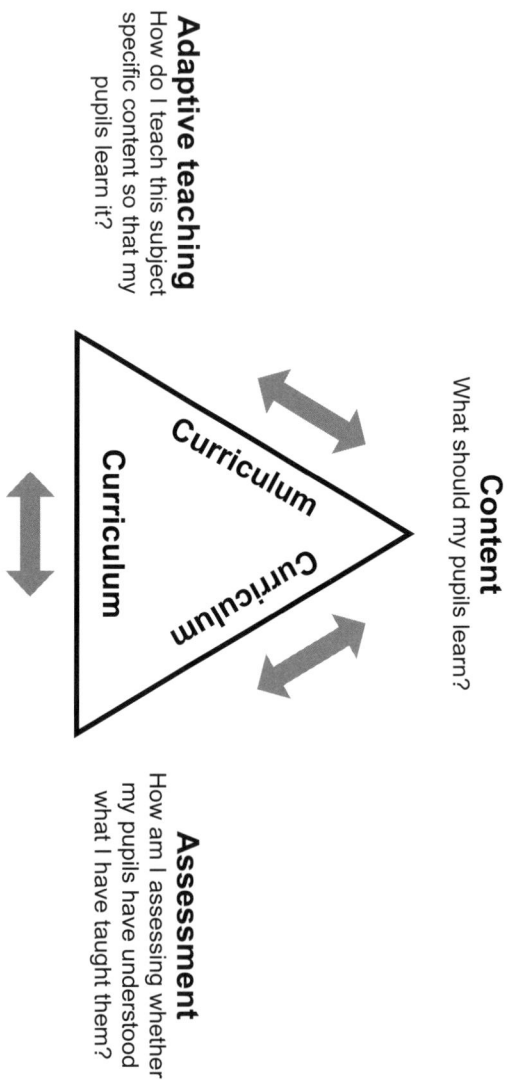

Adaptive teaching
How do I teach this subject specific content so that my pupils learn it?

Content
What should my pupils learn?

Curriculum

Curriculum

Curriculum

Assessment
How am I assessing whether my pupils have understood what I have taught them?

When developing the curriculum, all three elements of the triumvirate need to be considered simultaneously. What we have seen, however, is content privileged over pedagogy and assessment.

Arguably, two key figures laid the foundations for redesigning the curriculum in England: Dylan Wiliam and Michael Young. In 2013 Wiliam wrote that, 'A great intended curriculum badly taught is likely to be a much worse experience for young people than a bad intended curriculum well taught. Pedagogy trumps curriculum.'[8] Wiliam was clear that content alone is not enough.

Michael Young's book, *Knowledge and the Future School: Curriculum and Social Justice*, published in 2014, was highly influential in the drive towards a knowledge-rich curriculum.[9] It is important to point out at this point, that I am not arguing against a knowledge-rich curriculum. What concerns me is merely *giving* pupils content, without thinking about how to present the content so they find it irresistible.

Knowledge organisers and glue sticks are a modern educational curse!

In an important, yet little noticed article Michael Young reflected upon the development of the knowledge curriculum in England, some eight years after publishing his seminal book.[10] His comments – which I have cited, on occasion, earlier in the book and at length below – seem incredibly important to me:

'Lev Vygotsky [wrote] that acquiring knowledge in school has to be the voluntary act of a learner. You can't actually teach anybody anything; they have to learn it. You can help them, but they've got to have that desire to know. If you haven't encouraged pupils to engage in the process of acquiring knowledge, which is a very difficult process, then all you get is memorisation and reproduction in tests. I think this

8   D. Wiliam, *Redesigning Schooling: Principled Curriculum Design: 3* (London: SSAT (The Schools Network), 2013).

9   M. Young, D. Lambert, C. Roberts and M. Roberts, *Knowledge and the Future School: Curriculum and Social Justice* (London: Bloomsbury, 2014).

10 G. Duoblys, Michael Young: What we've got wrong about knowledge and curriculum, *TES* (21 September 2022). Available at: https://www.tes.com/magazine/teaching-learning/general/michael-young-powerful-knowledge-curriculum.

is why a lot of kids actually lose the desire to know during their time at school, whereas if we somehow found a way of enabling kids to discover that desire, which is inherent in all of them, schooling would be quite different. It would be a lovely thing to be a teacher, and not a struggle for much of the time. That's been quite a revealing thought to me. The current interest in the curriculum overlooks this point. It's so concerned with saying, "Have we got the knowledge?" that it forgets to ask, "How is the knowledge being acquired?" The curriculum is not just a body of knowledge; it's a group of communities we must encourage our students to join. That's how we have to look at it. We have to keep open the idea of a curriculum that is pedagogic, in the sense of it being accessible knowledge. It's difficult to access, but accessible nonetheless.'

Our education system is suffering, post-COVID, from low pupil attendance rates and poor pupil behaviour, and parents and children no longer live by the imperative that pupils must attend school. This is a world where a university education is no longer a guarantee of meaningful employment and where the internet is seen, all too often, as the easy-to-access source of all knowledge. Is it possible we have forgotten just how crucial it is to entice pupils into the learning process; that we no longer feel an obligation to encourage them to join our learning communities; that we think we can just give them a knowledge organiser, a glue stick and five hours of low-level administrative tasks and call that *teaching*?

Both Wiliam and Young emphasise the importance of teachers' pedagogy in the learning process. They trust the content specialists to know how to teach the nuances of the subject.

The thing is, you have got to make learning irresistible, and one way to do that is to let the expert teachers fly. I go fishing with my mate Tom. He is a truly great teacher. He has his own highly successful methodology. His students love his teaching style and they make great progress, evidenced in their GCSE progress scores. When I told him about this project, and one teacher in particular whose pupils have astronomically high progress scores, Tom said, without hesitation, 'I bet they are just left to get on with it.' And, of course, he is right.

The *well-trained, professionally thoughtful and evidence-informed* truly great teachers featured in this book have earned a level of autonomy. None is fettered by pedagogic diktat from above. They have fun, they enjoy what they do, and their pupils learn a great deal. As Tom Sherrington says, 'Teaching has to be joyful – and it can be if we let it.'[11] And what comes next was true for these primary teachers as it was for the secondary teachers I feature in its accompanying title (*This Much I Know About Truly Great Secondary Teachers*), namely, that being in those classrooms was – and I hesitate to use the word because I think it is overused to the point of redundancy, but I genuinely mean it and will use it anyway – an absolute *privilege*. Not once did a lesson drag, not once did I lose interest and rarely did I ever see a pupil off-task. The learning process is joyful. Watching them teach, one can only conclude that it is 'a lovely thing to be a teacher'.

The major common features of these truly great primary teachers

Much of what we can learn from these truly great teachers comes from the detail of the lesson visit records and the interviews. That said, I thought it would be useful to position my suggested findings within an evidence-based context. Barak Rosenshine's meta-analysis, Research on teacher performance criteria, written with the help of Norma Furst in 1971, identified eleven teacher behaviours that led to high levels of pupil learning:[12]

---

11 T. Sherrington, Evidence-informed teaching has to be built around each teacher's personality and desire for autonomy; let's celebrate that, *Teacherhead* [blog] (7 January 2024). Available at: https://teacherhead.com/2024/01/07/evidence-informed-teaching-has-to-be-built-around-each-teachers-personality-and-desire-for-autonomy-lets-celebrate-that/.

12 B. Rosenshine and N. Furst, Research on teacher performance criteria, In B. O. Smith (ed.), *Research in Teacher Education* (Englewood Cliffs, NJ: Prentice Hall), pp. 37–72, cited in R. K. Barrick and A. C. Thoron, Teaching Behavior and Student Achievement: AEC582 WC244, 1 (2016). EDIS 2016 (1). Gainesville, FL:6. https://doi.org/10.32473/edis-wc244-2016.

- Clarity
- Variability
- Enthusiasm
- Task-oriented and/or Business-like Behaviour
- Student Opportunity to Learn Criterion Material
- Use of Student Ideas and General Indirectness
- Criticism
- Use of Structuring Comments
- Types of Questions
- Probing
- Level of Difficulty of Instruction

I would argue that the first four in Rosenshine's list are common features of our truly great primary teachers. The most obvious is how every single teacher taught with unbridled, infectious *enthusiasm*. It's impossible not to share Josh Pike's delight in seeing his charges make progress. It's hard to be disinterested in Nicola Curran's fake dead leopard! Only a cardboard cut-out could fail to be excited about writing one of Megan Bull's Christmas riddles. What they were teaching was, according to their enthusiastic selves, irresistible. Now, they were, of course, putting on their best children's TV presenter personas; yet it is possible to act as though you are enthused. I would argue that you *have* to be enthused, it's part of your job to be enthused; if you're dulled by what you're teaching, what chance do the pupils have? Pritesh Raichura, in his spellbinding talk at the researchED London conference, acknowledged that you needed to learn how to have presence, how to perform in the classroom, how to vary your voice and exaggerate your facial expressions in order to appear enthused and make what you are teaching appealing to the pupils. He was certain you could learn to develop that elusive thing called 'class-room presence' and I cannot help but agree. Watching our truly great teachers, I wonder whether being enthused becomes a habit. These teachers are *actually* enthused. Maddie Jacques' energy for long division, Dean Salisbury's excitement about the class visit to Blists Hill, Molly Medhurst's verve for subtracting fractions, are all – it seemed to me as I sat in their classrooms – genuine.

Many enthusiasts would make poor teachers, however, because they would not be able to explain the object of their enthusiasm with any *clarity*. Not so with these truly great teachers, whose teaching is characterised by clarity in two main ways. It appears that narrating the direction of the lesson creates a safe environment for children. It was clear, in so many classrooms, exactly where we are now, what we are doing next and where we will end up. Mary Cawley, who, more than most teachers, needs to create a classroom that is a psychologically safe place, outlines the tasks for the day before they begin, with each activity on a small card, velcroed to the metal cupboard at the front of the room. Every time an activity is completed, Ahmed will take down the corresponding card. Teachers like Faariah Jamil and Helen Digger narrate each step of the lesson with total clarity and their pupils enact what has been narrated to the letter.

Rosenshine suggested that teachers who were able to explain content and frame questions with clarity, were more effective.[13] Indeed, clarity in communicating curriculum content is a crucial element of effective teaching. Without exception, the teachers modelled their thinking to the class. One extraordinary example was Megan Bull, who modelled her thinking in an '*I do, we do, you do*' writing activity. The fact that her pupils could explain to me that her modelling helped them understand how to do things, confirmed for me the effectiveness of her work. Dean Salisbury's modelling of the writing process was equally clear, as was Maddie Jacques' long division process, explained using a visualiser. Live modelling characterised by high-quality metacognitive talk clarifies for pupils – *makes visible* for them – the thinking processes of the teacher expert. Often the pupils were provided with clear heuristics, which meant, as Nicola Curran's pupils put it so wonderfully, that they

---

13 B. Rosenshine, *Teaching Behaviours and Student Achievement*, no. 1 (IEA studies) (Slough: National Foundation for Educational Research, 1 November 1971), p. 107.

could 'do hard sums but easy methods.' Indeed, what Rosenshine called *student opportunity to learn criterion material* sound suspiciously like teaching children how to think their way through applying what they know to new problems: 'Student achievement can be increased by teaching students how to resolve problems they encounter that are related to the content of the course but are not specific regurgitations of facts taught in the course.'[14] After watching these teachers at work, I have become utterly convinced that making our thinking visible is central to effective teaching and learning.

There is much to be said for *variability* when thinking about what constitutes a truly great teacher. Rosenshine suggests that, 'variation in the teacher's cognitive behaviour or the richness and variety of classroom materials and activities' were consistently significant in relation to student achievement.[15] That said, it is understandable why school leaders might prioritise consistency over variability, especially in a world where recruiting teachers is challenging. A vacancy cannot remain unfilled once term begins, because a vacancy cannot stand in front of 30 children and teach them. Yet a sentient human being with a set of slides, a script and a DBS can make a passable attempt to teach a class, but they are not going to be a truly great teacher. Pupils enjoy variability; in pedagogic terms, variability helps secure and maintain their attention. Take Mary Cawley's lesson, where, in 90 minutes, we had reading aloud, experimental learning, physical exercise, phonics, use of video, writing, speaking and listening, sign language and … and … Now, Mary's special needs class requires the ultimate in adaptive teaching where varying what you do, frequently and regularly, is essential. But, as Gary Aubin has often said, 'There are things that teachers can do that are useful for all pupils, while being particularly useful for some.'[16] Dean Salisbury's writing lesson included, amongst other things, watching a video, paired talk, teacher live modelling, oral presentations and writing. Pearl's rendition of the Henry VIII's wives song

14 Barrick and Thoron, Teaching Behavior and Student Achievement, p. 4.

15 Rosenshine, *Teaching Behaviours and Student Achievement*, no. 1, p. 147.

16 M. Myatt and J. Tomsett, *SEND Huh: Curriculum Conversations with SEND Leaders* (Woodbridge: John Catt Educational, 2023), p. 209.

was rooted in the varied approach to teaching and learning that characterises Molly Medhurst's practice. When you speak to them, variability in lessons is important to pupils; turning up every day to the same old, same old, is hardly likely to make learning irresistible.

Business-like behaviour, aka *being organised and purposeful*, is an essential feature of the truly great teacher. Rosenshine found 'a consistent, positive trend in favour of' achievement-orientated or business-like teacher behaviour.[17] Pupils especially enjoy being taught by someone who is well-organised and wants them to achieve, who focus their teaching on what is needed for pupils to be successful. They invariably commented upon the focused, organisational skills of their teachers. Take what one of Dean Salisbury's pupils said of him: 'What I like is that he is well-organised. When in lessons, he always has everything ready. There's no wasting time. I like teachers being organised, and when teachers aren't it wastes time. It's easier to concentrate when they are organised like Mr Salisbury.' Dean's pupils could have been talking about any of the other teachers featured in this book. For instance, according to her pupils Faariah Jamil is, 'really well-organised and she makes sure where everything is'. There is no point being enthused, clear and varied when you teach, if you cannot organise yourself and your resources to target your pupils' achievement.

While the teachers profiled in this book demonstrate many aspects of the other behaviours identified by Rosenshine and Furst, *enthusiasm*, *clarity*, *variability*, and *being organised and purposeful* are the main ones. Beyond those, there are five further common traits that emerged as I reflected upon what makes these teachers truly great. They all had *genuinely high expectations* of the pupils, both behaviourally and academically. Expectations of pupils is a complex area of research according to Rosenshine, who says, nonetheless, that there is 'significant correlation between teacher attitudes towards student achievement and actual student achievement'. This might be influenced by who teachers are teaching. It may be affected by the quality of curriculum materials;

---

17 Rosenshine, *Teaching Behaviours and Student Achievement*, no. 1, p. 96.

poor curriculum materials mean poorer achievement.[18] What I have come to know in my travels, is that it's easy to assert, quite glibly, that you have high expectations of those you teach; it is another thing entirely to see high expectations riven through classroom practice like the words through a stick of seaside rock. Take Josh Pike, for example. His teaching of ratio saw pupils reach levels of understanding they had no apparent right to reach based on their prior attainment. Or Megan Bull, whose pupils behaved impeccably even though it was three days before Christmas and at the end of a long term, and were utterly enthused by their studies. Or Faariah Jamil, who insists relentlessly that her pupils think for themselves when faced with a challenge, in order to develop their levels of independence as they approach secondary age. These truly great teachers epitomise what it is to have high expectations of their pupils.

Whilst I have named the third triumvirate of the curriculum, 'assessment', the term encompasses any activity that *checks for understanding*, something these teachers do relentlessly. Someone like Maddie Jacques has excellent situational assessment. She has her radar on *all* the time, building an insight map across the class as to what learning is happening, pupil-by-pupil. Moment after moment sees these teachers check whether their pupils have learnt what they have been taught. Molly Medhurst's *volte face* at the end of her lesson on subtracting fractions was genius. Because she teaches between the desks, she knows what has been understood by whom and to what degree. When she set her class the challenge of subtracting a fraction from a whole, she made tangible a misconception she had perceived as she had looked over her charges' shoulders. Once surfaced, she was then able to disabuse them of their misconception and the foundations of future learning were secured. Without Molly's constant checking for understanding, that crucial misconception would have been baked into the pupils' grasp of fractions. All of which brings us back to the dynamic relationship between content-adaptive pedagogy-assessment. Whether it is via teaching between the desks, disciplined use of show-me boards, expert questioning techniques or the responses of bellwether pupils, truly great

---

18 Rosenshine, *Teaching Behaviours and Student Achievement*, no. 1, p. 218.

teachers have a forensic comprehension of who can do what and, consequently, the direction in which they need to take their teaching next.

Closely linked to checking for understanding is the commitment to give *help to individual pupils*. Such precisely targeted support takes huge amounts of energy, but watching these teachers (and those I feature in its accompanying title, *This Much I Know About Truly Great Secondary Teachers*, help the individual pupils who need just that little extra guidance, I swear they were energised rather than depleted by the process. Nicola Curran's pupils, for example, were hugely praiseworthy of her efforts to support them: 'She has made my sums better. She'll come over to you and help you if you get stuck. We do hard sums but easy methods.' To the accusation that such individualised support fosters learned helplessness, I would merely say that when these teachers provide a pupil with support, that is all it is, support. They don't tell them the answers, they clarify their thinking. In fact, the individualised help is more like *probing*, another of Rosenshine's identified behaviours: 'probing; that is, teacher responding to students with further clarifying questions … may lead a student towards a more comprehensive answer than the initial one s/he gave'.[19] Individualised support is most often part of extending pupils' thinking and not telling pupils the answer. Megan Bull's pupil was clear in this respect: 'she doesn't tell you the answer to things'. Nicola Curran teaches her pupils to be curious, to think for themselves. It just takes some children longer than others. As I make clear in her profile, Nicola is encouraging, but gives nothing away. 'Let's not use the word "worried" Liam. I'm not worried about you getting it "right". I'm more interested in you trying to figure it out. I like that much better. Dig a little deeper for me.' As she says herself, her aim is to make her pupils independent of her, to get them to think for themselves so that 'they don't need me anymore'.

Truly great teachers have a *confident understanding of the content* they are teaching – indeed, it is a prerequisite for intellectually challenging the pupils. Rosenshine found that 'achievement gains were higher in classes of teachers who provided intellectual emphasis (over whether

---

19 Rosenshine, *Teaching Behaviours and Student Achievement*, no. 1, p. 136.

students enjoy themselves), something only possible if the teacher is confident about their curriculum content'.[20] Primary teachers have a unique challenge, in that they are faced with being an expert in every subject. What I found from meeting the teachers featured here, is their commitment to learning new academic content out of their specialism. I thought Nicola Curran *had* to be a sports teacher in a previous life, so expert was her dribbling with a hockey stick, but I was wrong! Josh Pike's understanding of ratio suggested to me that he was a mathematician, but his first degree is, ironically, in sports coaching! Megan Bull stepped up to be the co-mathematics lead even though her degree is in linguistics. Molly Medhurst is a dramatist, yet she has worked hard at becoming an expert teacher of maths. Maddie Jacques, historian, had worked hard at understanding the technicalities of long division before she taught the process with utter clarity to her Year 6 pupils. Several teachers were primary trained in their first degree; *all* the teachers continue to work hard on understanding, to a mastery level, the content they teach. Not one of them relied on a bought-in scheme and a clicker.

The final common feature of all the truly great teachers featured in this book, is that they take time to find out about each child and *build positive working relationships*. When I visited Alexandra Park to meet Megan Bull, her deputy head teacher, Claire Williams, was crystal clear about the importance of this aspect of school life and its crucial relationship to high-quality teaching and learning: 'We make sure that the teachers know our school values, and the first one, "Care", is the first thing that you work on. If you get relationships with children and parents right, everything else comes after that.' Megan was able to support Lisa when she was in danger of dysregulating because she knew that Lisa liked rabbits and she was able to ask Lisa who she thought would be softer and furrier, Rudolph the Red Nosed Reindeer or her rabbits? Megan had taken the trouble to find out about what makes Lisa tick and used that to diffuse a potential mini-crisis moment. Molly Medhurst was equally committed to seeing beyond the pupil and treating the children with deep humanity. Her motivation for teaching back where she

---

20 Rosenshine, *Teaching Behaviours and Student Achievement*, no. 1, p. 93.

began was founded in a genuine respect for her pupils and a desire to improve their lot. The pupils I spoke to about Molly could not have been more praiseworthy of her and her commitment to them.

The primacy for these teachers of building foundational relationships with their pupils is open to challenge. The famous line by Rita Pierson, 'Every child deserves a champion, an adult who will never give up on them, who understands the power of connection, and insists that they become the best that they can possibly be', is sometimes derided.[21] When I challenged Molly Medhurst about the primacy of relationship building, her response was robust and convincing:

John Tomsett (JT): What did you learn in your first year about teaching?

Molly Medhurst (MM): You're constantly having to adapt. Things get thrown at you, the curriculum changes, your day-to-day changes. What I think I learnt the most was the relationship with the children is number one, always.

JT: Tell me what you mean by that. Let's dig into that. Nearly everybody says that. I'm really interested in what that looks like.

MM: My teachers at school were so fantastic at making me feel valued. My priority is making these children feel valued. Obviously, progress data are important and making sure they leave school with subject knowledge is important and being ready to go onto secondary, college, university, whatever, that's really important, but I think if these children can leave at the end of the day and feel they've had a good day and feel happy, that's what I'd want.

JT: What do you say when people say your job is to educate and challenge academically, because I've just watched you teach hard and press them to understand subtracting fractions?

21 R. Pierson, Every kid needs a champion, *TED* (3 May 2013). Available at: https://www.youtube.com/watch?v=SFnMTHhKdkw.

MM: Of course the academic is key, but I don't think I'd be able to teach like that and have such great levels of attention, if I didn't have such positive relationships with those children. Getting to know them on a personal level, treating them like people, building those relationships first.

JT: **You do that beautifully.**

MM: Oh, thank you. I don't know everything, I don't know the curriculum inside out, I don't know all about pedagogy because I'm still learning, but I think I really take the time with these children and form those foundational relationships.

It's hard to argue with Molly – and Nicola and Megan and Mary and Josh and Maddie and Dean and Faariah and Helen – because they all are truly great teachers and they all subscribe to the notion that without getting to know your pupils as people and forging respectful, trusting relationships with them and their parents, it is difficult to teach as well as they do and for their pupils to learn as much as they possibly can.

Final reflections: two sides of the same coin, or something more?

So, here are nine behaviours of the nine truly great teachers featured in this book:

1   *Teach with enthusiasm*

2   *Explain things with clarity*

3   *Vary your pedagogic practices*

4   *Be organised and purposeful*

5   *Have genuinely high expectations*

6   *Check for understanding*

7   *Have a confident understanding of the content*

8   *Help individual pupils*

9   *Build positive working relationships*

Many readers will say that they could have listed these nine behaviours of truly great teachers for me before I began my work and saved me the days spent beetling around the country visiting schools and the hours it has taken to write this book. I am sure that Professor Rob Coe, both my collaborator and provocateur, will point out that all I had to do was look at these teachers' pupils' progress data to know that they must be truly great teachers who do the nine things listed above on a daily basis. But, as Rosenshine says, 'student achievement is inadequate as a sole measure of teacher effectiveness,'[22] a sentiment supported by Matthew A. Kraft, who wrote recently in the *TES*: 'We know that we can't boil down a teacher into a simplistic uniform measure of their performance. It is much more complex.'[23]

That said, are my findings and Rob's single pupil progress data point just two sides of the same coin? They probably are, to a great extent. That is, if you exhibit those nine teacher behaviours, as night follows day, your pupils will make good progress, and if your pupils have made good academic progress, it is highly likely that you will be exhibiting those nine teacher behaviours. But it is nuanced and it is, as Kraft says, *complex*. The thing about the Rosenshine book, is that it begins by saying this field of research is damned tricky. I led Huntington School in York, which is a Research School. I know, through bitter experience, how tracking the golden thread from teacher behaviours to pupil outcomes is complexity personified. I remember asking my last Year 13 economics class, in their final lesson, what it was they liked best about the way I taught – was it the pre-reading process, questioning, modelling answers, the role play to illustrate the law of diminishing returns of the factors of production, group presentations, research tasks … ? And the lad who went on to attain an A* grade at A level in the summer examinations replied, 'I liked it best when you read through the textbook and explained it to us'. All that effort, and that was all I

22 Rosenshine, *Teaching Behaviours and Student Achievement*, no. 1, p. 13.

23 Z. Niemtus, Matthew A. Kraft: The struggle to spot (and develop) effective teachers, *TES* (6 November 2024). Available at: https://www.tes.com/magazine/teaching-learning/general/how-to-spot-and-develop-effective-teachers.

needed to have done! But what the Year 13 student was actually saying, was that he liked clear explanations and the work to be targeted precisely upon what he needed to know to be successful. Since the textbook was endorsed by the examination board and written by the chief examiner, his reflection made complete sense.

But education has to be about more than examination outcomes. Whilst I can see the sense of Rob's quest to find a single pupil progress data point to represent individual teacher efficacy, teachers do more than just help pupils make academic progress. They create communities. So, I think, there are a couple of further learning points to be taken from these teacher profiles.

I was very clear that I wanted to enjoy myself at work. As a head teacher I was in school for 10–12 hours a day, every day, for 18 years. The core part of my waking life was spent at work. I needed to enjoy myself. I never subscribed to the concept of a work/life balance. If work is the opposite of life, then work is logically, being equated with death. I called it a work/home balance since both are part of my life, and to acknowledge how important my work was as a major element of who I am.

Mahatma Gandhi said, 'Happiness is when what you think, what you say, and what you do are in harmony.' So, when at work, you have to be yourself and enjoy being there. The teachers I visited were visibly enjoying their lives in the classroom. Both teachers and pupils were happy to be there. Truly. These teachers were being themselves. Pupil behaviour was great. I never heard a teacher shout. Those foundational relationships that Molly Medhurst talked about were established so very firmly in all the classrooms I visited. They responded to individual need and they cared deeply about every single child. They were not limited by a regimented, didactic teaching and learning policy; indeed, the way they were happy to adapt what they did within a loose pedagogic framework surely raises questions for the current practice in some settings where the approach to teaching and learning emphasises consistency beyond all else. As my mate Tom suggested, they were trusted to get on with it.

Schools are, arguably, the most important social centres in our crumbling neighbourhoods and their output goes beyond an examination value-added score. They are comprised of classroom communities built by truly great teachers like those featured in this book. The sense of obligation to each other that these teachers create in their classrooms leads to great things, one of which is the way pupils mimic their teachers' behaviours and attitudes. When those foundational relationships are established, whatever the teacher does, the pupils will do too. Most importantly, it was as clear as one of Josh Pike's explanations of ratio that every single truly great teacher worked demonstrably hard for the pupils. I have always harboured the odd doubt about what you can actually learn from pupil voice exercises, but the conversations with the pupils were utterly illuminating. So many – if not all – of them said that they worked hard because their teacher worked hard and they didn't want to let their teacher down. I had a sense that this was important; I knew that I worked hard for my old English teacher, Dave Williams, some 40-odd years ago, because he cared enough to work hard for me. I once met one of my former A level students, now in his forties, who said the class had worked hard because Karl Elwell, my co-teacher, and I had worked hard, but I never thought the level of reciprocity was quite so marked. Consequently, if we need a final teacher behaviour to make it a neat ten, it would be *work hard for your pupils*.

Providing a high-quality education for every child in our country is an amazingly ambitious endeavour. I marvel at the whole enterprise. It depends upon dedicated professionals – like the teachers featured here – in the corners of our schools, in every village, town and city, maintaining high standards, giving their all for our children, day-in, day-out, when no one is looking. The whole thing is selfless heroism, personified. If it were easy – as some of the cynics might crow – the profession wouldn't have a recruitment and retention crisis.

I will end with Nicola Curran, across the water in Larne, who finished her email to me with this: 'I'm off to collect my little ones for another fab day of learning. Who knows what the day will bring with their curious minds?! It's exciting!'

.

Select Bibliography

Andrews, B. (2025). How 'efficiency' derailed education, *TES* (25 February). Available at: https://www.tes.com/magazine/teaching-learning/general/how-efficiency-derailed-education.

Barrick, R. K. and Thoron, A. C. (2016). Teaching Behavior and Student Achievement: AEC582 WC244, 1 2016. EDIS 2016 (1). Gainesville, FL:6. https://doi.org/10.32473/edis-wc244-2016.

Barth, R. S. (1991). *Improving Schools from Within: Teachers, Parents, and Principals Can Make the Difference* (San Francisco, CA: Jossey-Bass).

Coe, R. (2014). Classroom observation: it's harder than you think, *Cambridge Insight* [blog] (9 January). Available at: https://www.cem.org/blog/classroom-observation.

Coe, R., Aloisi, C., Higgins, S. and Elliot Major, L. (2014). *What Makes Great Teaching? Review of the Underpinning Research* (London: Sutton Trust). Available at: https://www.suttontrust.com/wp-content/uploads/2014/10/What-Makes-Great-Teaching-REPORT.pdf.

Coe, R., Rauch, C. J., Kime, S. and Singleton, D. (2020). *The Great Teaching Toolkit: Evidence Review* (Sunderland: Evidence Based Education). Available at: https://evidencebased.education/great-teaching-toolkit-evidence-review/.

Devine, D., Fahie, D. and Mcgillicuddy, D. (2013). What is 'good' teaching? Teacher beliefs and practices about their teaching, *Irish Educational Studies*, 32(1): 83–108. https://doi.org/10.1080/03323315.2013.773228

Duoblys, G. (2022). Michael Young: What we've got wrong about knowledge and curriculum, *TES* (21 September). Available at: https://www.tes.com/magazine/teaching-learning/general/michael-young-powerful-knowledge-curriculum.

Husbands, C. (2013). Great teachers or great teaching? Why McKinsey got it wrong, *IOE blog* (10 October). Available at: https://blogs.ucl.ac.uk/ioe/2013/10/10/great-teachers-or-great-teaching-why-mckinsey-got-it-wrong/.

Kirschner, P. A. and Hendrick, C. (2020). *How Learning Happens: Seminal Works in Educational Psychology and What They Mean in Practice* (Abingdon and New York: Routledge).

Kirschner, P., Hendrick, C. and Heal, J. (2022). *How Teaching Happens: Seminal Works in Teaching and Teacher Effectiveness and What They Mean in Practice* (Abingdon and New York: Routledge).

Lemov, D. (2021). *Teach Like a Champion 3.0: 63 Techniques that Put Students on the Path to College* (San Francisco, CA: Jossey-Bass).

McCourt, M. (2019). *Teaching for Mastery* (Woodbridge: John Catt Educational).

Muijs, D. and Reynolds, D. (2010). *Effective Teaching: Evidence and Practice* (London: SAGE Publications).

Myatt, M. (2016). *High Challenge, Low Threat: How the Best Leaders Find the Balance* (Woodbridge: John Catt Educational).

Myatt, M. (2018). *The Curriculum: Gallimaufry to Coherence* (Woodbridge: John Catt Educational).

Myatt, M. and Tomsett, J. (2021). *Huh: Curriculum Conversations Between Senior and Subject Leaders* (Woodbridge: John Catt Educational).

Myatt, M. and Tomsett, J. (2022a). *Primary Huh: Curriculum Conversations with Subject Leaders in Primary Schools* (Woodbridge: John Catt Educational).

Myatt, M. and Tomsett, J. (2022b). *Primary Huh 2: Primary Curriculum Leadership Conversations* (Woodbridge: John Catt Educational).

Myatt, M. and Tomsett, J. (2023). *SEND Huh: Curriculum Conversations with SEND Leaders* (Woodbridge: John Catt Educational).

Myatt, M. and Tomsett, J. (2024). *AP Huh: Curriculum Conversations with Alternative Provision Leaders* (Woodbridge: John Catt Educational).

Niemtus, Z. (2024). Matthew A. Kraft: The struggle to spot (and develop) effective teachers, *TES* (6 November). Available at: https://www.tes.com/magazine/teaching-learning/general/how-to-spot-and-develop-effective-teachers.

Nuthall, G. (2007). *The Hidden Lives of Learners* (Wellington: NZCER Press).

Rosenshine, B. (2012). Principles of instruction: research-based strategies that all teachers should know, *American Educator*, 38(1): 12–19, 39. Available at: https://www.aft.org/sites/default/files/periodicals/Rosenshine.pdf.

Rosenshine, B. (1971). *Teaching Behaviours and Student Achievement*, no. 1 (IEA studies) (Slough: National Foundation for Educational Research).

Rosenshine, B. and Furst, N. (1971). Research on teacher performance criteria. In B. O. Smith (ed.), *Research in Teacher Education*, pp. 37–72 (Englewood Cliffs, NJ: Prentice Hall).

Sherrington, T. (2017). *The Learning Rainforest: Great Teaching in Real Classrooms* (Woodbridge: John Catt Educational).

Sherrington, T. (2019). *Rosenshine's Principles in Action* (Woodbridge: John Catt Educational).

Sherrington, T. (2021). Reviewing lessons from the perspective of the least confident. Are you reaching them? *Teacherhead* [blog] (27 December). Available at: https://teacherhead.com/2022/12/27/reviewing-lessons-from-the-perspective-of-the-least-confident-are-you-reaching-them/.

Sherrington, T. and Caviglioli, O. (2020). *Teaching WalkThrus: Five-Step Guides to Instructional Coaching: Visual Step-By-Step Guides to Essential Teaching Techniques* (Woodbridge: John Catt Educational).

Sherrington, T. and Caviglioli, O. (2021). *Teaching WalkThrus 2: Five-Step Guides to Instructional Coaching* (Woodbridge: John Catt Educational).

Sherrington, T. and Caviglioli, O. (2022). *Teaching WalkThrus 3: Five-Step Guides to Instructional Coaching* (Woodbridge: John Catt Educational).

Sherrington, T. and Caviglioli, O. (2024). *Learning WalkThrus: Students and Parents – Better Learning, Step by Step* (Woodbridge: John Catt Educational).

Siegel, M. A. (1977). Teacher behaviors and curriculum packages: Implications for research and teacher education. In L. Rubin (ed.), *Curriculum Handbook: Administration and Theory* (Boston, MA: Allyn & Bacon Publishers) (ERIC Document Reproduction Service No. ED 134 932).

Tabberer, R. (1994). *School and Teacher Effectiveness* (Slough: NFER and Staffordshire LEA). Available at: https://www.nfer.ac.uk/media/2lgkpzs4/school_and_teacher_effectiveness.pdf.

Tomsett, J. (2015). *This Much I Know About Love Over Fear ... Creating a Culture for Truly Great Teaching* (Carmarthen: Crown House Publishing).

Wiliam, D. (2016). *Leadership for Teacher Learning* (Blairsville, PA: Learning Sciences International).

Willingham, D. T. (2021). *Why Don't Students Like School? A Cognitive Scientist Answers Questions About How the Mind Works and What It Means for the Classroom*, 2nd edn (San Francisco, CA: Jossey-Bass).

Young, M., Lambert, D., Roberts, C. and Roberts, M. (2014). *Knowledge and the Future School: Curriculum and Social Justice* (London: Bloomsbury Publishing).

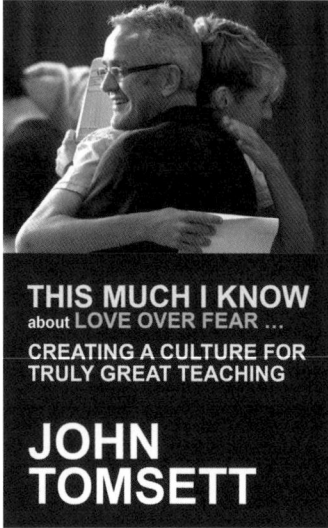

This Much I Know About Love Over Fear …

Creating a culture for truly great teaching

THIS MUCH I KNOW
about LOVE OVER FEAR …
CREATING A CULTURE FOR
TRULY GREAT TEACHING

JOHN
TOMSETT

This Much I Know About Love Over Fear is a compelling account of leading a values-driven school where people matter above all else. Weaving autobiography with an account of his experience of headship, Tomsett explains how, in an increasingly pressurised education system, he creates the conditions in which staff and students can thrive. Too many of our state schools have become scared, soulless places. Tomsett draws on his extensive experience and knowledge and calls for all those involved in education to find the courage to develop a leadership-wisdom which emphasises love over fear. Creating a truly great school takes patience. Ultimately, truly great schools don't suddenly exist. You grow great teachers first, who, in turn, grow a truly great school.

There is a huge fork in the road for head teachers: one route leads to executive headship across a number of schools and the other takes head teachers back into the classroom to be the head teacher. John strongly believes that if the head teacher is not teaching, or engaged in helping others to improve their teaching, in their school, then they are missing the point. The only thing head teachers need obsess themselves with is improving the quality of teaching, both their colleagues' and their own.

An authentic personal narrative of teaching, leadership and discovering what really matters. It gets to the heart of what is valuable in education and offers advice for those working in schools.

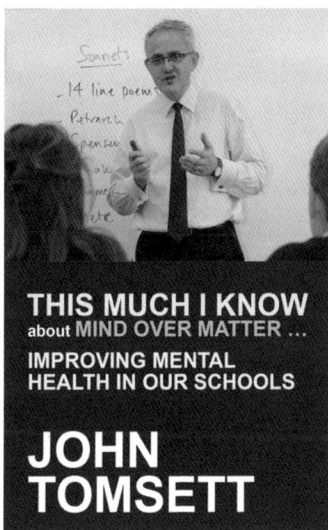

This Much I Know About Mind Over Matter …

Improving mental health in our schools

ISBN 978-178583168-3

John Tomsett's second book, *This Much I Know About Mind Over Matter,* is replete with truths about the mental well-being of children in state schools, about creating a school culture where everyone can not just survive, but thrive, and about life around manic depression. With his typical mixture of experience, wisdom and research-based evidence, Tomsett explains how he manages the pressure of modern-day state-school headship. He interweaves his authentic personal experience of a childhood traumatised by his mother's manic depression with his strategies for turning the tide of students' mental health problems and surviving as a head teacher in a climate where you are only as good as your last set of examination results. He addresses the growing issue of children's mental health issues with refreshing honesty, offering up a plan for averting a mental health crisis in our schools. The autobiographical narrative modulates between self-effacing humour and heart-wrenching stories of his mother's life, blighted by mental illness. His professional reflections are a wisdom-filled blend of evidence-based policy and decades of experience in teaching and school leadership. Tomsett writes with genuine humility. His prose is beautiful in its seeming simplicity. When you pick up one of his books you will find you have read the first fifty pages before you have even noticed: surely the hallmark of truly great writing.

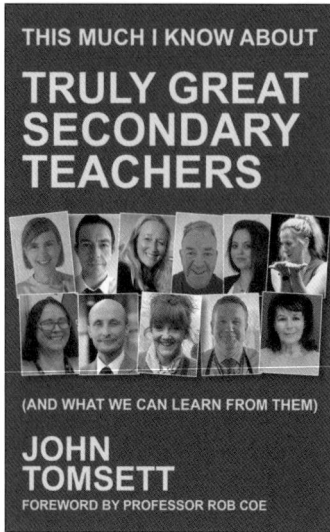

This much I know About Truly Great Secondary Teachers

(and what we can learn from them)

ISBN 978-178583741-8

Foreword by Professor Rob Coe

Through a set of in-depth case studies, *This Much I Know About Truly Great Secondary Teachers (and what we can learn from them)* by John Tomsett brings to life how eleven outstanding secondary teachers cultivate great learning in their classrooms.

Covering a range of school types, social contexts, pupil ages and subjects, each detailed vignette is based on observing the teachers teach, and discussions with them, their colleagues and pupils. The conversations that form the heart of this book provide a picture of not just what these teachers do, but why they do it: the choices and adaptations they make, and the pedagogic and philosophical principles that guide them.

Each teacher is unique in the way they teach and in how they talk about teaching, but they also have some common behaviours and attitudes that make them truly great. John draws together these characteristics, summarising what we can all learn from their utter dedication, enthusiasm and commitment to preparing the next generation for a bright future.

Essential reading for all secondary school teachers, school leaders, teacher trainers and education researchers.